# THE LUMINOUS BRUSH

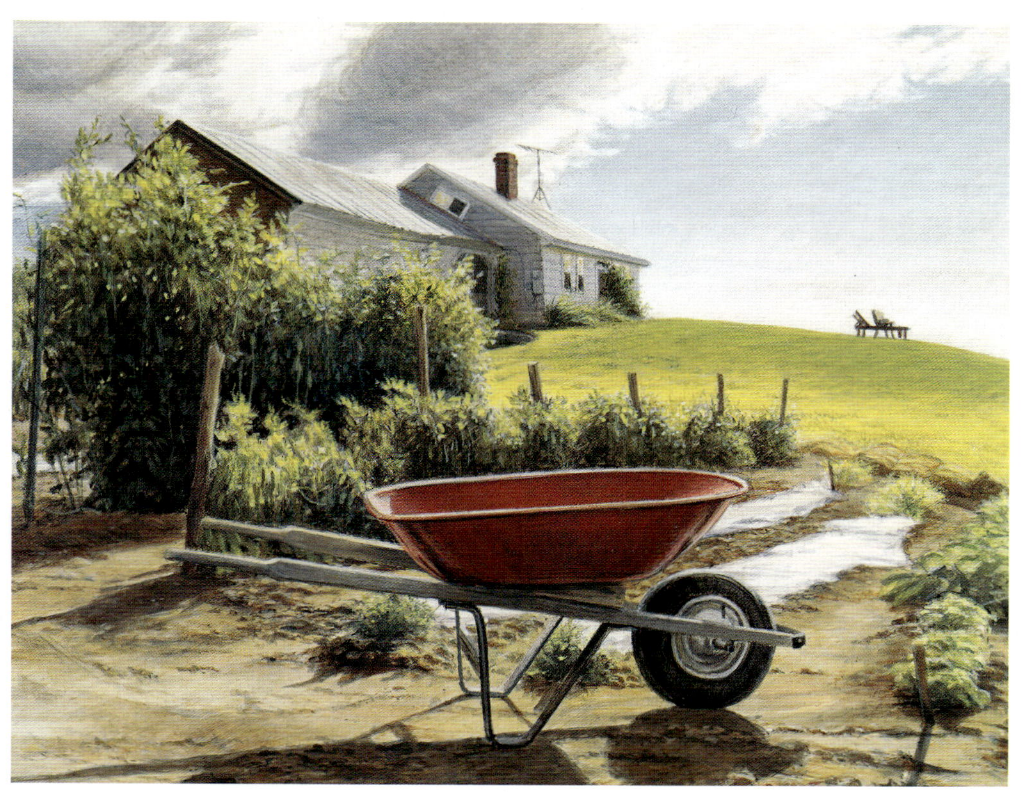

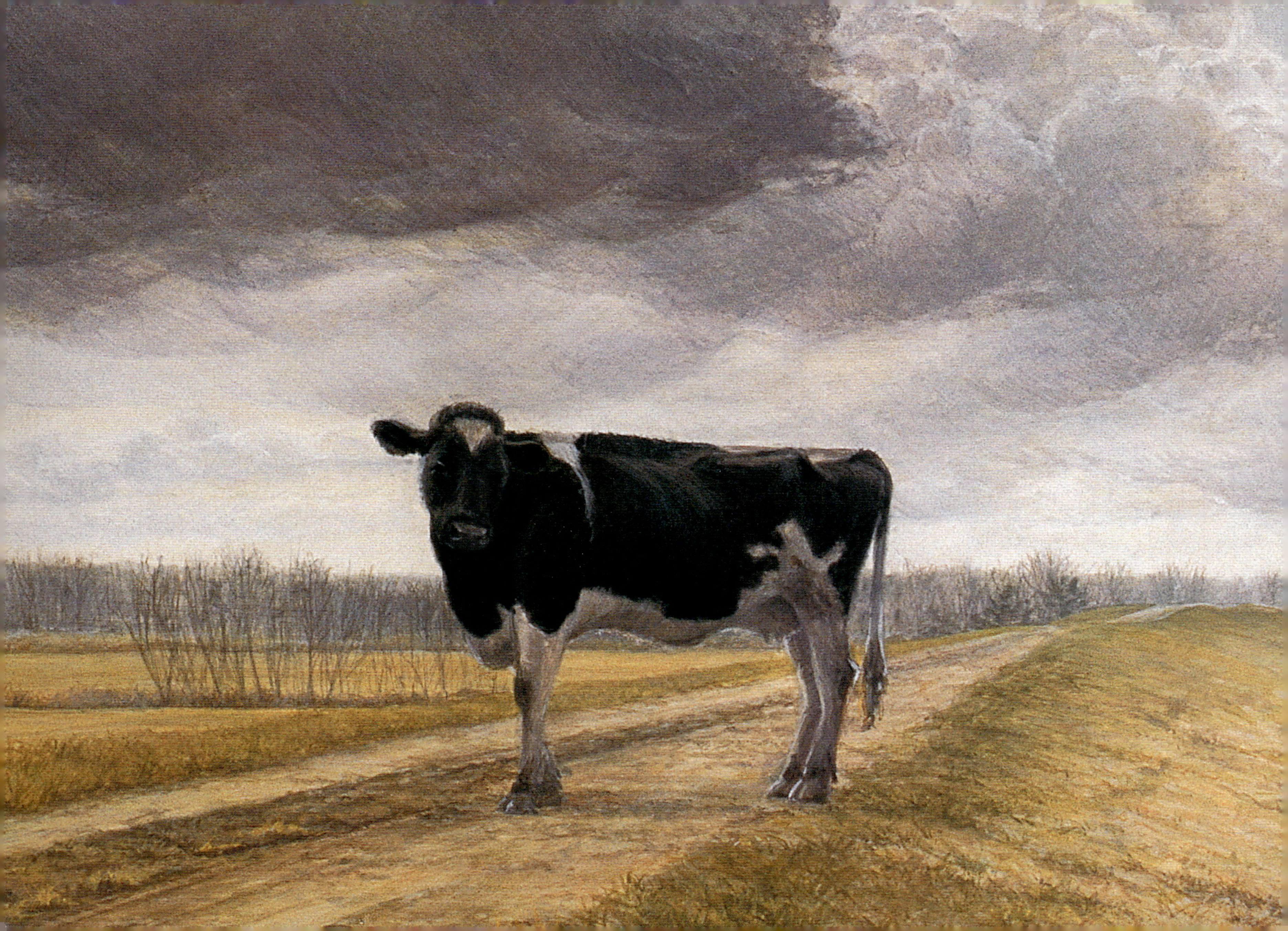

# THE LUMINOUS BRUSH

## PAINTING · WITH · EGG · TEMPERA

Altoon Sultan

WATSON-GUPTILL PUBLICATIONS/NEW YORK

FOR MY PARENTS

FRONT COVER: Altoon Sultan
ROUND BALES, HAZY DAY,
RYEGATE, VERMONT
$10^1/_2 \times 19^1/_2$ inches

PAGE 1: Altoon Sultan
RED WHEELBARROW
GROTON, VERMONT
$9 \times 12$ inches

PAGES 2-3: Altoon Sultan
COW ON THE LEVEE,
BATON ROUGE, LOUISIANA
$7^1/_2 \times 20$ inches

Copyright © 1999 by Altoon Sultan

First published in 1999 in the United States
by Watson-Guptill Publications,
a division of BPI Communications, Inc.
1515 Broadway, New York, N.Y. 10036

**Library of Congress Cataloging-in-Publication Data**

Sultan, Altoon.
    The luminous brush : painting with egg tempera / Altoon Sultan.
        p.    cm.
    Includes bibliographical references and index.
    ISBN 0-8230-2888-7
    1. Tempera painting—Technique.   I. Title.
ND2468.S85    1999
751.4'3—dc21                                   99-37390
                                                    CIP

All rights reserved. No part of this publication may be reproduced or
used in any form or by any means—graphic, electronic, or mechanical,
including photocopying, recording, taping, or information storage and
retrieval systems—without the written permission of the publisher.

Printed in Hong Kong

First printing, 1999

1 2 3 4 5 6 7 8 9 / 05 04 03 02 01 00 99

# Acknowledgments

I would like to thank the people who have contributed in various ways to this book. Special appreciation goes to the artists who shared their working processes. George Tooker was wonderfully generous with his time. I thank him for allowing me to photograph his underpainting and for all the technical information that he provided. Stan Berning, Michael Bergt, and Carol Mothner took the time to photograph and chronicle their work in progress—contributing to a greater understanding of the possibilities of the tempera technique. Michael's technical expertise was especially appreciated. Rick Levy spent a great deal of time in my kitchen, photographing my preparations of paint and gesso; his wonderful photographs are the result. Leonard Dufresne, with his passion for art instruction books, gave invaluable advice on the manuscript. My research on egg tempera painting was aided by the rich resources of the Sherman Art Library at Dartmouth College. Thanks to everyone at Watson-Guptill with whom I've worked: I am grateful to Candace Raney who supported this project, Margaret Sobel who helped to make this a better book, Areta Buk for the beautiful design work, and Ellen Greene for her great production work. And thanks to G. for being so patient during all those hours I spent at the computer.

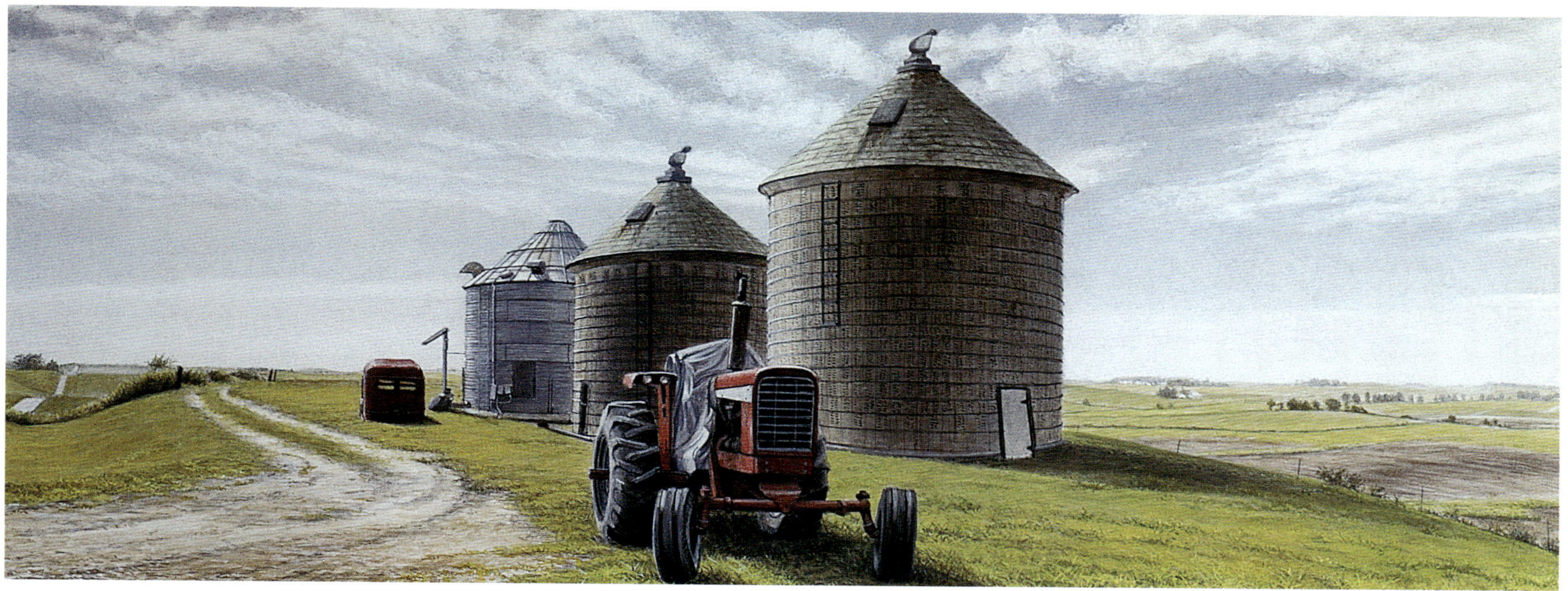

GRAIN BINS, BLAIRSTOWN, IOWA
8½ × 23 inches

# Contents

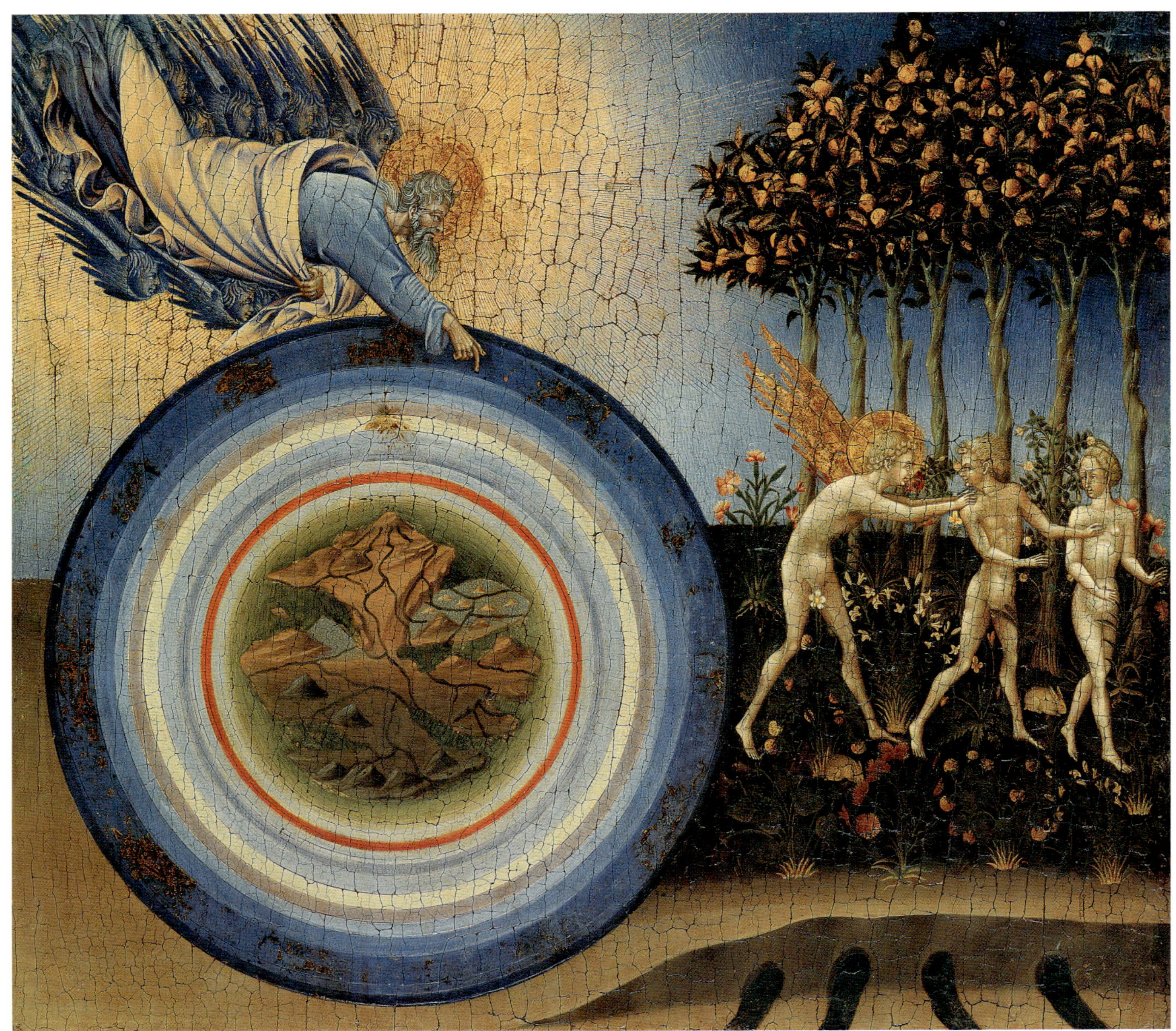

Giovanni di Paolo
## THE CREATION AND THE EXPULSION OF ADAM AND EVE FROM PARADISE

This *predella* panel painted with egg tempera is a masterpiece of Sienese painting. It has remarkable imagery, with many layers of iconographic meanings. God has created the heavens—shown as Dante's celestial wheels—and the earth with its four rivers and its seas. Adam and Eve are being cast out of a paradise of symbolic flowers and fruits.

# Preface

When I first visited Italy in 1971, my great painting loves were the giants of the High Renaissance—Raphael, Titian, Michelangelo, and Caravaggio. At the time, I was painting large narrative figure compositions and looked to these masters for lessons in composition and form, and also in ambition. Seeing humankind as the measure of all things seemed to be the only way to interpret the world.

It was in Siena in 1984 that I discovered that my tastes had changed. I was profoundly moved by the Duccio *Maesta,* and spent enchanted hours in front of fourteenth- and fifteenth-century panel paintings. It was not only the glowing color and clarity of these paintings that attracted me, but also a deep sense of faith. It is odd that I would be interested in this very religious work, since I am a secular and practical person. Perhaps the fact that I started to work more as a landscape painter and spent many hours observing the world around me allowed me to accept the spirituality in our lives. At any rate, I could no longer see human beings as the center of existence.

My enchantment with the *predella* panels also included the process by which they were made. These pictures were painted using egg tempera, before the wide use of oil paint started in the late fifteenth century. For ten years after my visit to Italy, I closely studied early Renaissance panel paintings and thought more and more about learning to use tempera, especially after seeing the "Painting in Renaissance Siena" exhibition at the Metropolitan Museum of Art in New York, in 1988.

In 1994, I finally gathered all the necessary supplies, and with the guidance of the book by Daniel Thompson, *The Practice of Tempera Painting,* began to learn to use egg tempera. I feel greatly rewarded by my foray into this ancient medium. It is an easy and beautiful paint to handle: the color is sparkling, the form is clear, and the details are crisp.

I truly love using egg tempera, and would like to see it have wider use among today's artists. This book is intended to help those interested in this lesser-known medium, by providing clear step-by-step instructions, with lots of illustrations. Don't be intimidated by the seemingly endless preparations before actual painting can begin—they are not difficult. These preparatory steps actually enhance our connection to our work as we make paint and gesso.

Finally, I want to point out that although the book uses my own work as illustrations for the tempera painting process, everyone has a different approach to their painting—each with a unique touch, color sense, and idea of form. My work is intended simply as a guide, not a formula. I hope that this book will encourage you to start on your own journey with egg tempera painting.

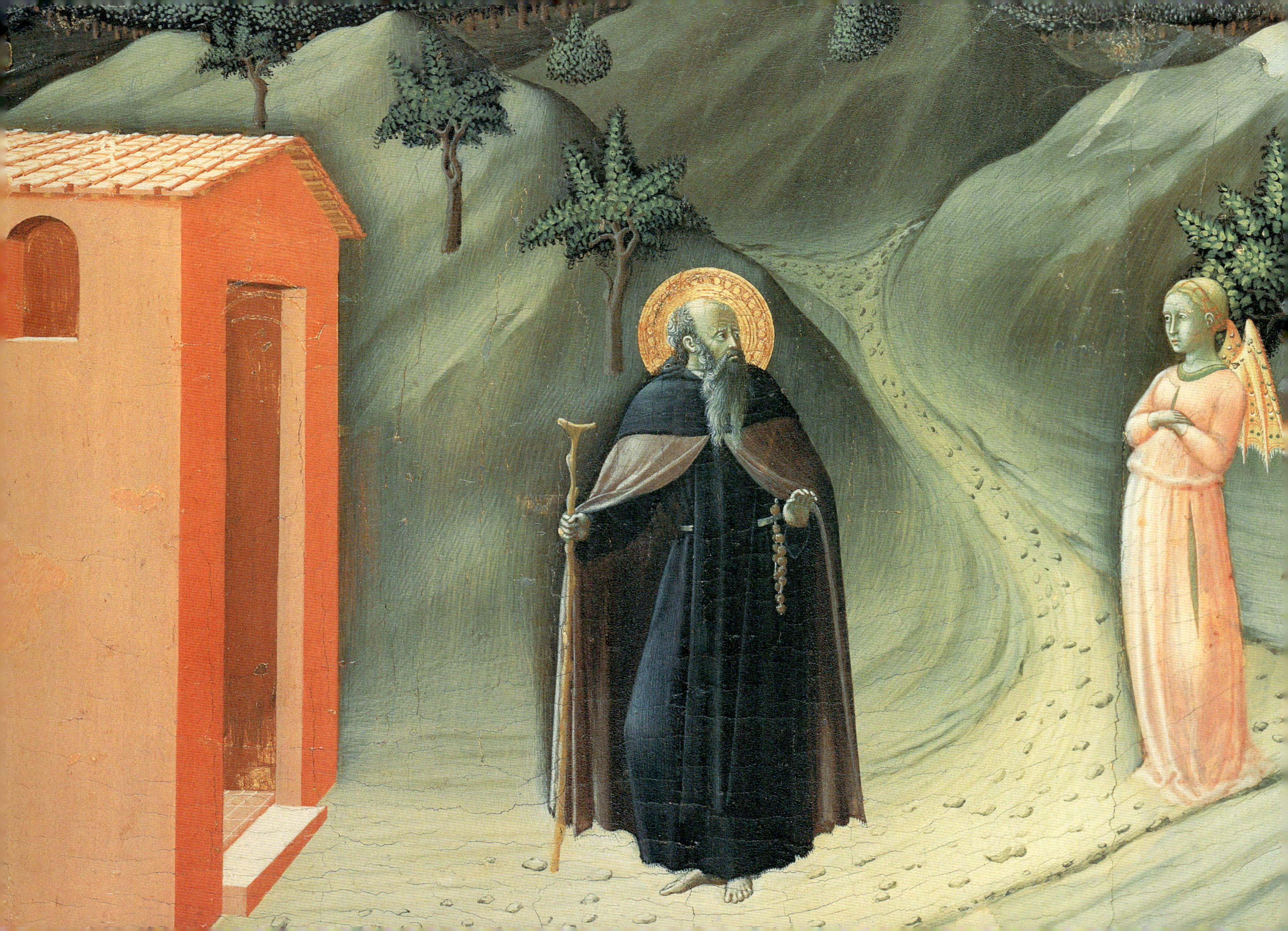

# AN INTRODUCTION TO EGG TEMPERA PAINTING

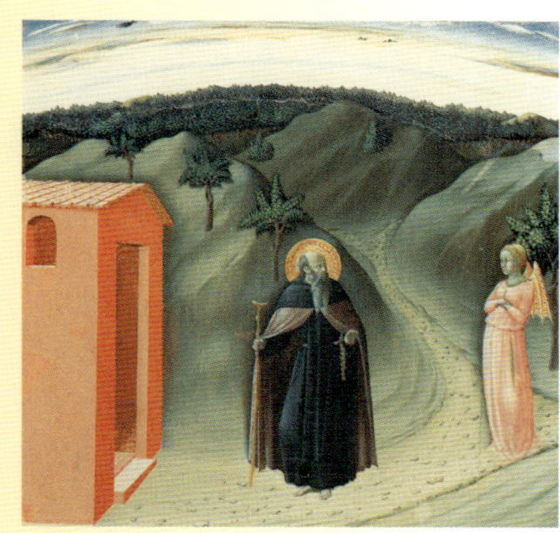

Osservanza Master
TEMPTATION OF
SAINT ANTHONY
1430

The Osservanza Master is my favorite of the Sienese panel painters. I love the drama of his compositions, along with the stark but beautiful landscape, clearly rendered form, and vivid color.

In our personal lives we try to temper our emotions, in industry we temper steel. We attempt to bring out the best qualities in ourselves, and in the materials that we use. The definition of the verb to "temper" derives from the Medieval Latin—*temperare* meaning "blending or mixing." In ancient painting practice, to temper pigment powders meant to mix them with a medium, also called a binder, in order to make a paint that would adhere to a surface. A tempera painting was differentiated from a fresco, in which pigments were applied to a wet plaster wall without a binder, and became embedded in the dried surface.

In order to paint on canvas or a wooden panel, a binding medium is necessary. A binder that is an *emulsion*—a stable mixture of a watery substance and a fatty substance—is now called a *tempera*. Usually oil and water do not mix, as the old adage says. But in some natural substances, such as milk, the juice of the milkweed, and the yolk of an egg, fatty globules are suspended in liquid. Mayonnaise is an example of an artificial emulsion, a combination of egg and oil. There are a variety of natural and artificial temperas used for painting: egg tempera which uses only the yolk of the egg, egg-oil emulsions, emulsions with gum (the hardened sap of trees) and casein (the curd of soured milk). In art history books, the works that are described as tempera paintings, especially early Renaissance Italian panel paintings, are usually egg temperas. For this book, I will use the word "tempera" to mean "egg tempera."

# The Beginnings of Tempera Painting

In Georgia O'Keefe's paintings of the hills of New Mexico, we see multi-colored bands of earth. From ancient times, earth and minerals of varying colors have been pulverized to make pigments for paintings. Since these pigments are simply powders, the pigments have to somehow adhere to the painting surface. The earliest paintings known to us, prehistoric cave paintings, were painted without any binding medium. Earth in a variety of colors was gathered, mixed with water, and applied to the wall. The fortuitous natural action of water on rock created a thin layer of limestone that bound the pigment to the surface, as a natural fresco. Ancient Egyptian painters used a watercolor paint on stone or mud plaster walls, with gum or a glue size (a solution of an animal glue and water) as the binder.

We can imagine that an egg must have seemed just the right thing when artists of the distant past were looking for a binder for their pigments—eggs mixed easily with water and dried to a water-resistant finish. Pliny, writing in the first century AD about Greek painting methods, mentions egg yolk as a binder for wall and panel painting. Unfortunately, there are no surviving panel paintings from classical Greece or Rome. The earliest existing egg tempera panels are the Fayum mummy portraits, painted in Egypt by Greek artists from the first through fourth centuries AD. I had thought that these beautiful paintings were all painted with encaustic (a paint made with color pigment and melted beeswax), but several were done in egg tempera.

Throughout the Byzantine and medieval periods, most painting was done for manuscripts or on walls. The exceptions were icons—devotional images painted on wooden panels. These icons were painted with either a tempera made up of beeswax, alkali (a substance that will neutralize an acid, such as baking soda) and size, or with egg tempera. There were clear rules for the painting of these images which had religious significance—for instance, colors were applied from dark to light. Contemporary icon painters continue to use egg tempera, since the egg is a symbol of renewed life.

The study of art history asks the *why* of paintings; what was their purpose—religious, civic, or personal. This social history determined the *how*—the technical history. In Italy, it wasn't until a change in the church liturgy in 1215 when the doctrine of transubstantiation (the transformation of the bread and wine into the body and blood of Christ) was formalized and the priest turned his back on the congregation to conceal the mystery of transformation, that altarpieces painted on wooden panels came into use as a proper background for the elevation of the Host. Also, towards the end of the thirteenth century there was an upsurge of religious feeling which resulted in the construction of many new churches in towns throughout Italy, all requiring altarpieces which would exalt the parishioners by illustrating the stories of Christ, the Virgin, and the saints. There was a great deal of new artistic activity—the painting workshops were busy with many orders for panel paintings to be used as altarpieces. The medium for these paintings was egg tempera.

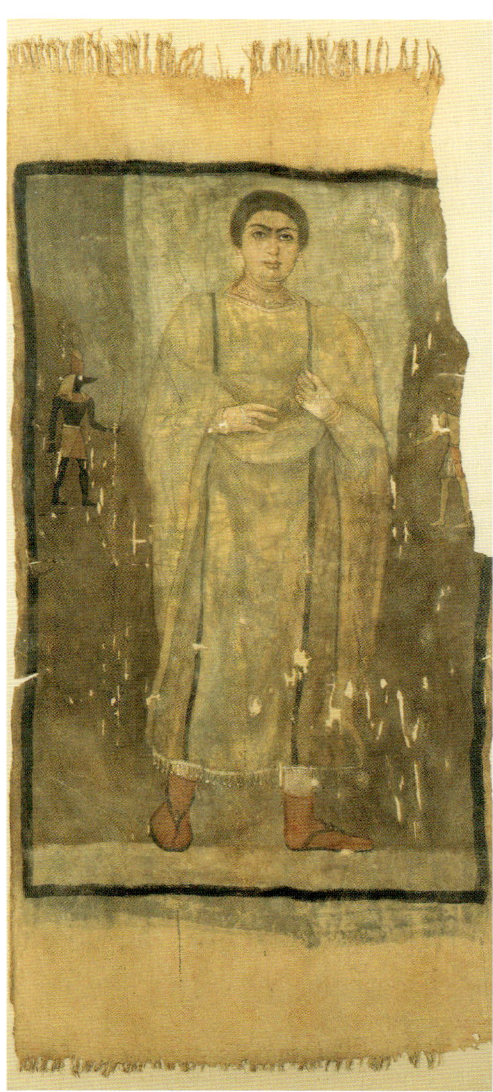

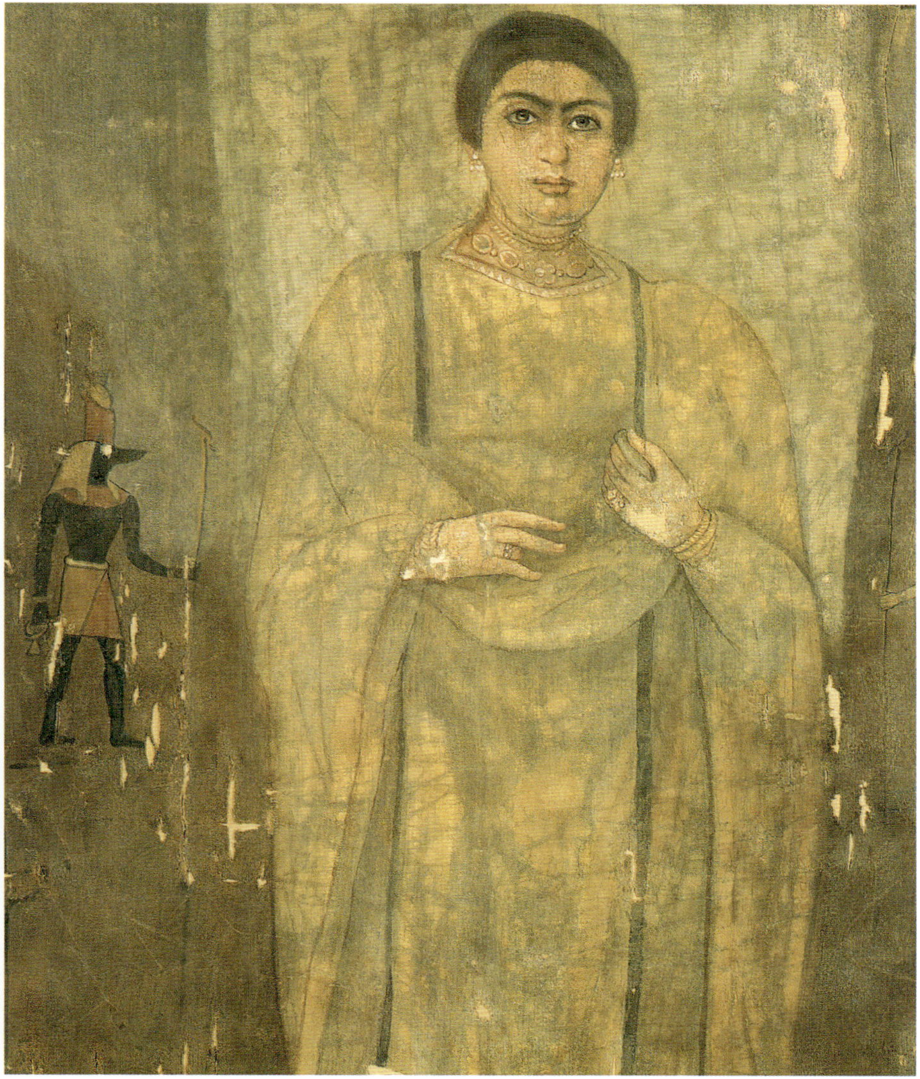

This is one of the earliest examples of egg tempera painting. The portrait is painted in a classic style. Shrouds were often placed on top of mummy masks.

# Italian Panel Painting of the Early Renaissance

The panel paintings made in Italy from the late thirteenth through the mid-fifteenth centuries are, to my eyes, some of the most beautiful and affecting images ever painted. There is magic in these paintings that illicits a different response than the wonder produced by the palpable life in a Velázquez oil painting. Instead there is a widening-of-the-eyes type of marvel at a world ordered by faith. In these works, color is lively and rich, form is simple and clear, and there are wondrous details in the gilding, architectural depictions, and landscape. The portrayal of human emotion, though sometimes exaggerated, seems somehow powerfully true. Practically all the artwork produced during this period was of religious subjects, and paintings were seen to have an important function in the religious life of the community. Because one of the primary purposes of these paintings was to tell stories, all aspects of the painting support the narrative structure. In the late thirteenth century, the clergyman John of Genoa's *Catholicon* explained that there were three reasons for the use of images in churches: as an instructional tool for illiterate parishioners; as an aid to memory, because images remain in the mind more vividly than words; and to enhance devotion. The worshiper can read the story of a saint's miracles in the series of paintings on a horizontal predella, or altar step, which is under the main panels of the altarpiece. Predella panels, with their carefully wrought and intimate images, are for me the most wonderful features of the paintings of this period.

During this period, painters were considered artisans; they worked on commission, fulfilling very specific contracts that stipulated the subjects of the paintings, the materials to be used, and the amount of work to be completed by the master's (the head of the workshop's) hand. Yet, as Cennino Cennini, who traces his painterly lineage back to Giotto, wrote in *The Craftsman's Handbook* (a manual for artists written about 1400) the praiseworthy painter was the one who entered the profession with enthusiasm, devotion, and an elevation of spirit. His book remains a valuable source of information and much of what we know of painting techniques of the period come from Cennini. Modern high-tech analyses of paintings of the period support his descriptions of panel preparation, pigments, gilding, and egg tempera painting technique.

The panels for tempera painting were generally made of poplar and were quite thick because poplar is a soft wood. They were prepared with two types of gesso: *gesso grosso,* and *gesso sottile,* a coarse underlayer and a fine finishing layer, sometimes with an open-weave linen cloth laid on the panel before the gesso was applied. The gesso sottile was laid on in at least eight thin coats on the flat part of the panels. The artist then indicated the composition of the painting with an underdrawing in ink, using a brush or a pen. He scratched the gesso lightly to delineate the areas to be gilded. Sometimes the painters had to make their own pigments, something we luckily don't have to do. The pigments were carefully ground with water and mixed with egg yolk that acted as a binder. This resulting paint was then thinned with more water.

When we look closely at a fifteenth-century egg tempera painting, we see that the paint was applied with layers of discrete brush strokes; the form is described in parallel or hatched lines. This technique was determined by the properties of the tempera medium—if applied properly, it dries to the touch almost immediately, making blending impossible. The color was layered gradually, sometimes in three different values over the white gesso ground, sometimes over a different color that would influence the final color. The translucence of the tempera allowed for this mixing of color in the eye of the viewer, or "optical mixing." For example, a purple robe might be underpainted with yellow to add interesting variations of color; and when painting flesh, the practice was to underpaint with a green earth color to create cool half-tones.

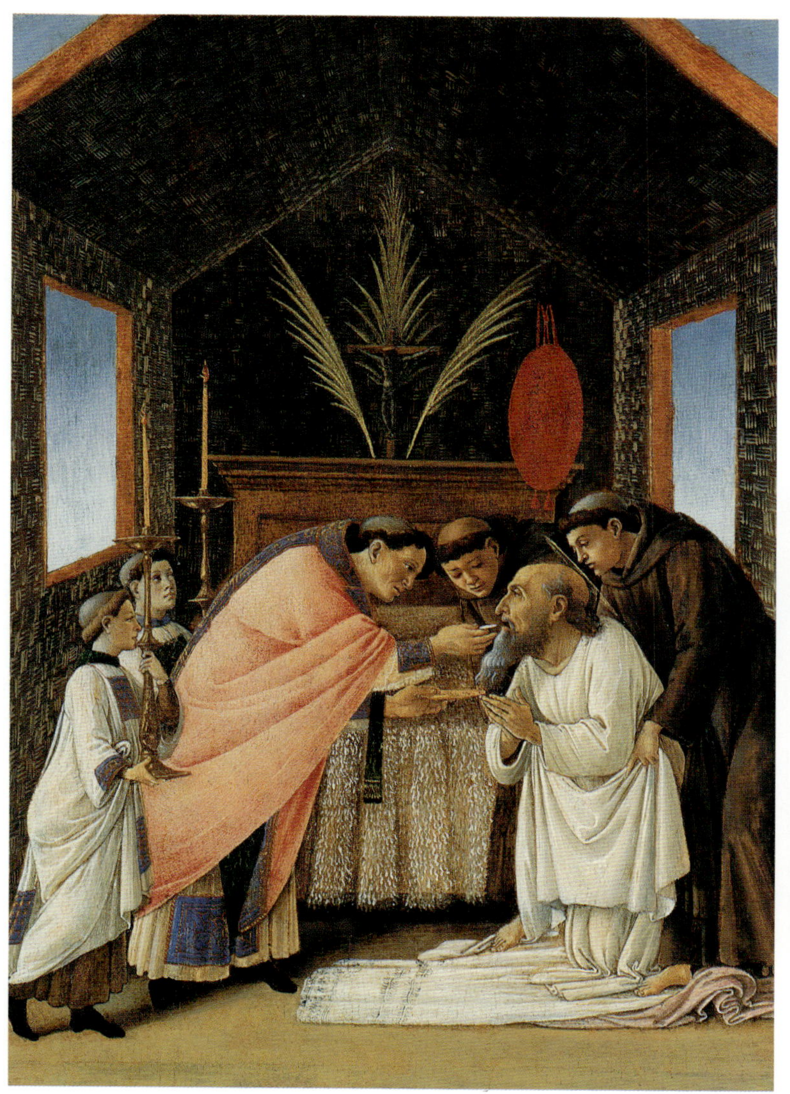

This deliberate, linear technique was the perfect one for the spiritual, conceptual approach of medieval and early Renaissance artists who practiced an art of ideas, not of appearances. As the fifteenth century advanced and humanism became the dominant cultural force, artists looked for a way to enhance the naturalism of their work. They wanted to be able to blend colors and soften the edges of forms. Starting in the early fifteenth century, drying oils (oils that don't stay tacky forever, but dry into a waterproof film) came into use which allowed for easier manipulation of paint. At first, oil paint was used in a mixed technique with tempera—tempera underpaintings were glazed with pigments ground in oil or egg-oil emulsions. But the use of egg tempera gradually declined, and after 1600, oil paint was used almost exclusively.

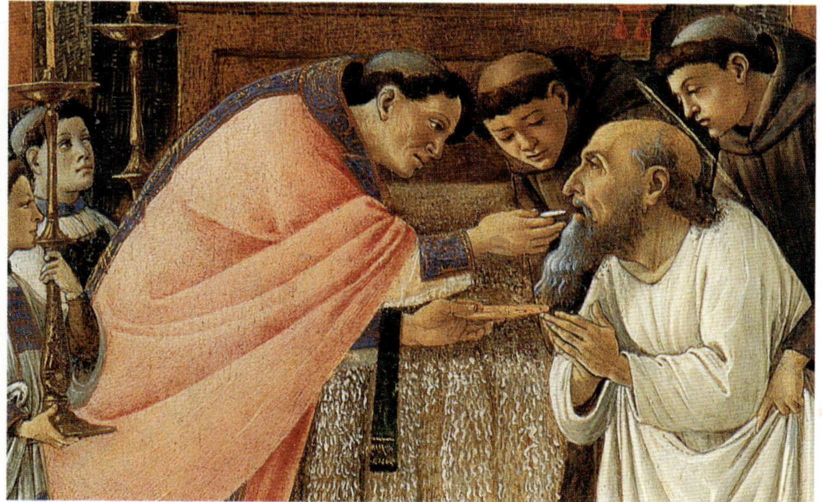

Botticelli

THE LAST COMMUNION OF SAINT JEROME

This small devotional panel was painted for a merchant. Its exquisite refinement marks the height of the tempera painting technique.

# Egg Tempera in the Twentieth Century

During the mid-nineteenth century, there was a revival of interest in historical painting methods. In 1844, Mary Merrifield published the first translation in English of Cennini's treatise on painting. Sir Charles Eastlake wrote *Materials for a History of Oil Painting* in 1847, citing many manuscript sources from the Renaissance. Another translation of Cennini by Christiana J. Herringham appeared in 1899, sparking a resurgence of interest in the technique of egg tempera painting.

In 1933, Yale University Press published yet another translation of Cennini by Daniel Thompson. Thompson also wrote an egg tempera manual, *The Practice of Tempera Painting,* published in 1936, which

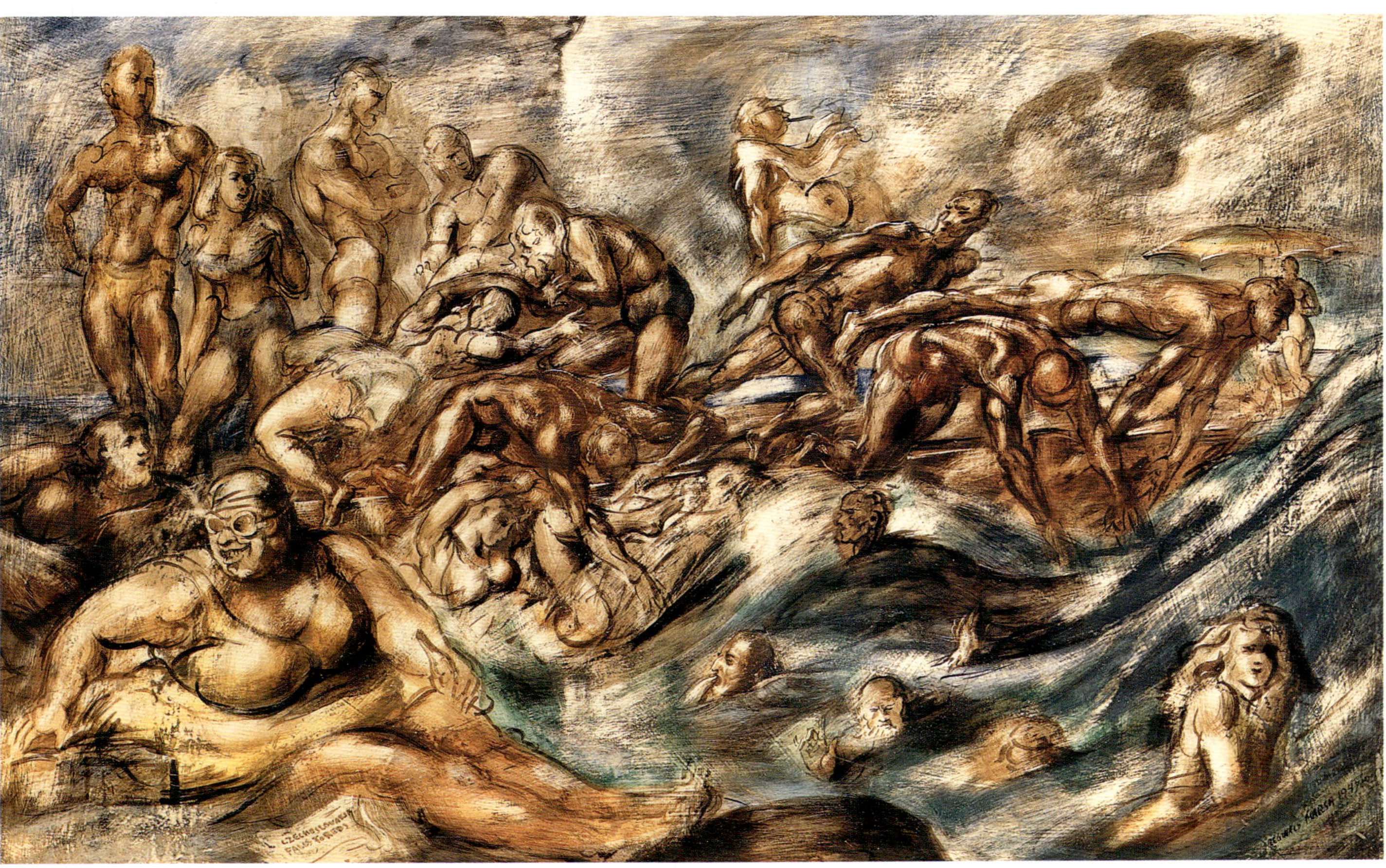



Reginald Marsh
CONEY ISLAND
BEACH
1947

This is an example of a painterly use of tempera where the paint is transparent and applied very fluidly. In some areas the paint has been scratched or wiped away.

made Cennini's traditional egg tempera technique accessible to American artists. Both Thomas Hart Benton and Reginald Marsh used tempera before this date, but they handled the medium fluidly, more like watercolor. Peter Hurd, an artist from New Mexico who studied with N.C. Wyeth and married his daughter, learned to use egg tempera from Cennini's text in 1935. He in turn taught the technique to Andrew Wyeth, his young brother-in-law. Wyeth's primary medium, along with watercolor, is egg tempera. He was originally attracted to the medium by the naturalness of the tempera color. His temperas are initially painted broadly and are then built slowly with many layers of paint. The tempera medium, along with drybrush watercolor, allows Wyeth full play with both fluidity and precision, as well as his combination of abstraction and realism.

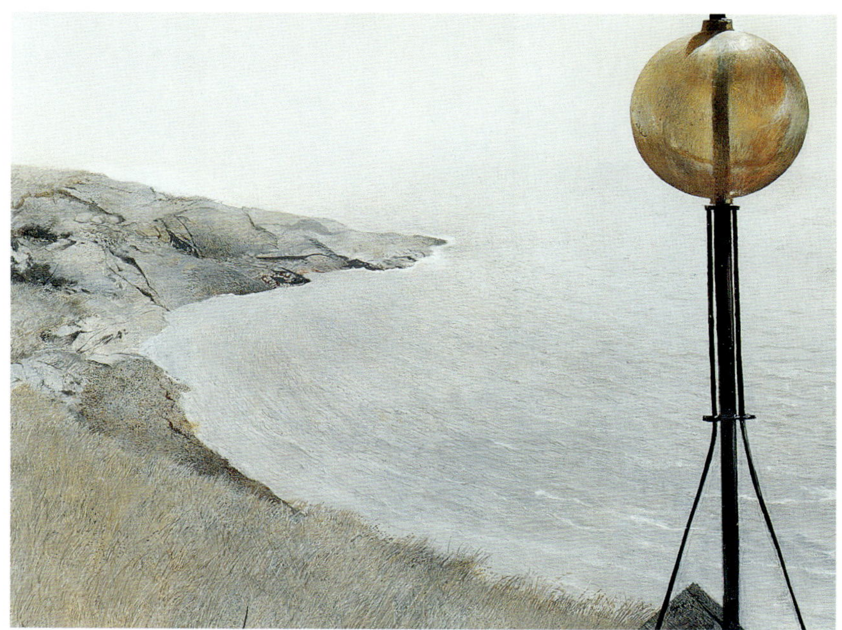

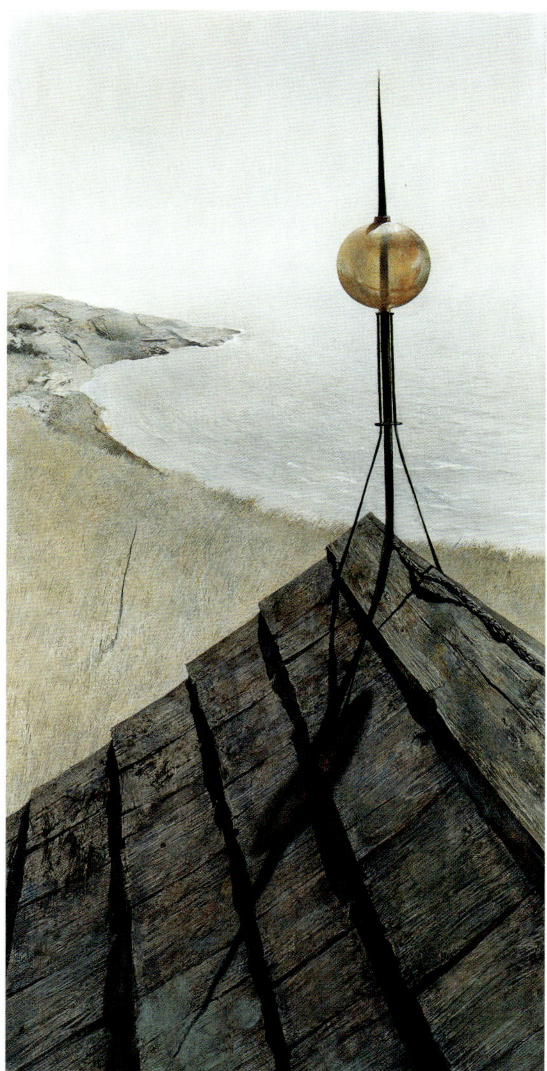



The tempera technique is used to great effect in this strongly abstracted composition. Note the translucence of the ball of the lightning rod, the transparent grays of the water, and the textures of the roof created by scumbles and by scratching the paint.

The three most important twentieth-century artists who have worked almost exclusively in egg tempera are Paul Cadmus, Jared French, and George Tooker. The three were friends who passed along painting ideas to each other. French learned the technique of egg tempera in 1939, and introduced it to Cadmus. After 1940, both artists worked solely in this medium, except for some recent paintings by Cadmus in acrylic. George Tooker first worked with tempera while studying with Reginald Marsh at the Art Students League, but like Marsh he used tempera in more of a watercolor fashion. When he met Cadmus and French in 1944, they told him about the Thompson book, *The Practice of Tempera Painting*. He soon found that this seemingly demanding medium suited him perfectly, and since then all of his paintings have been in egg tempera.

All three of these artists work primarily with the figure, but each has very different sensibilities. Paul Cadmus is a remarkably fluid draftsman, and his paintings are pulsing with contemporary life and energy. He uses a robust crosshatching technique which he used in oils before he began to use tempera, and he models forms with great animation. Jared French builds his classical forms much more delicately, since he is interested in creating an archetypal reality. His color is rich, saturated, and symbolic. A sense of a reality beyond the one pictured also pervades the paintings of George Tooker. His beautifully simplified figures, bathed in glowing light, are reticent yet allude to a spiritual life.

The egg tempera technique has worked very well for these three different painters. The paintings were made on gessoed pressed-wood panels and the color layered by individual strokes of the brush. Contrary to its supposed difficulty, egg tempera has made picture making easier for them. For George Tooker it is ideal because "it is a slow method that allows for changes, modifications of color and form, and a slow development." Cadmus, French, and Tooker, though not in the artistic mainstream, are thoroughly modern artists who, along with Wyeth, have brought the fifteenth-century practice of egg tempera painting solidly into the twentieth century.

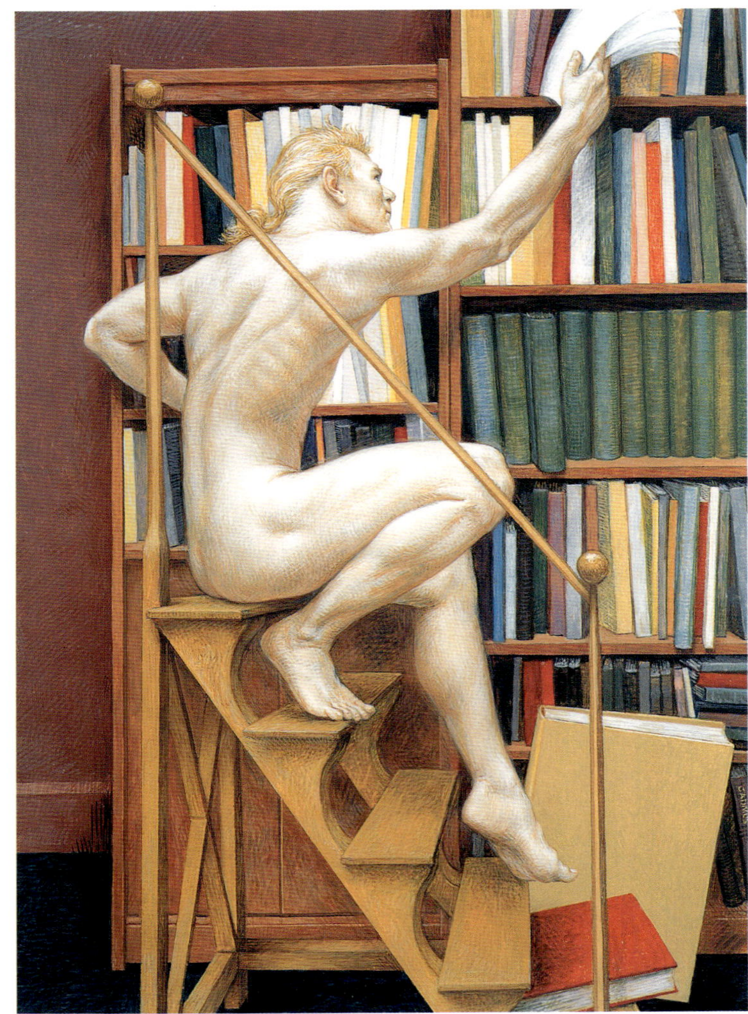

Paul Cadmus
BOOK BUFF
1994

Cadmus uses distinct strokes of the brush to build form, which enliven the surface of the painting.

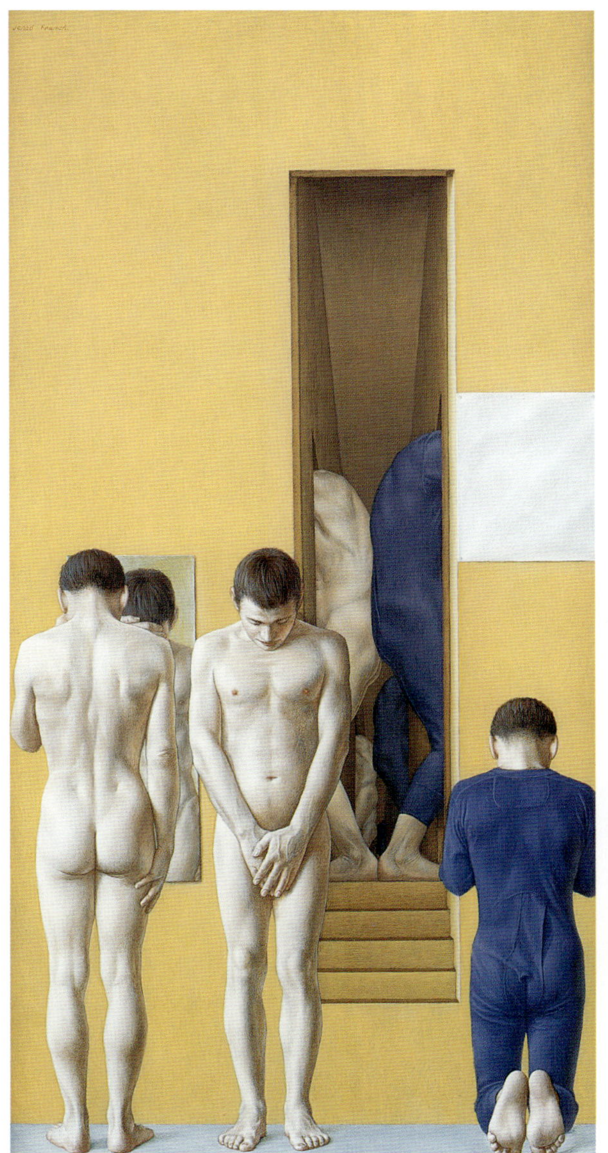

Jared French
EVASION
1947

The brilliant color of this painting is almost startling and, along with the mysterious figures, points to a personal symbolism.

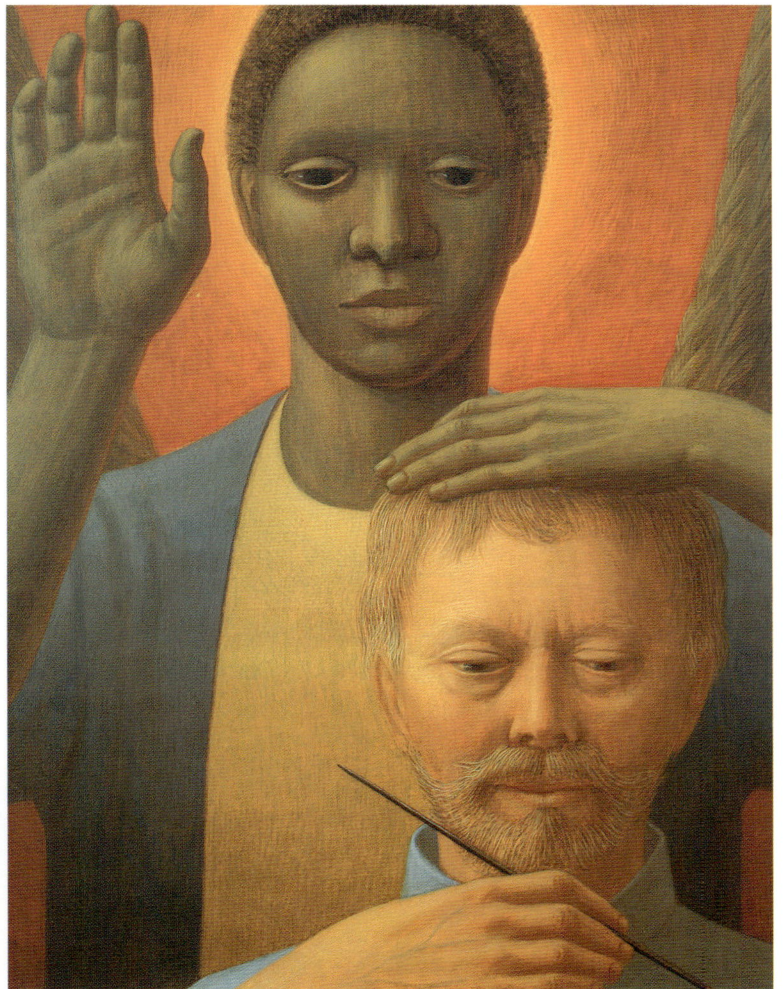

George Tooker
DARK ANGEL
1996

Tooker's brush strokes follow the form of the figures. They are open enough to give the skin the effect of translucence and depth.

# The Distinctive Qualities of Tempera Painting

First of all I would like to quote George Tooker, who has told many people that "egg tempera is not difficult, it's just slow." Once you get used to its properties, tempera is deeply pleasurable to work with. I still remember the excitement of layering color on the underdrawing when I was working on my first egg tempera—a Colorado landscape with hay bales and mountains. With the application of thin layers of paint of different values and hues, beautiful color was emerging. Because this water-based paint dried almost immediately, I was able to quickly paint layers of colors, each layer subtly changing the color. It was similar to my first experience in a darkroom, watching an image magically appear on blank paper.

Egg tempera does have some real limitations, however. It is a paint that dries quickly, so is best-handled with lines and crosshatching, similar to a drawing technique. The soft blending that is so easy with slow-drying oil paint is not possible with the quick drying tempera. Oil paint is perfectly suited for thick impasto effects, but egg tempera will crack or peel if used thickly. Tempera's tonality is somewhere between that of oil paint and gouache—it cannot achieve the rich darks of oil, but its colors are deeper and more brilliant than the blond tones of gouache. It is not a medium for bravura or *alla prima* brushwork—although some artists have used it in that unconventional way—but the unique depth and luminosity of egg tempera color is lost if the paint is not layered. And most important, it is not an improvisational medium—egg tempera works best within a conceptual framework: with a clear underdrawing and an understanding of how to make light, form, and space. This is not to say that changes can never be made—color can be easily altered by overpainting, and mistakes can be wiped off with a damp rag—but tempera is a medium that encourages planning. It reminds us that painting is more than self-expression; it is also a craft and a discipline.

The medium whose technique is most similar to that of egg tempera is drybrush watercolor, which was used in the past by Albrecht Dürer and also by contemporary artist Andrew Wyeth. Drybrush watercolor is handled slowly; the color is laid down with the point of a brush wiped almost dry. Egg tempera, another water-based paint, is also handled with a dry brush, but the layering of color in the tempera technique gives the color great depth. Also, it is translucent rather than transparent like watercolor, allowing for deeper color effects. And tempera is a much more forgiving medium than watercolor—it is quite easy to correct any mistakes.

When I first began painting with tempera, I took to it right away—it was so easy to manipulate color, and I loved its clear form and precise detail. I must admit that I was prepared for the paint handling of tempera by my previous use of gouache (another fast-drying water-based paint) and drypoint (prints made from a copper plate on which I developed a drawing by careful crosshatching with a diamond-point needle.) Tempera gives quick results. Because the paint dries almost immediately, my brush can move rapidly over the panel. The underpainting doesn't mix or lift off with new layers, as it does with gouache, allowing for a rapid layering of color. But tempera is quick on a small scale—when I want to make a six-foot painting, I use oil paint.

I certainly don't think that egg tempera is suited only to representational painters; anyone who loves color and has a careful approach to their work would enjoy this medium. For example, I think that it would be an excellent medium for minimalist abstraction. Style should not be a determining factor in the use of tempera; it is more a matter of the sensibility of the artist. Anyone who has a deliberate and meditative approach to art making will enjoy using egg tempera.

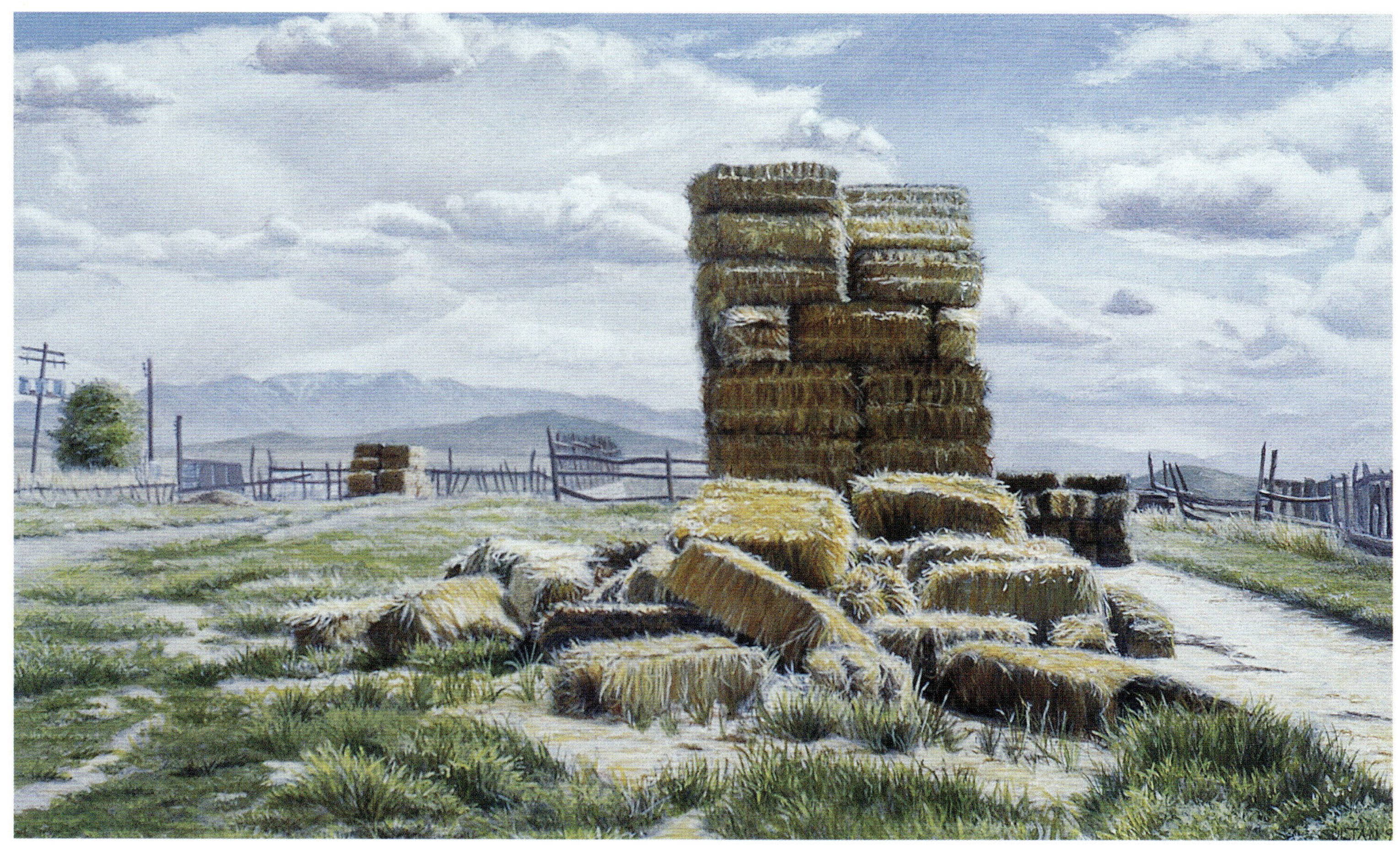

HAY, DELTA, COLORADO
7 1/2 × 12 5/8 inches

This is the first painting that I completed using egg tempera. The translucency of the tempera medium echoed the translucency of the sky, so I was able to achieve a quality of light and depth in the sky that is impossible to reproduce in *alla prima* oil painting. It was so easy to paint the textures of hay and grass because the paint dried right away—each stroke of color remained distinct. I then unified these distinct strokes by painting a very thin layer of color over them.

We've grown accustomed to the widespread use of plastic in our lives and it is ubiquitous in the agricultural landscape. In this setting, plastic is actually quite beautiful because of its brilliant colors and translucency. Egg tempera is the perfect medium for conveying the effect of light passing through an object, since light passes through the layers of paint.

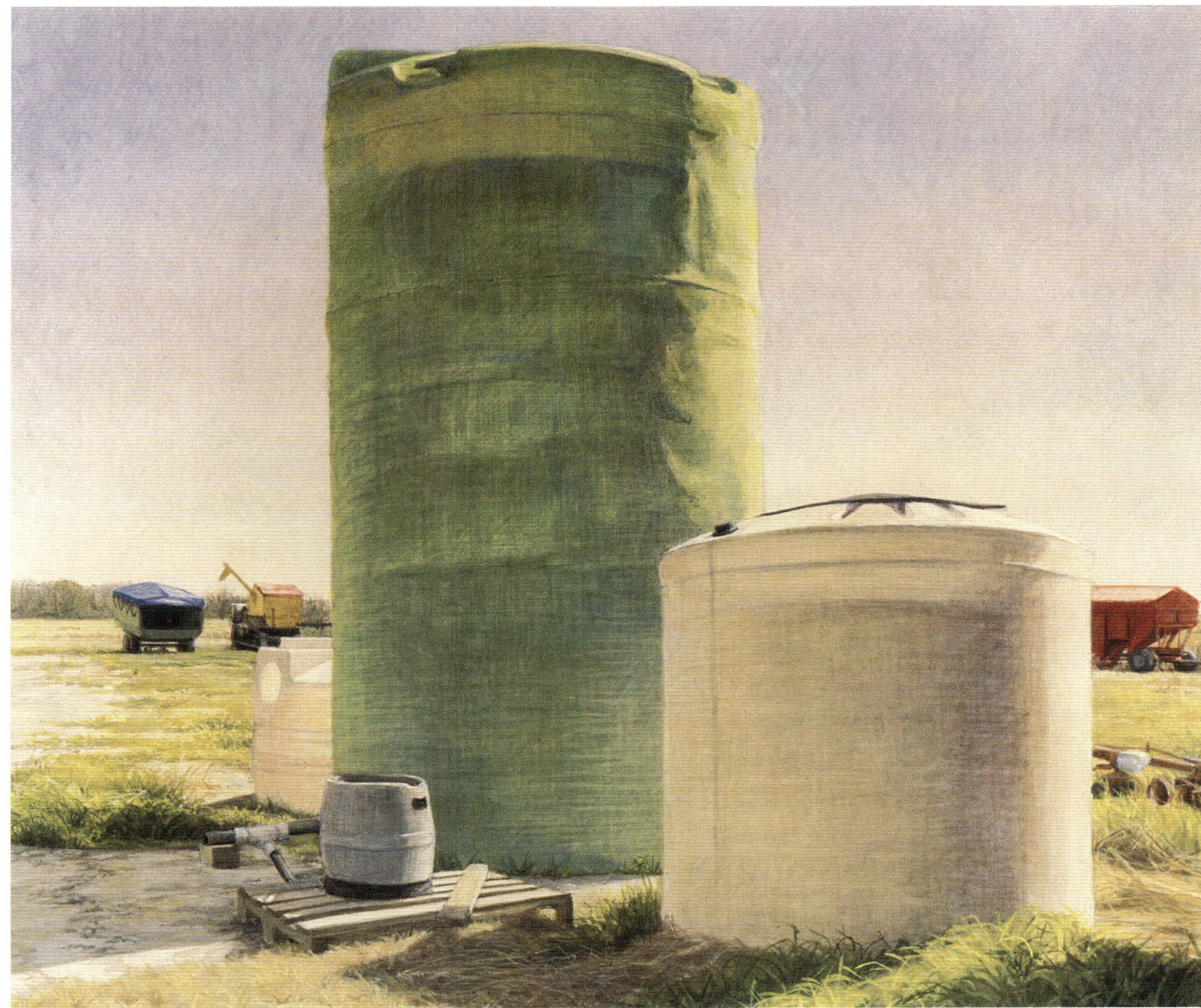

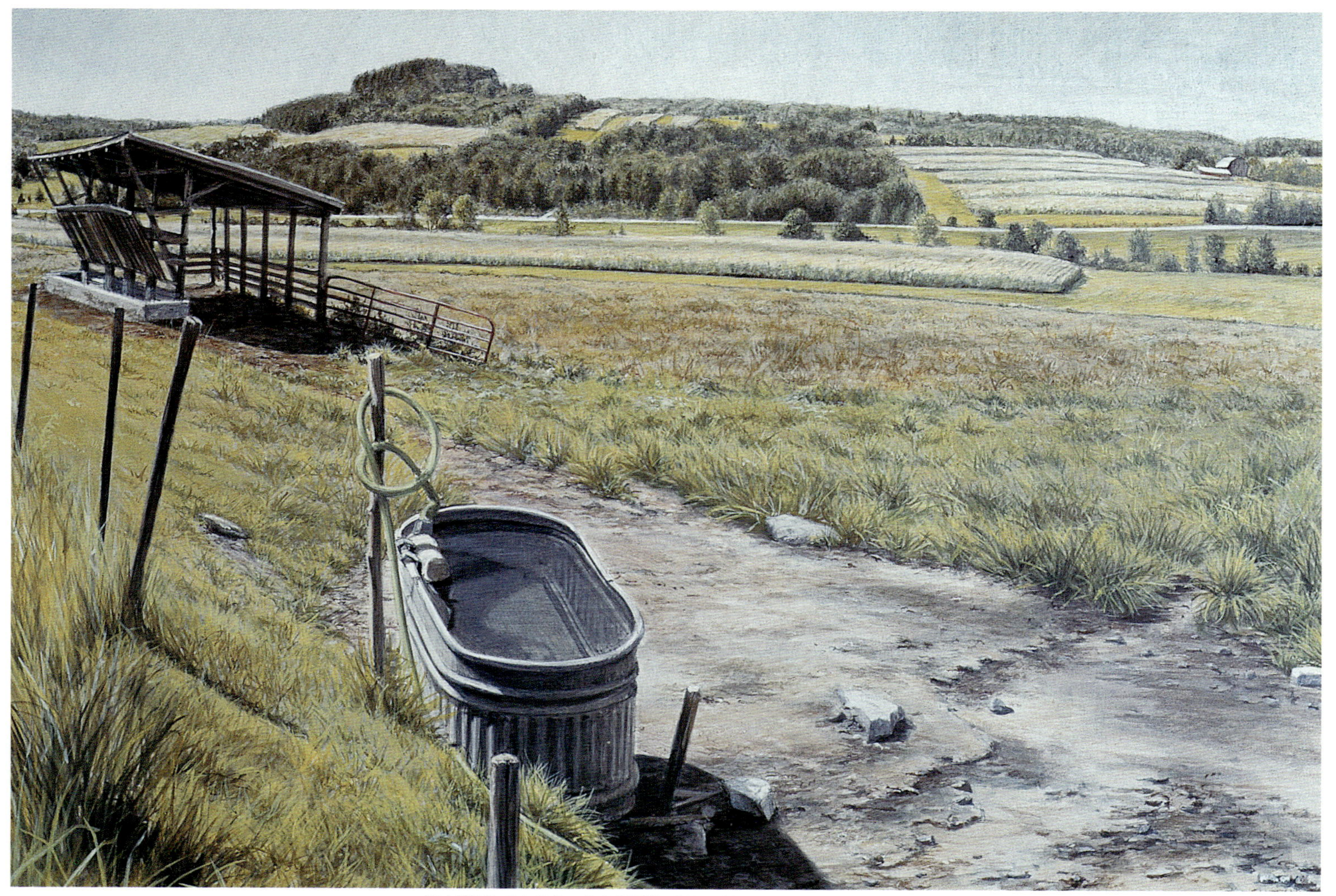

WATER TANK, SOUTH PEACHAM, VERMONT
10 × 15 inches

In this painting, the problem of painting the varied layers of water was made simple by the quick-drying translucency of the paint. I was able to play with lighter and darker tones, mimicking the reflective and transparent qualities of water.

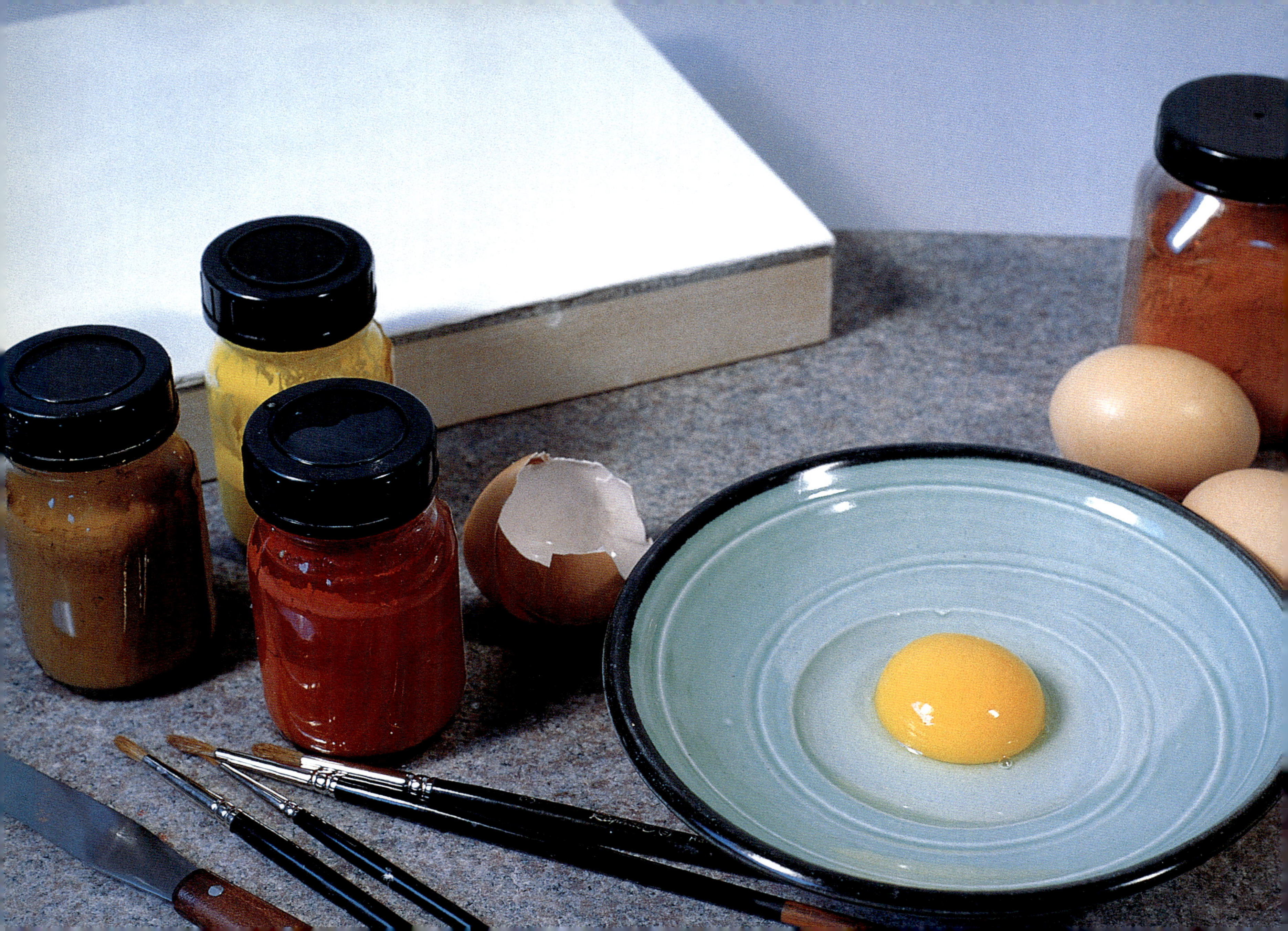

# GETTING STARTED: MATERIALS FOR TEMPERA PAINTING

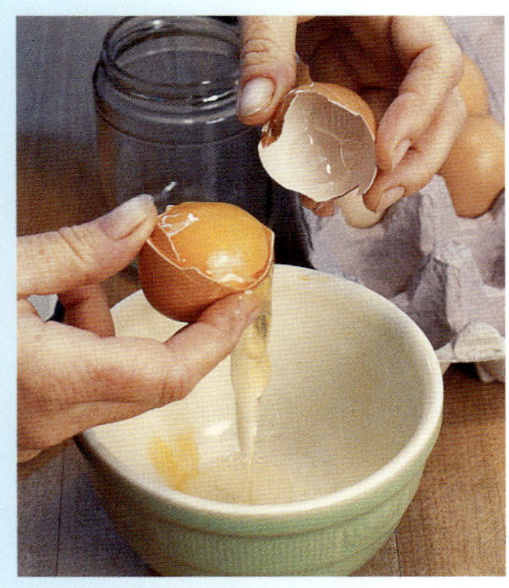

Opposite: Some of the materials needed for egg tempera are an egg yolk, brushes, pigments, and a gessoed panel. Above: The key ingredient.

I have always loved looking at pigments in art supply stores—the rich and brilliant colors are so enticing since they are not hidden in tubes. Using the wide range of colors available in powdered pigments is one of the great pleasures of tempera painting.

In addition to buying pigments, working with egg tempera requires a small investment in some new art supplies. After this initial expenditure, egg tempera is a very thrifty medium. I am still using the same pigments that I ground in water five years ago. The chalk and gelatin used for making gesso are inexpensive, as are the pressed-wood panels. Brushes will be the most expensive items of your egg tempera supplies—but they are worth it since you will have much better results with high quality brushes.

Tempera also requires an investment of time for the preparation of pigments and panels. Although at first they may seem daunting, once you get used to these processes, they become a simple matter. If you're not quite ready for grinding pigment and making gesso, you may also choose to use some of the ready-made products on the market to get a feel for the medium. If you find that you enjoy the egg tempera technique, you may want to prepare your own pigments and panels.

# Pigments for Tempera

During the Renaissance, the number of pigments available to artists was limited. There were natural colors from earth or mineral sources, artificially prepared colors, and organic colors from plants or animals. Yellow ochre and green earth are earth colors. Ultramarine blue is an example of a mineral source; the pigment is extracted by a rather complicated process from the very expensive semi-precious stone lapis lazuli, imported from Afghanistan. Vermilion, the most important red used in the Renaissance, was artificially produced by heating mercury and sulfur. Blacks made from charcoal and the lake pigments or dyes made from insects or dyewoods, such as rose madder, are examples of organic pigments.

Today we are fortunate to have hundreds of natural and manufactured pigments at our disposal, and they are relatively inexpensive. We now have the manufactured ultramarine blue, instead of the expensive mineral lapis lazuli. If you are interested in trying historic pigments, many of them are available from Kremer Pigments (see Sources), including various grades of lapis lazuli.

I don't make a fuss over pigments; I use the same basic palette that I use for oil or gouache, with the addition of some interesting earth colors. It is important that the white that we use for egg tempera is an opaque pigment. Lead white was the traditional pigment used for tempera, but it is extremely toxic, so it has been replaced by titanium white, which is opaque. For black, I use ivory black. I find the cadmium colors indispensable because of their brilliance and opacity, and use a range of reds, yellows, and oranges, as well as a rich cadmium brown, which is reddish in hue. The cadmium pigments must be handled carefully because they are toxic. I use four blues: ultramarine, cobalt, cerulean, and manganese, a very cool intense blue, especially useful for skies. I most often mix my greens, but I also use chrome oxide green, an opaque color with good tinting strength. Earth colors are wonderful for tempera, and I use yellow and brown ochres, raw and burnt siennas, and umbers. Kremer Pigments has a long list of earth colors; they are cheap and fun to experiment with. You will find that some colors are transparent and have low tinting strength, so they are useful for glazes (or, in the case of green earth, underpainting flesh), but are not as good for color mixing. The choice of colors is very personal— as you paint, you will get a sense of which colors work well for you.

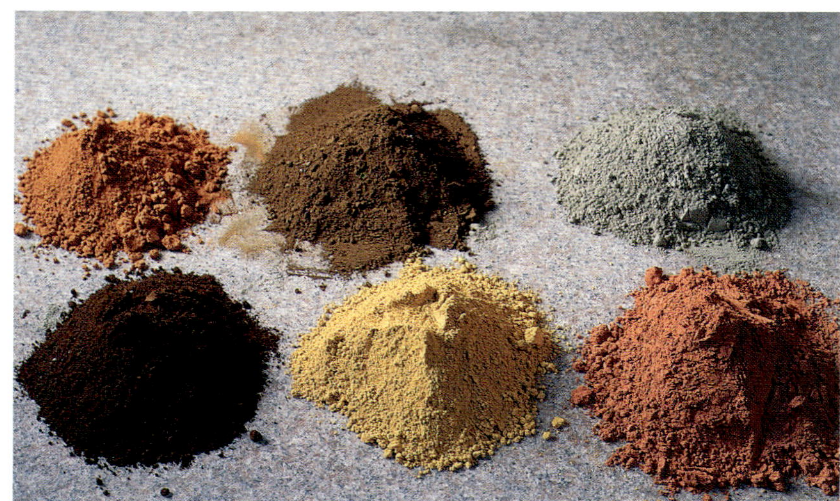

Here is a selection of earth colors (from Kremer Pigments) for the tempera palette. Clockwise from upper left: French ochre red, satin ochre German, green earth Italian, Venetian red Italian, yellow ochre Italian, and burnt umber cypress.

# Grinding the Pigments

To work with tempera, powdered color pigments must be ground with water to make a pigment paste. Some artists, such as George Tooker and Paul Cadmus, mix their pigments with water on a white glazed ceramic tile as needed each day, using a palette knife as the grinding implement. You can also use a piece of ground glass. I prefer to have my color paste ready for daily use, so I grind my pigments with water using a muller and slab and store them in wide-mouthed glass jars. The grinding isn't difficult because the pigments available today have fairly fine particles. One exception is the earth colors, which can be a bit gritty. Some pigments are toxic and hazardous, such as the cadmium colors, but even with non-hazardous colors you should always wear a dust mask and rubber gloves when handling pigments.

To make the pigment paste, you need either a mortar and pestle or a muller and slab. I live in Vermont, where there are many granite quarries, so it was easy and cheap for me to get a granite slab—ideal for grinding pigments. You can also use a piece of ground plate glass or a piece of marble, although it is a much softer stone. The slab should be about sixteen inches square. The muller, made out of glass, has a flat rough surface; it should be at least three inches in diameter. A ceramic mortar and pestle, which are readily available in art supply stores, are fine tools for the job of grinding colors but their smaller size requires working with a smaller amount of pigment. If you buy a mortar and pestle from a supplier other than an art store, be sure that the bowl and the end of the pestle are *un*glazed for proper grinding.

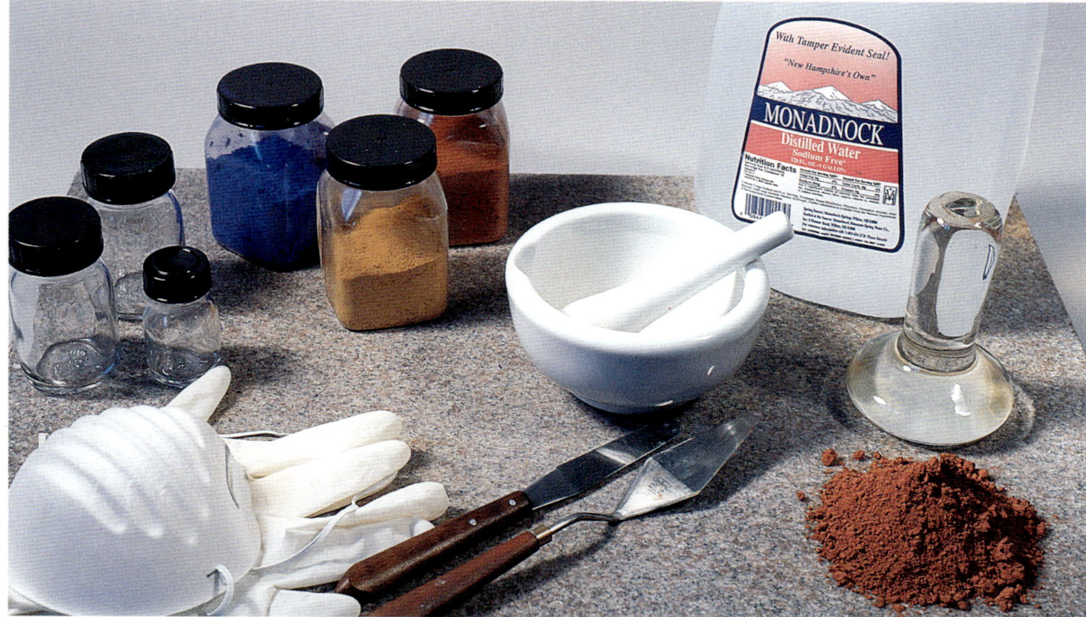

Materials for grinding pigments (clockwise from upper left): Wide-mouthed glass jars for containing the pigments ground in water, plastic jars containing powdered pigments, a mortar and pestle, distilled water, muller, a pile of powdered pigment, palette knives, dust mask, and rubber gloves; all lying on top of a slab of granite.

Since ground pigments can be stored in jars for a very long time, it is a good idea to use distilled water for the grinding process. If your water contains minerals or bacteria, they could contaminate the pigments. To use the mortar and pestle, put a couple of tablespoons of pigment into the mortar, and add a few drops of distilled water, enough to make a thin paste. Using the pestle with some pressure, grind the pigment paste (don't just stir it) for a few minutes. I usually grind each pigment for about five minutes. You want to have the pigment thoroughly blended with the water. If you are grinding an earth color, feel a bit of the paste between two fingers to be sure that it is smooth—if not, continue grinding.

If you are using a muller and slab, you can put a few tablespoons of pigment on the slab. Add distilled water to make a thin paste, and work the muller in a slightly rocking, circular motion over the pigment mixture. The paste will spread over the surface of the slab, so move your muller over the whole surface, round and round. If the pigment paste builds up on the edges of the muller, scrape it off with your palette knife and place it on the slab. As with the mortar and pestle, you should be grinding and not simply mixing the pigment.

Gather the ground pigment with a palette knife and put it into a wide-mouthed glass jar. Cover the pigment paste with distilled water—this prevents the paste from drying out, in which case you would have to regrind the pigment. Wash the grinding implements thoroughly with soap and water after each color is ground. An abrasive cleanser used with a scouring pad will clean off any pigment remaining on the slab and muller.

The only color that I've found difficult to grind is ultramarine blue. The pigment gets gooey when water is added to it, and it settles into a hard mass in the jar. So, you can grind it at the beginning of each workday, or, like me, buy a color concentrate—the pigment ground in water with a dispersal agent added to keep the pigment fluid. I also use a titanium white color concentrate, since I was told that titanium was difficult to grind. These concentrates are available from Kremer Pigments and Guerra Paint and Pigment.

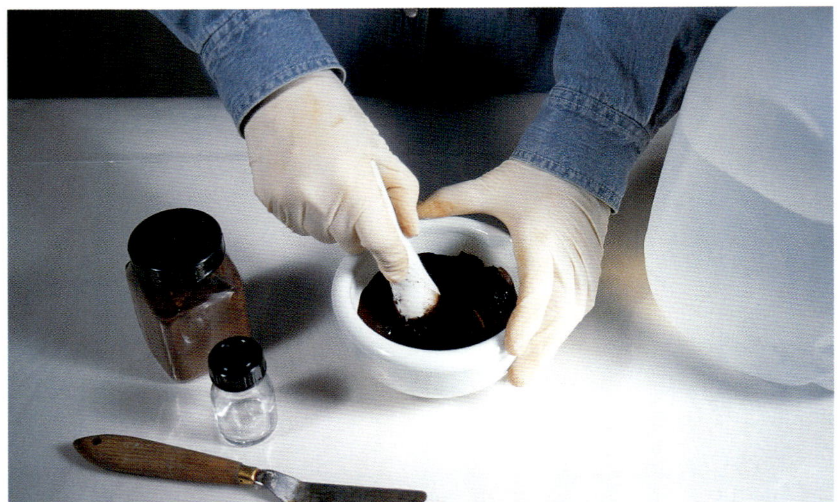

Grinding pigment with a mortar and pestle.

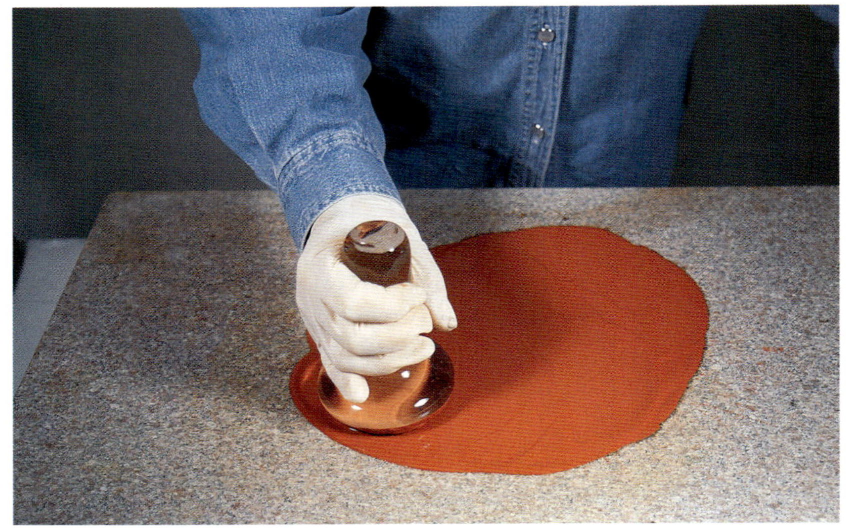

Grinding pigment with a muller and slab.

# Painting Materials

We all have our favorite painting materials: the kind of palette, shape of brush, type of rag or paper towel that we like to use. Although I offer some guidelines for the materials that you will need for tempera, they can be adjusted for your particular preference.

Since tempera paint is used very thinly, the best palette to use is one designed for watercolor that has separate wells for holding paint, along with a flat area for additional color mixing. If you want to mix a large amount of color you can use plastic or porcelain saucers.

It really pays to spend money on good brushes for tempera painting—you want to be able to make several strokes with a fine point before having to recharge the brush. I have found that sable brushes are necessary for painting with egg tempera, and Kolinsky sables are the best of all. Kolinsky sables hold their shape better than ordinary sable brushes; they have more spring, finer points, and hold more paint, so their extra expense is justified. These brushes will last a long time if they are washed carefully with a mild soap after a day's work.

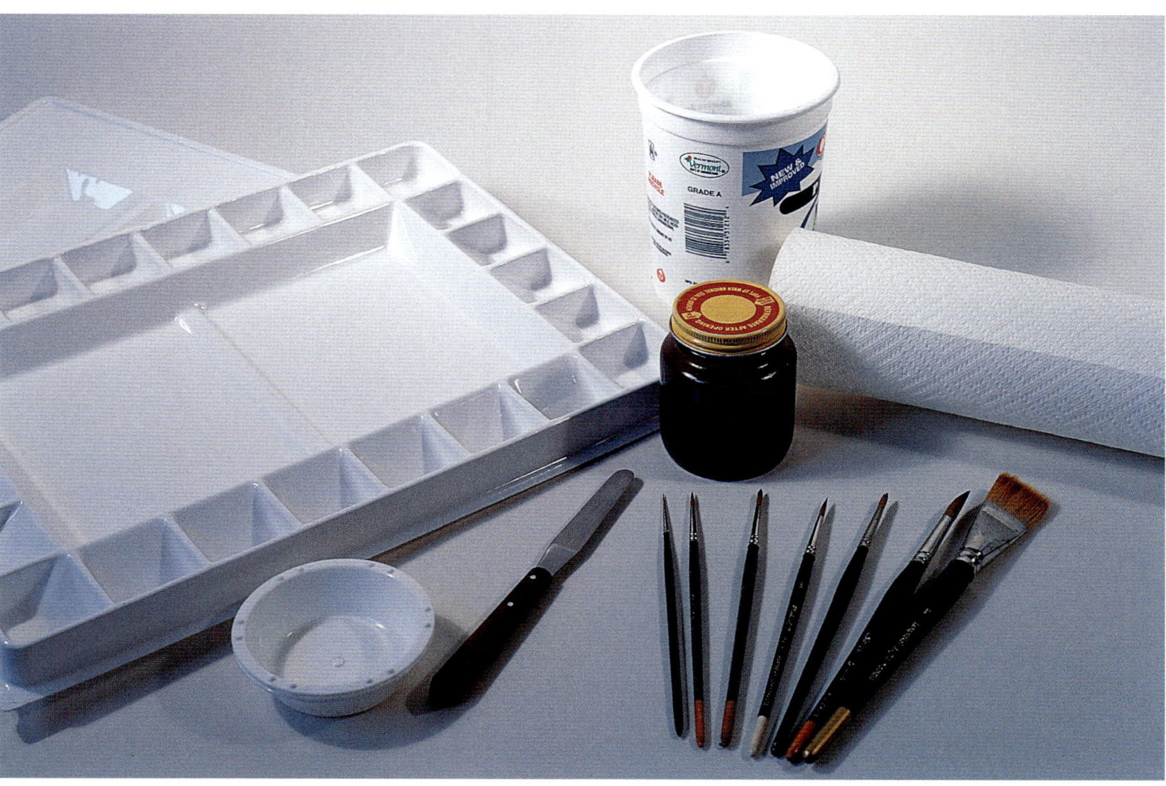

Painting materials (clockwise from upper left): Plastic palette with individual mixing wells, container for water, paper towels, small jar for the egg yolk, an assortment of brushes, palette knife, small saucer for color mixing.

Throughout the painting process, I work with the point of a brush wiped almost dry, whether layering a light, semi-opaque color—scumbling, or a transparent color—glazing. I paint with round watercolor brushes of various shapes—some have a wider belly or point than others—for different parts of the painting. For instance, I use a brush with a narrow belly and very fine point for detail work; for painting skies, I use a larger brush that has a wide belly and a somewhat blunter point. This broader point allows me to apply the color more quickly while still using hatched lines. It's a good idea to try different brush shapes made by one company—Raphael makes a few differently shaped Kolinsky sable watercolor brushes—or experiment with several companies. In that way you will discover which brushes work well for you. It is not necessary to have tiny brushes—a good #1 or #2 brush that comes to a fine point will work for most precise detail (though I also use a #00). The largest brush that I use is a #3. For broadly laying in large areas of underpainting, a flat sable brush, 3/4-inch-wide, may come in handy.

I rinse the brushes thoroughly with water when I change colors. At the end of the workday, I wash them thoroughly with a gentle soap, carefully cleaning the egg yolk medium from the brushes. These are expensive brushes, so it is important to take good care of them.

I use a narrow palette knife for removing pigment paste from jars. If you grind your pigments each day, you may want to use a wider knife. The other necessary supplies are things that are found around the house: a small jar to contain the egg yolk medium and paper towels or rags for wiping the brush after it has been dipped in paint. And, since we use water to thin the paint and to rinse brushes, a large container for water.

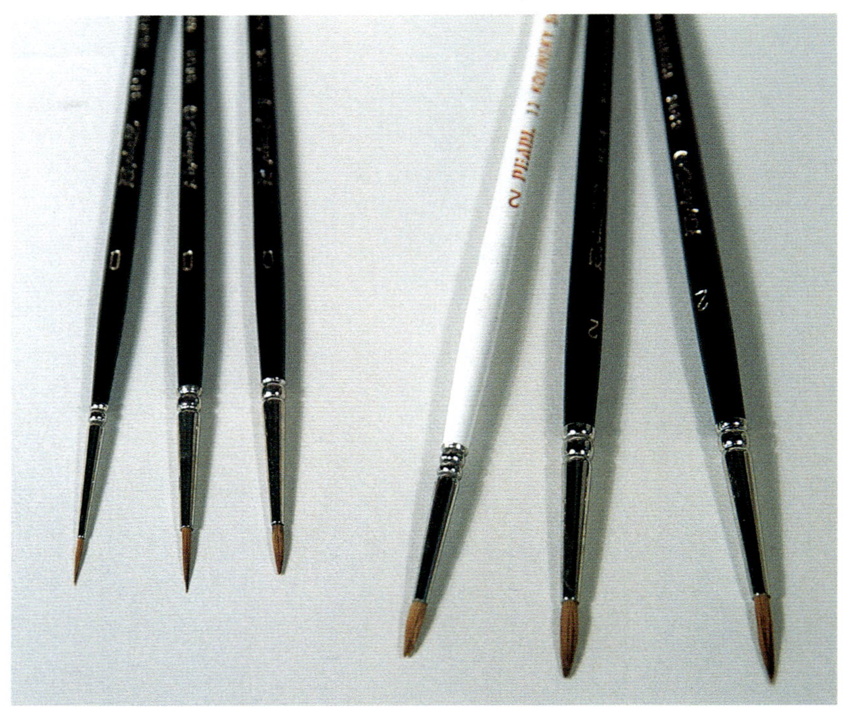

Here are several differently shaped Kolinsky sable brushes. On the left are three #0 brushes made by Rafael. From left to right they are a #8413 with a thin belly and very fine point, good for painting precise details; a #8408 with a full belly and a fine point; and a #8404 with a full belly and round point. On the right are three #2 brushes. First is a brush made by Pearl Paint, a #11 with a full belly and a short point, and then two Rafael brushes, a #8404 and a #8408 with the same shapes as the #0 brushes. When I am painting precise detail, I use a brush with a fine point, such as the #8413 or the #8408. To paint large areas I will use the rounder point of the Pearl paintbrush or the Rafael #8404.

# Preparing the Egg Yolk Medium

The yolk acts as the medium, or binder, for tempera, as linseed oil does for oil paint—the particles of paint are bound to each other and to the painting surface. The egg yolk contains a fatty oil which is emulsified, or suspended, in a watery solution of egg proteins, or albumen. Egg tempera paint dries quickly as the water evaporates. Then the proteins coagulate when exposed to air and light and form a waterproof film. Egg oil hardens but does not dry completely which adds strength to the tempera.

You need to handle the egg yolk to clean it of the egg white and membrane. Because of this, the egg must be as fresh as possible, or the yolk will break apart before being completely separated. Most supermarket eggs are produced on large egg farms and have pale yellow yolks that lie flat when broken on a surface. The membrane surrounding the yolk of these eggs is quite weak. Free-range eggs, on the other hand, have deep orange-yellow yolks that stand up roundly on a surface. If they are reasonably fresh, they won't break apart when handled. If you are not fortunate enough to have a local supply of farm-fresh eggs, health food stores are generally a good source for free-range eggs. In his painting manual, Cennini differentiated between town eggs and country eggs by their difference in color. In practice it really doesn't matter what color the yolk is, because the yellow color that seems to affect the pigments will bleach out in a few days.

The first steps for cleaning the yolk are familiar to anyone who cooks—the initial separation of yolk from white. Break the eggshell on a counter or bowl edge, letting the white fall out into a bowl while keeping the yolk in one half of the shell. Pass the yolk back and forth a few times from one half of the shell to the other, letting the white continue to drip into the bowl.

Passing the yolk back and forth between the two shell-halves.

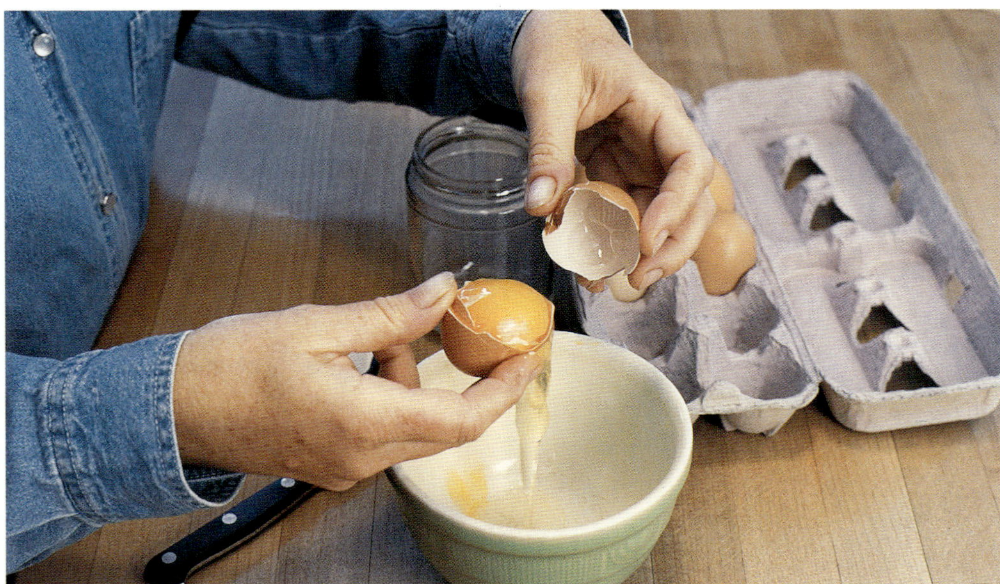

Then put the yolk in the cupped palm of one hand and pass it back and forth from hand to hand, wiping your hand each time on a towel. This removes more of the white. Then, holding the yolk in cupped fingers, pierce the membrane with a pointed object—the tip of a small knife is perfect. Let the filling of the yolk drop into a small glass jar, leaving the membrane in your hand. Discard the membrane or add to the white for cooking or feeding your dog, which is what I do with it. To the yolk in the jar, add one teaspoon of water and mix thoroughly with anything handy—a spoon, knife, or chopstick, which is what I use. This is your medium. It will remain fresh for two or three days if refrigerated when you are not using it. I prepare one egg yolk at a time, which usually lasts for two or three days of painting. Since a painting may take two weeks to complete, I generally need five or six eggs to make my medium over that time.

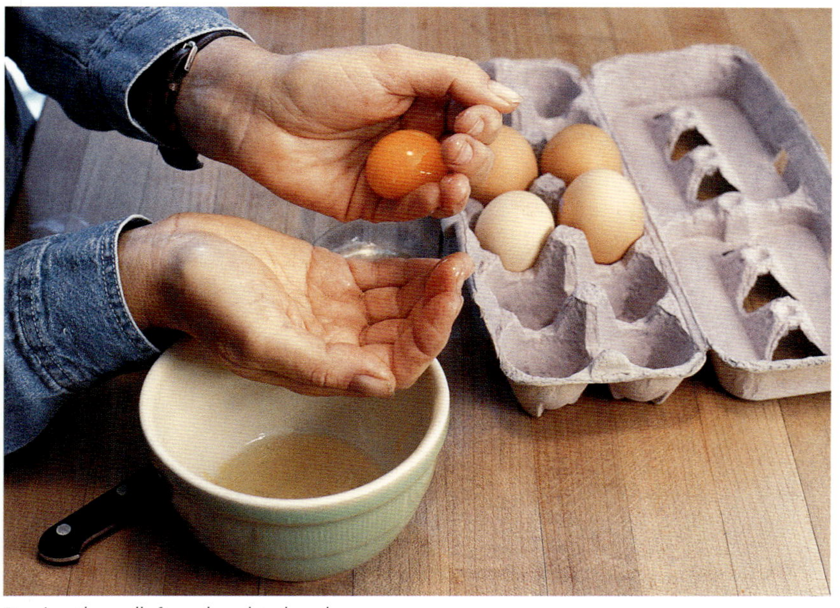

Passing the yolk from hand to hand.

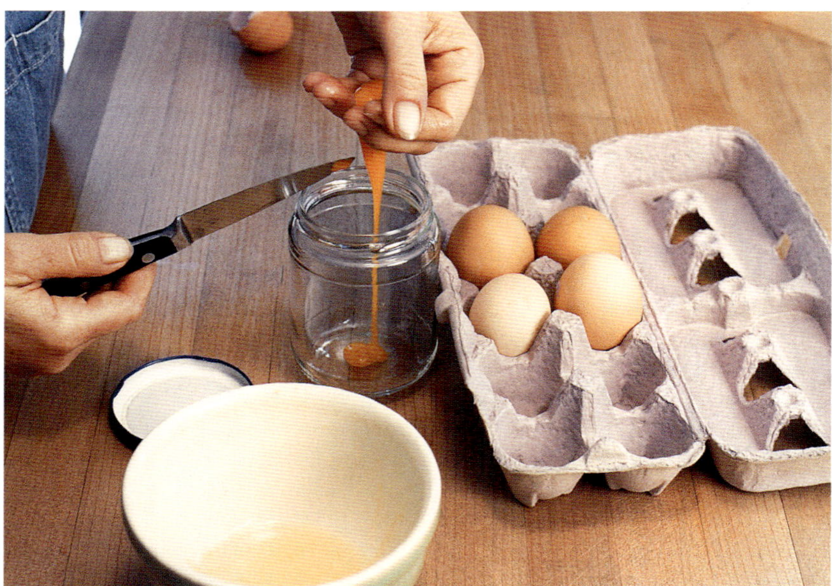

Piercing the yolk membrane.

# Ready-Made Materials

If you want to try the technique of egg tempera painting, but don't want to prepare anything, there are tube temperas and prepared panels that you can buy. If you find that you like the technique, you may then be ready to make your own materials. Rowney, Sennelier, and Old Holland make egg tempera paints. The egg tempera in tubes is not strictly egg tempera, but an egg-oil emulsion. If thinned to a watery consistency, it will handle like pure egg tempera. Put a small amount of paint in the well of your palette, in the same way that you would place the pigment paste, and thin with water to the consistency of India ink. Use the paint as you would the tempered pigments. If you don't want to grind pigments, but want to work with egg yolk, two suppliers sell pigments already ground in water, called pigment dispersions or color concentrates: Guerra Paint and Pigment and Kremer Pigments.

*Clayboard* is a thin pressed-wood panel that has been coated with kaolin clay mixed with polymer binding agents. The surface is very white and smooth. It is somewhat absorbent, which is necessary for tempera. Because Clayboard is not as absorbent as traditional gesso, you must allow more time for the paint layers to dry between coats or the underlayers will lift with the application of a new layer. I do not recommend this product for beginners—it can be very frustrating to see the underpainting lift from the surface. Clayboard is inexpensive, and comes in several sizes.

You can buy very high quality panels that are ready for sizing and gessoing. ArtPanel makes a medium density fiberboard that is 3/8-inch thick and comes in several sizes. The panels come with keyslots for hanging. ArtPanel will also make custom panels. They are available from art suppliers or directly from the manufacturer (see Sources).

There are several pre-mixed dry gessos available, which only require adding water. I have tried the mix made by Fredrix, which didn't seem to be absorbent enough for my needs, although other artists have had good results with it. The mix by Grumbacher was too thick when mixed

according to directions, but makes a fine gesso for egg tempera, if you thin it with water to make it the consistency of house paint. You should apply pre-mixed gessos as described in the following chapter under "Applying the Gesso." Do not sand between coats as recommended on the gesso containers—the layers of gesso should bond with each other. Acrylic gesso will not work at all for egg tempera painting because it is not absorbent, which is necessary for a good egg tempera ground. You may be able to find someone near you who will make gessoed panels; ask at an art school or art supply store.

If you use any of these products, experimenting with egg tempera becomes a simple matter, eliminating the preparation of panels and pigments. If you enjoy the technique, you may be ready to make your own gesso panels and grind some pigments, since many more colors are available as pigments than as concentrates or in tubes. Your mind can be busy thinking about the next painting as you calmly grind pigment or layer homemade gesso on pressed-wood panels.

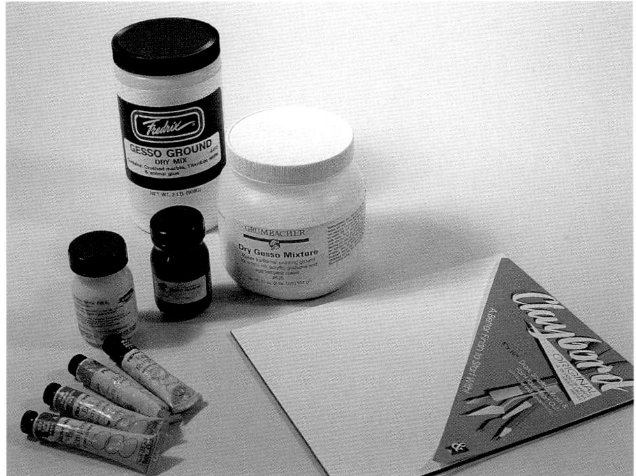

Ready-made materials (clockwise from top): Dry gesso mixes, Clayboard panel, tube egg temperas, color concentrates (also called pigment dispersions).

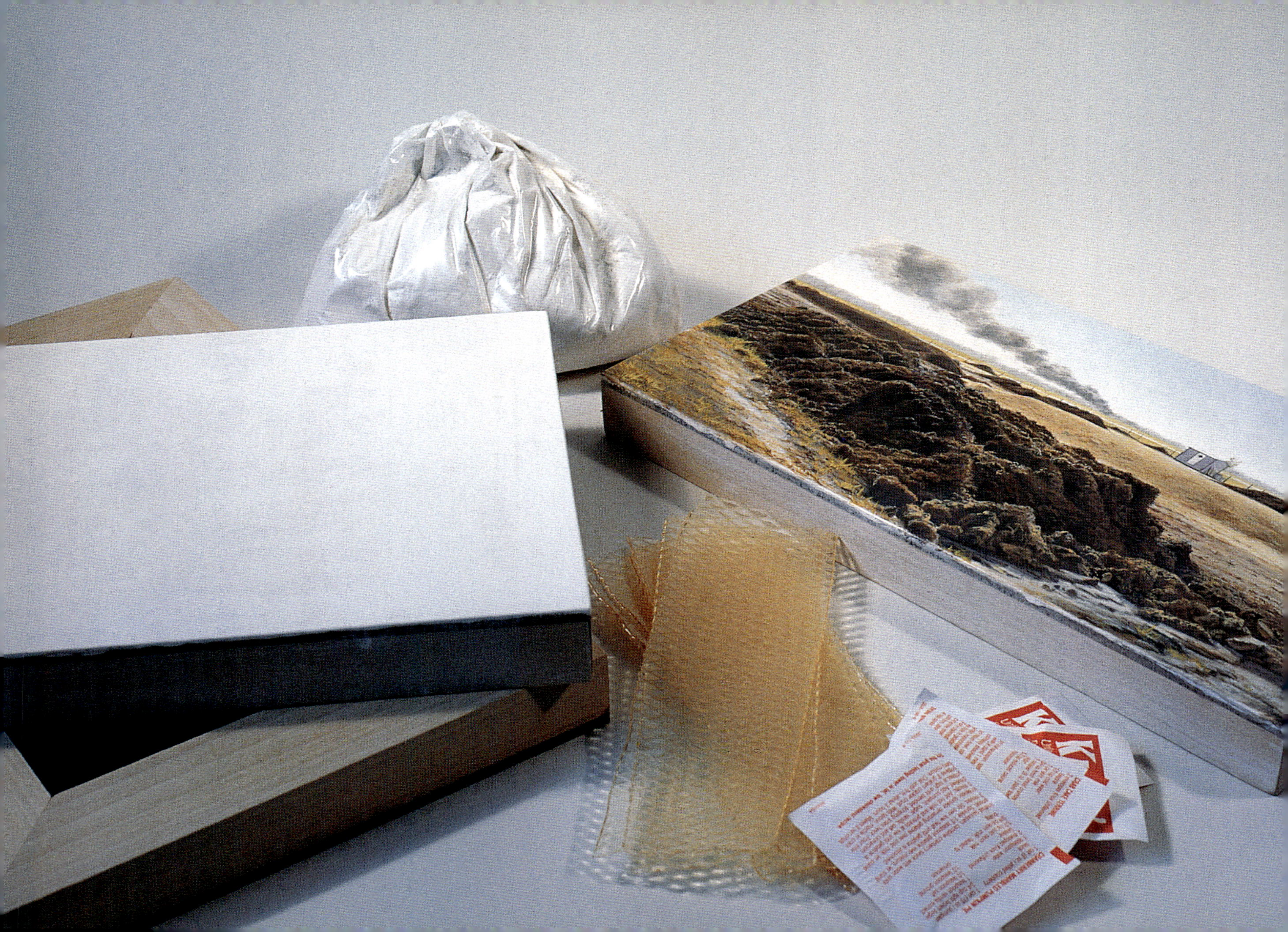

# PREPARING THE PAINTING PANELS

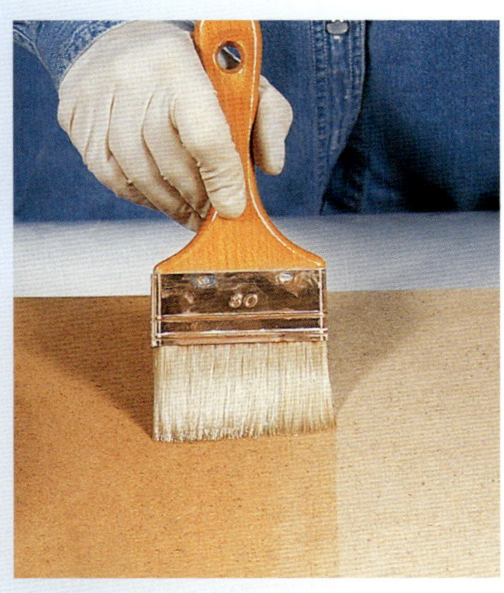

Opposite: Along with a painting on a cradled panel are panels, gelatin, and chalk for preparing gesso. Above: Sizing the panel.

During the Renaissance, artists painted on solid wood panels—poplar was used in Italy, oak in northern Europe. The best planks were those cut from the center of the log, because they would have less of a tendency to warp. They were dried for a long period of time. Large paintings were made up of several planks of wood fastened together, supported on the back by horizontal and vertical strips of wood. Any defects on the surface had to be repaired. A glue size was prepared by boiling parchment clippings, and was applied to the surface. Sometimes a thin linen fabric was applied with size. Then gesso (which is the Italian word for gypsum, or calcium sulphate) was prepared and applied over the moldings and the flat of the panel in several layers: first *gesso grosso*, or thick gesso, then *gesso sottile,* the thin gesso. Gesso sottile was made with slaked plaster of Paris, which was plaster that had soaked in water for a month, and stirred every day. After the panel dried, the gesso coating was carefully scraped smooth and the panel was ready for painting. After this fairly complicated process, the way we prepare panels for painting today will seem very simple and straightforward.

# Materials for Panels

The absorbent gesso ground that we use for tempera is brittle and therefore must be applied to a rigid support like wood, not a flexible canvas; gesso will crack if applied to a canvas support. It is probably impossible these days to find well-seasoned, solid wood panels that will not warp terribly over a relatively short time. Plywood, because of its thin veneer, may split and crack with the application of gesso. When I tried using plywood, small cracks appeared in the gesso after several months. Therefore, I have found that the best support for egg tempera paintings are pressed-wood panels made of wood fibers subjected to pressure, commonly known under the brand name of Masonite. It is also referred to as fiberboard. This surface is stable and will not crack or split. Pressed wood is available in either tempered or untempered forms. The tempered product is strengthened by the addition of oily resins, which may affect the painting, so it is best to use untempered pressed-wood panels. If your lumberyard does not carry the untempered board, it can be ordered in $4 \times 8$-foot sheets.

In order to prevent warping, you should use panels that are $1/4$ inch thick. If you work on large paintings, it is a good idea to cradle or stabilize the panels by gluing strips of wood at least $1 \times 2$-inches thick to the backs. These strips of wood are laid around the edges of the panel, and on large panels, are cross-braced through the center. I prefer to cradle my panels *before* painting on them. This way, I only need to gesso one surface instead of both sides of the uncradled panel. I also don't have to worry about damaging the painting while cradling the panel, and the painting will be ready for framing when completed.

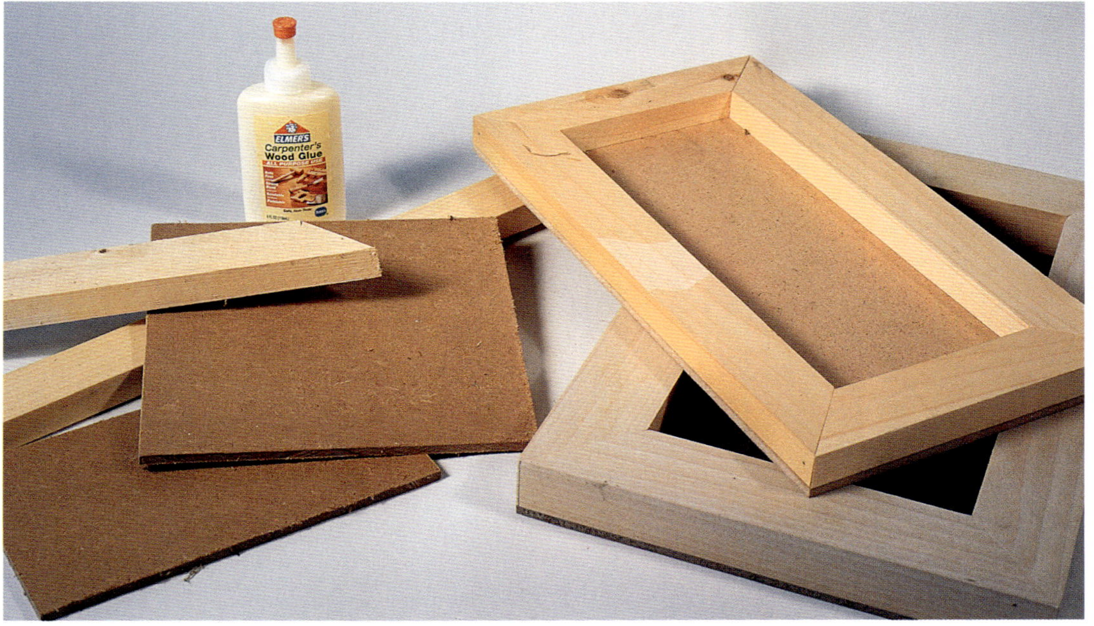

Materials for panels (from left): $1 \times 2$-inch strips of pine, $1/4$-inch untempered Masonite panels, wood glue, two cradled Masonite panels, on top cradled with pine, beneath cradled with poplar.

# Materials for Gesso

Egg tempera works best on a slightly absorbent traditional gesso ground. To make the gesso, you need a chalk and a glue. During the Renaissance, gesso was made with gypsum, which is calcium sulphate. Terra Alba, available from art suppliers today, is a natural gypsum that makes a bright white gesso. Today, most artists use gilder's whiting, or chalk. There is chalk from Bologna (a natural carbonate sulfate) and chalk from France (natural calcium carbonate). The choice is a matter of personal preference, since they will all make good gesso. Terra Alba makes a beautifully white painting surface, but I have more trouble with air bubbles when I make gesso with it. So, I prefer to use the chalk from France, because it is whiter than the Bologna chalk.

The other ingredient in gesso is glue. Rabbitskin glue is often used in recipes for gesso, as is gelatin, another animal glue. Various books discuss the pros and cons of the different glues and there are differing opinions about proportions of glue to water. I use gelatin since Thompson's recipe in *The Practice of Tempera Painting* recommends it. Gelatin comes in sheets or in granulated form. I buy granulated food gelatin at the supermarket; it is easy to measure for the gesso recipe because it is sold in one-ounce boxes—the four envelopes inside the box total one ounce. Various tests of glue strength in art manuals show that food-grade gelatin has adequate strength for gesso. My gesso surfaces, using gelatin, have always had the correct hardness and absorbency for tempera.

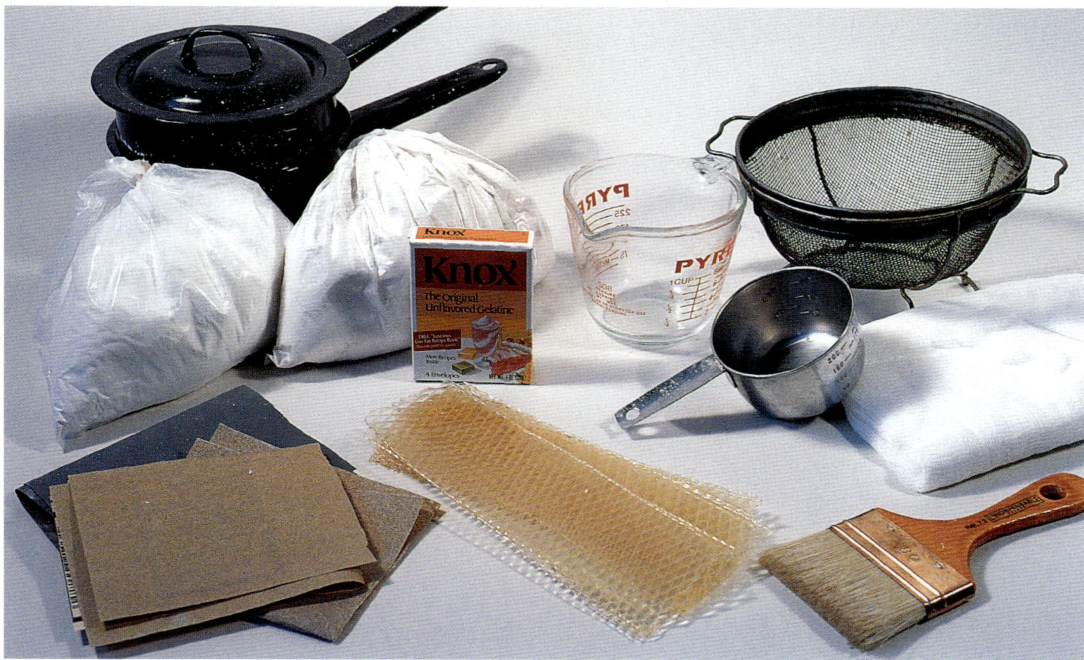


Materials for the preparation of gesso (top row): Double boiler, bags filled with chalk from Champagne, France, package of gelatin, liquid measuring cup, dry measuring cup, strainer, cheesecloth. Bottom row: Sandpaper, sheet gelatin, gesso brush.

# Sizing the Panels

The first step in getting the pressed-wood panel ready for the gesso is to lightly sand the surface of the panel with a medium sandpaper. This removes its shine and makes the panel more receptive to the glue size, which is applied before the gesso. Size is a solution of an animal glue and water. Rabbitskin glue is often used for this purpose. Oil painting canvases are sized with a rabbitskin glue size before painting begins because sizing protects the canvas from the damaging effects of the oil. In a like manner, the layer of size on the gesso panel both seals the panel and prepares it to accept the gesso. The materials that you need to make and apply the size are gelatin, a double boiler (or suitable substitute), a heat source (your stove or hot plate), a liquid measuring cup, and a soft bristle brush, about 3 inches wide.

Take one ounce (30 grams) of gelatin and add it to 16 fluid ounces, which is two cups (470 milliliters) of cold water in the top of a small double boiler. The gelatin should be left to soak for about 15 minutes if you are using the granulated form, longer if you are using the sheet form. The gelatin will swell and get soft. Bring a moderate amount of water to a boil in the bottom pot of the double boiler, and place the top section with the softened glue over it. The rising steam will melt the gelatin, and soon it will become a clear solution in water. Do not try to heat the gelatin solution over direct heat, because it will burn. Stir the gelatin solution with the brush, to be sure that it is completely dissolved.

I place the panels that I am preparing on a plastic tarp to keep my table clean. Take the entire double boiler to your worktable to keep the size hot. Fill your brush with the hot size, and brush the size with even strokes, horizontal or vertical, over the surface of the panel. Wipe the brush against the edge of the glue pot and with this dry brush, smooth out the strokes in the opposite direction to which they were applied. When working on large surfaces, you should brush out the size in one-foot squares so that it doesn't begin to dry before it is smoothed. If you use large, uncradled panels, they need to be sized on both sides to prevent warping, then left to dry leaning against a wall. Let the sized panels dry overnight.

If you have any gelatin solution remaining, you can store it in a covered container in the refrigerator in plastic freezer containers. The solution will remain fresh for several days if kept refrigerated.

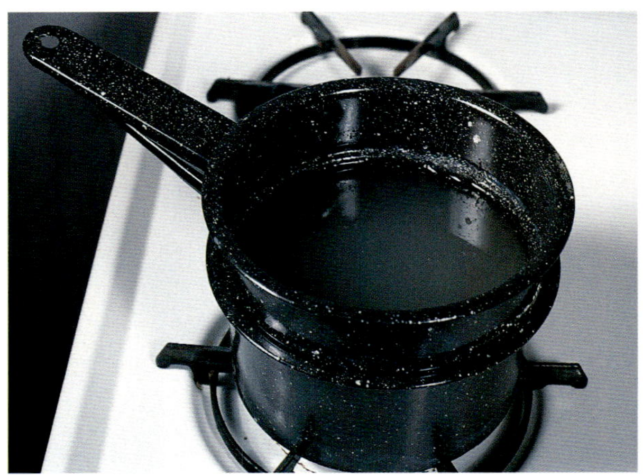

The gelatin is softening after being added to cold water. Its cloudy appearance will change to a clear liquid when it is heated over boiling water.

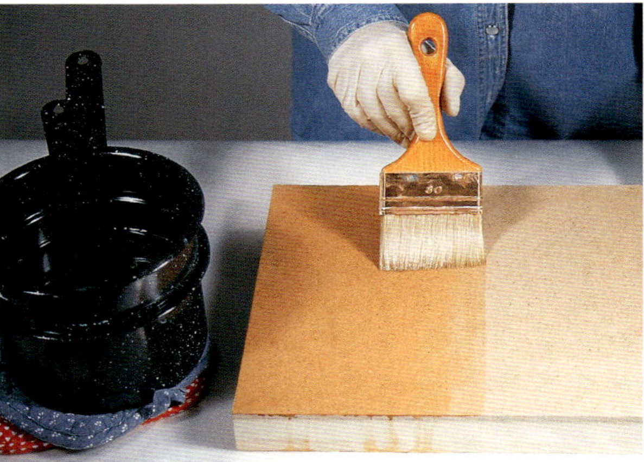

Applying the size to the panel.

# Making the Gesso

To make gesso, we begin with the same gelatin solution that we use for the size—one ounce (30 grams) of gelatin in 16 fluid ounces of water (470 milliliters), prepared in the same way as the size in the above section. If you have some gelatin solution remaining, you can reliquefy it over steam in the top of the double boiler. Measure out one and one-half cups of whiting for every one cup of gelatin solution—or one and one-half parts whiting to one part size. Sixteen ounces of water are two cups, so you will need three cups of whiting. If you are using the remainder of your size solution, reduce proportionally the amount of whiting added.

The hardest part of making gesso is mixing it without creating air bubbles which make tiny pinholes in the gesso surface. When I began making gesso, I found it very difficult. I had lots of air bubbles and the gesso was too thick and kept forming a solid skin in its surface. I now realize that one of the reasons for my troubles was that Thompson's gesso recipe called for the whiting to be one and one-half times the amount of size by *weight*. It should be one and one-half times the amount of size by *volume*.

I have discovered other elements that contribute to the process of making perfect gesso, described in this and the following section. Room temperature is an important element—it is best to work in a very warm, dry room and you should slowly mix the whiting into *warm,* not hot, size. After the gelatin has dissolved, remove the top part of the double boiler containing the gelatin solution from over the hot water, allowing it to cool slightly. The solution should not become cool or it will gel. Slowly add the whiting to the gelatin solution through a strainer or sifter, pushing it through with a spoon. It is important to slowly add the whiting, so air bubbles will not be dragged into the gesso. Try to distribute the whiting around the pot so that it doesn't all pile up in the middle, but is absorbed into the size solution. Any whiting not absorbed into the size solution can be brushed into it.

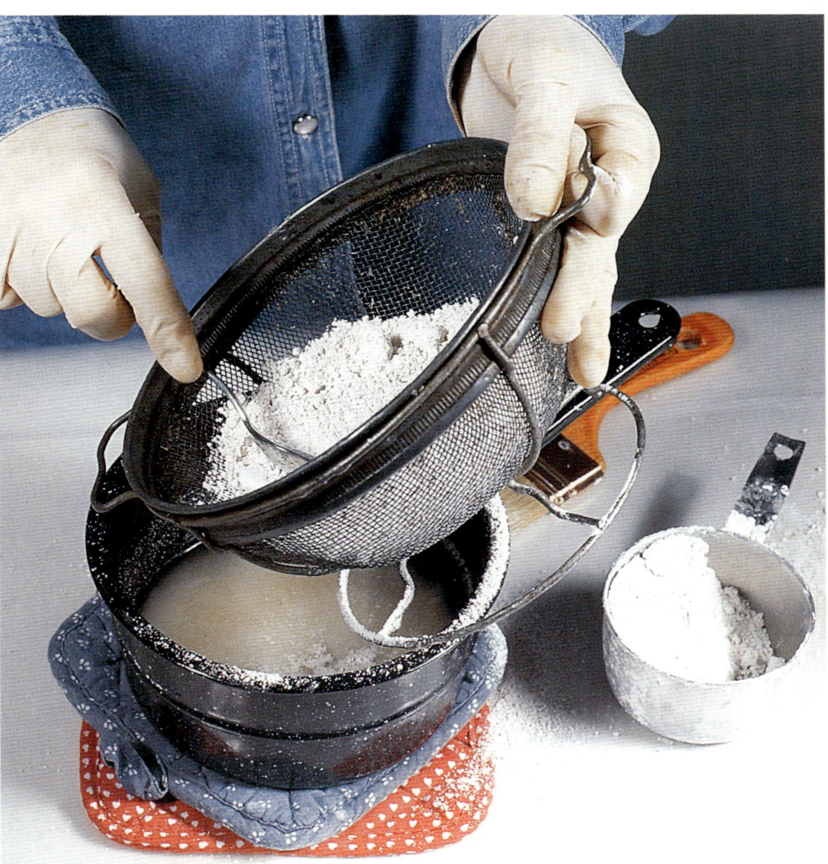

Sifting the whiting into the size solution.

After the whiting is added, *gently* stir the mixture with your gesso brush. Don't worry if it is not smooth—the straining process will take care of that. Slowly pour the gesso into another container. Clean the top part of the double boiler then fasten a double layer of cheesecloth over the pot using a large rubber band or string. You could also use a nylon paint strainer instead of the cheesecloth. Gradually pour the gesso through the cheesecloth, using the brush to press any lumps into the pot. The gesso will be about the consistency of heavy cream. If at any point while you are gessoing your panels the gesso begins to gel, *briefly* put it over hot water, stirring it gently with the brush, just until it liquefies again. If the gesso gets too hot, air bubbles will form.

If the gesso is too thick, you have to add more size solution to thin it; adding just water at this point would make the gesso too soft. However, if during the time that you are applying the gesso to the panel it becomes too thick to brush out easily, it is because water is evaporating—so you can add a bit of water to thin it.

Straining the gesso through the cheesecloth.

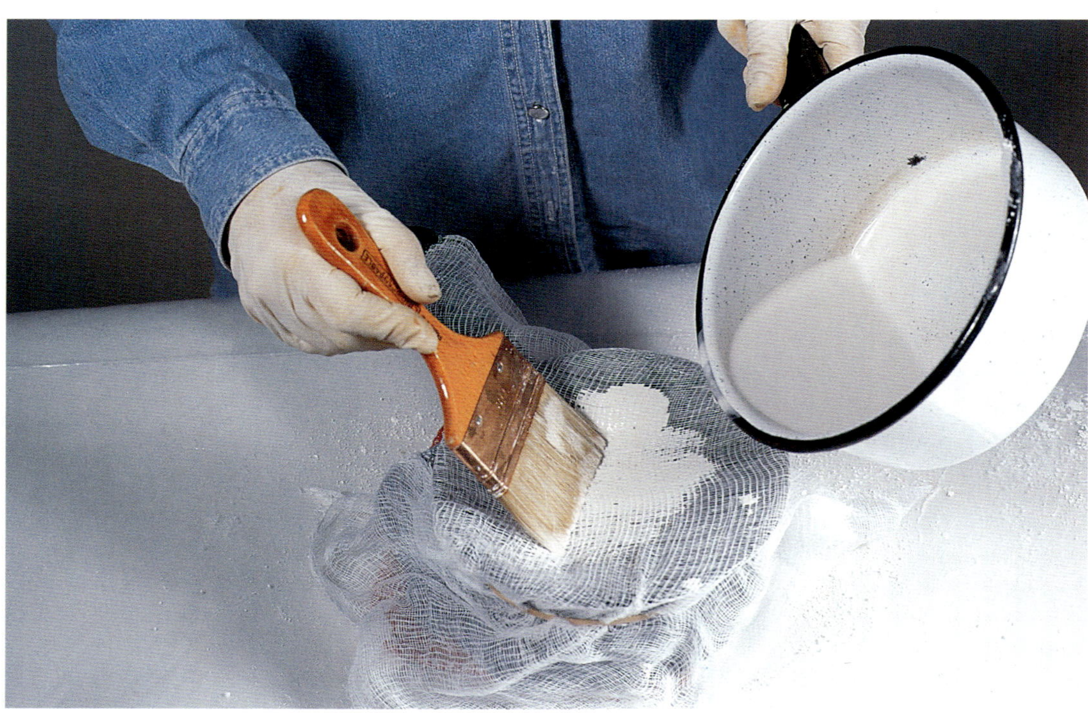

# Applying the Gesso

The gesso that you have made using two cups (16 ounces) of the gelatin solution should be enough to prepare five or six small (12 inches or so) panels with six to eight coats of gesso. Because there's a certain amount of waiting involved as each coat of gesso dries to the touch, it makes sense to prepare several panels at once, saving a good deal of preparation time. If you are using uncradled large panels, you will have to gesso them on both sides to prevent warping. An easy way to do this is to gesso one side first, which may warp. The next day, when the gesso is dry, prepare the other side of the panel. When this dries, the panel will straighten out. Gessoing both sides at once can be very messy, and you must let the gesso dry by leaning the panel against a wall, as you did for the coat of size.

For the first coat of gesso, load the brush, wipe off the excess gesso and apply the gesso across the panel. To make it adhere to the coat of size, rub your fingers over the wet gesso on the panel in a circular fashion. To apply subsequent coats, brush the gesso on to the panel in a horizontal or vertical direction, smoothing out the strokes in the opposite direction as you did with the size. The gesso should be applied smoothly and not too thickly. If you are working on a large panel, put the gesso on in squares, because you don't want the gesso to dry before smoothing it. Brush out an 8 or 12-inch square in a vertical direction, smooth it in a horizontal direction, then move to the next square.

In order for the gesso layers to bond with one another, they should not be completely dry before another layer is added—just dry to the touch. You will see the surface of the gesso begin to go from a shiny, wet sheen to a matte finish as it dries. At this point it is ready for another coat of gesso.

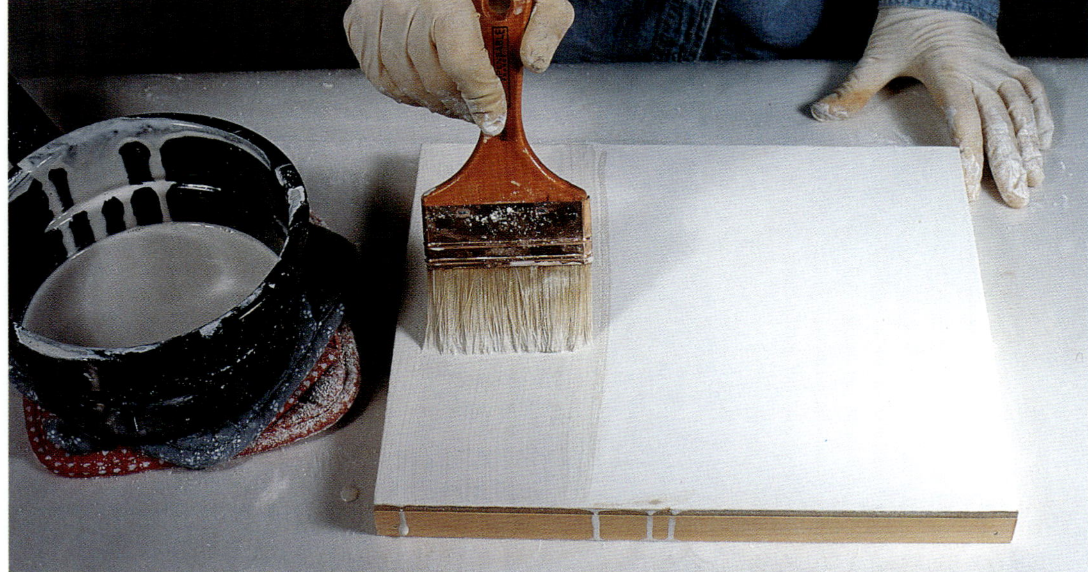

Applying the second coat of gesso.

Before each new coat of gesso, you should carefully and slowly stir the mixture in the pot with your brush, because the chalk may settle to the bottom. The next coat should be laid down in the opposite direction from the first coat—horizontal or vertical, and the squares should overlap one another—begin the new squares at the halfway point of the previous ones to create a smoother surface. Repeat this application in opposite directions for at least six coats. I prefer to put seven or eight coats of gesso on my panels.

If air bubbles appear in the gesso as I am applying it to the panels, I can eliminate most of them by gently stroking across the panel with the brush until the gesso begins to set. Use an even, soft stroke of the brush across the panel, especially on the edges; pressing against the edge of the panel with the brush will create more air bubbles. You will notice that I have used the words *gently, softly, carefully* in these instructions: these words are another key to making gesso that is free of imperfections, along with warm, not hot, size, and a warm room.

The amount of time that each layer of gesso will take to dry depends on the conditions in the room. A cool, damp day is not a good time to prepare panels, because the gesso will be slow in drying and the gesso in the pot will gel quickly. A very warm, dry room is ideal. I have my best results when working in a room heated by a wood stove—the temperature is 75 degrees and the air is very dry. Don't try to speed the drying by putting the panels in direct sunlight—this can cause the gesso to crack. Your first layers of gesso will probably dry to the touch in 15 to 30 minutes. The final layers may take longer. Again, if the gesso in the pot begins to gel, put it briefly over hot water to liquefy it. I find that if the room that I am working in is warm and dry, the gesso will not gel during the three or four hours necessary to complete the panels. As a matter of fact, I like to apply the gesso when it has become a bit thicker—it seems to have fewer air bubbles. I keep a lid on the gesso mixture between coats to help prevent it from forming a skin on its surface.

When your minimum of six coats of gesso have been laid down as smoothly as possible, let the panels dry overnight. They are then ready for finishing.

# Smoothing the Gesso Panels

One of the great pleasures of working with tempera is painting on traditional gesso panels. The gesso after sanding is silky smooth—a gorgeous, sensuous surface. Six coats of gesso are necessary to insure that there will be plenty of gesso left after sanding the panel smooth; we don't want the wood to show through the gesso.

Sanding the panels creates a lot of dust, so be sure to protect your work area or work outside, and wear gloves and a dust mask. Beginning with a sheet of medium-grit #120 sandpaper, folded in quarters, work in circular patterns over the surface of the gesso, smoothing out uneven brush marks. Be careful while you are sanding—if some dirt gets on the panel, it can leave bad scratches. Bevel the edges of the panel, which will help prevent them from chipping. When the panel is quite smooth, change to a fine #220 sandpaper. With circular movements, go over the panel until it is very smooth. For a final smoothing of the panel, use a #400 wet or dry sandpaper. Use it dry, sanding lightly in horizontal and vertical straight lines. This will make the gesso very silky and free of scratches. If you want a very glassy surface, you can wet this sandpaper and work lightly over the surface. After you wipe off the dust with a damp sponge, the gesso panel is ready for painting.

Another way to smooth the panel is to use a small sharpening stone— also called a whetstone—about three or four inches long. Dip the stone into cold water, and with the wet surface go over a section of the panel with a circular motion until the stone moves smoothly. Wipe off the excess gesso with a damp, not wet, sponge. Continue to dip the stone in water and work it over the surface of the panel, moving it from one area to another, until it is smooth. If you work too long in one spot, there is a danger that you will remove the gesso entirely, so be careful as you work. When the panel is smoothed, let it dry for a few hours. It is then ready for a final sandpapering with a fine #220 and then #400 sandpaper.

As before, sand the panel lightly with circular, then horizontal and vertical movements, and wipe off the dust with a damp sponge.

When the panel is completed, it will have a smooth and silky feel. The gesso should be hard enough for you to barely be able to scratch it with your fingernail, yet be absorbent enough to accept ink and paint. If it sands off too easily and dissolves with the application of paint, it is too soft. This is caused by not using enough gelatin in the mixture. Too much gelatin will create a gesso that is too hard, making it difficult to sand smooth. It will also not be absorbent and may crack. Any defects in the gesso will show up right away—I once mixed a batch with too little gelatin, and a couple of hours after completing the application, the too-soft gesso had cracked and separated from the panels. Using the recipe in this book, your gesso should be just right.

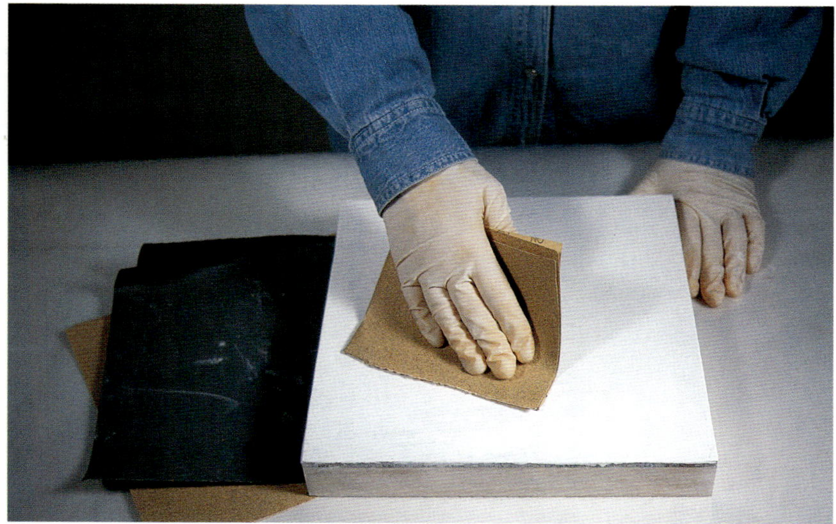

Sanding the gesso.

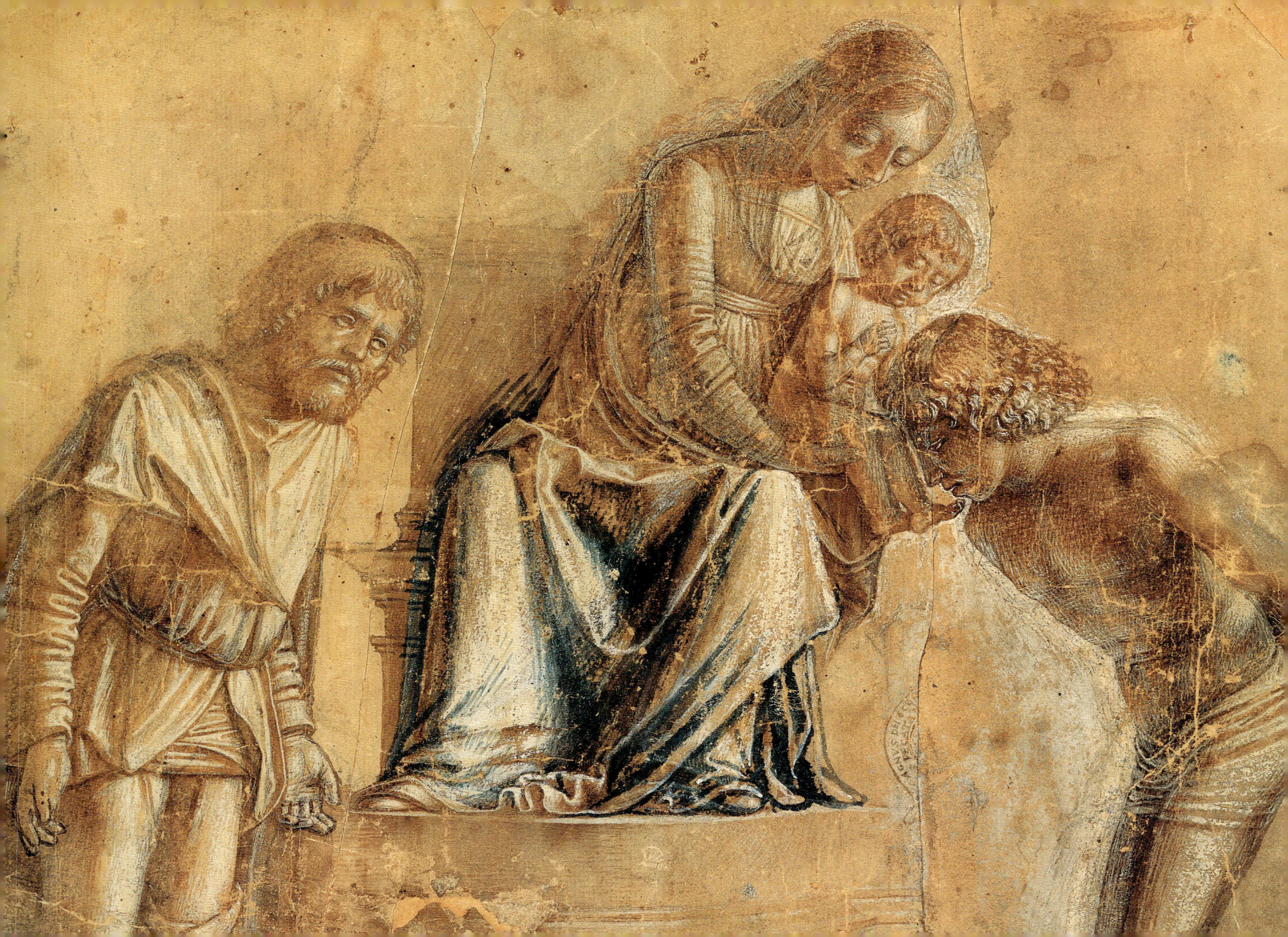

# DRAWING IS YOUR FOUNDATION

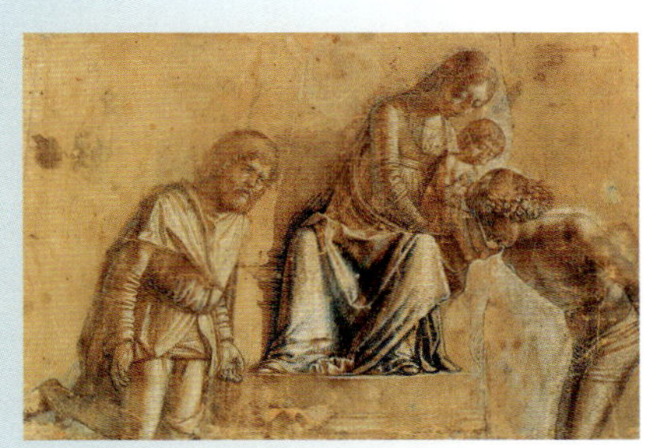



This very highly finished drawing was completed as a model for a painting.

No matter what kind of medium you work in as an artist, drawing is an essential element. Making a mark and placing it in relation to other marks, whether with paint, ink, or graphite, requires drawing skills. Good draftsmanship is essential for tempera painting because its nature is linear. When working with tempera we use clear lines that enclose forms with distinct edges. The blurring and softening of form that can be achieved with oil paint cannot be duplicated with tempera.

During the Renaissance, drawings were used as studies for paintings. Loose compositional studies were used to present ideas to the client who commissioned the artwork. After a composition was decided on, more studies were made of individual figures, developing their gestures and form. Finally, a highly finished drawing on toned paper, a *modello,* was often drawn as part of the contract for the painting. Drawing was integral to the process of making a painting.

When I first decided to paint with egg tempera, I felt a bit overwhelmed by its seeming complexity. So, I started by drawing with India ink and white gouache on hand-prepared toned paper. In this way, I got a feel for the materials by mixing the size and pigment for the paper and I also began to understand the technique of crosshatching with the point of an almost dry brush. By focusing on the process of drawing, I gradually worked my way up to painting, which is much easier than jumping directly into painting on a panel. This gradual approach is similar to that of the Renaissance workshop apprentices who slowly learned the skills of their trade, with painting as the pinnacle of their achievement.

I don't use my drawings on toned paper as studies for my paintings, but as artworks that stand on their own. I occasionally find motifs that have such dramatic value contrasts that I decide to make them into drawings rather than paintings. For my egg tempera paintings, I complete a careful line drawing on paper that I transfer to the gesso panel using tracing paper and a sheet of newsprint covered with charcoal (explained in the detailed demonstration). Many artists make very complete studies before beginning their painting so as to completely understand the challenge they have set for themselves. For this purpose, drawing with India ink and white paint (either gouache or white egg tempera) on toned paper is ideal.

Whether you make detailed studies or not, it is necessary to understand the technique of crosshatching with a dry brush, since this is the foundation of the tempera technique. In this chapter, I will explain and demonstrate the method of drawing with brush and ink on toned paper and on a gesso panel—the underdrawing for the egg tempera painting. If you practice with ink on paper, moving to color on panel will be easy.

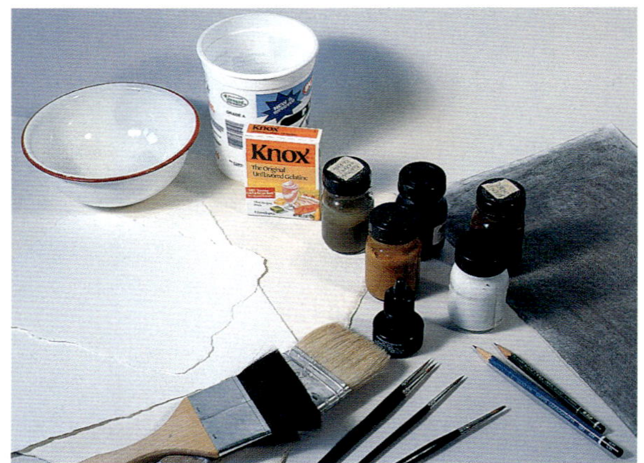

Drawing materials (clockwise from upper left): Bowl for mixing pigments, water container, gelatin for toning paper, pigments in jars, charcoal-coated transfer paper, pencils, brushes for drawing, India ink, brushes for toning paper, watercolor papers.

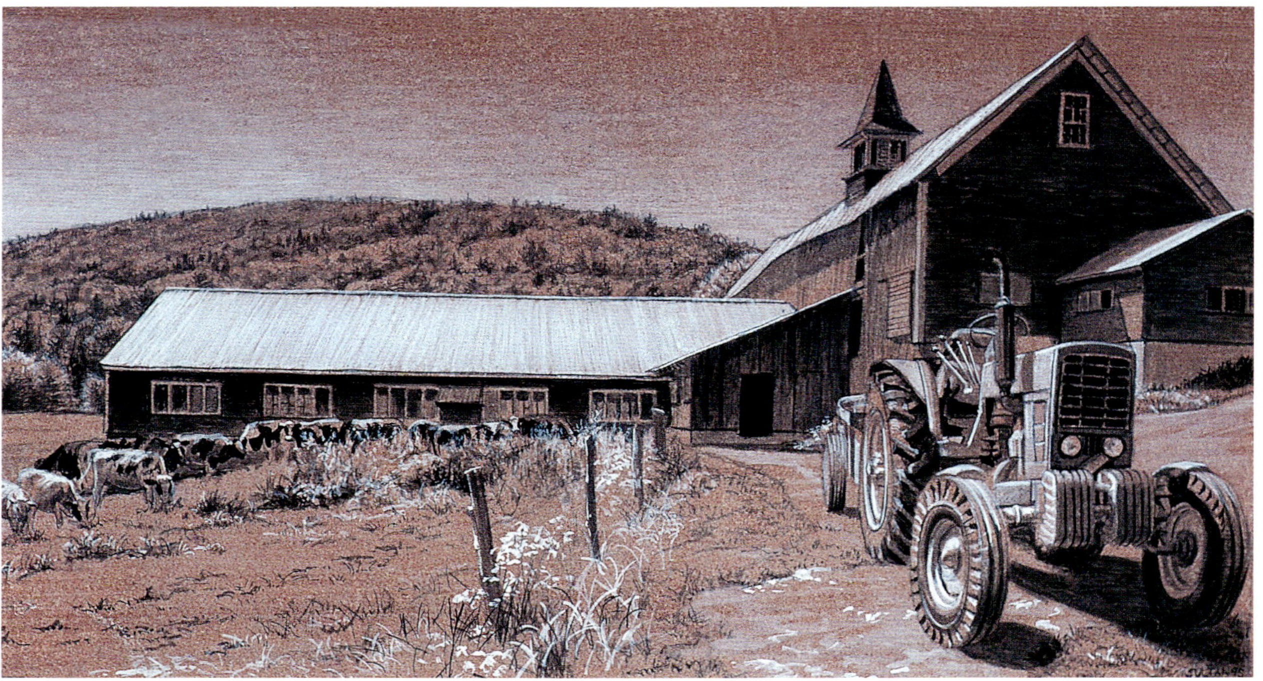

RUSSIAN TRACTOR, FAIRLEE, VERMONT
7¹/₄ × 15¹/₄ inches

I prepared a dark red paper for this drawing to emphasize the character of the tractor and New England barn. The tones were built slowly, with many layers of crosshatching.

# Handling Brush and Ink

The key to the mastery of the tempera technique is the *gradual* development of form. This is achieved in the underdrawing by using several different values of India ink, created by mixing the ink with different amounts of water, beginning with a light value and slowly adding darker tones where needed. Each value can be layered, crosshatching subtly or boldly, giving the illusion of a range of tones—only three values of ink can seem like many more.

With this hatching technique, the brush is used like a pen or pencil, with an almost-dry point. The brush is dipped in ink, the excess ink wiped off on the side of the palette well, and then the brush is wiped on a paper towel. This way, you will be able to make several strokes of the brush without having a little blob of ink at the end of each stroke. If you do have these drops of ink, it means that the brush wasn't wiped dry enough. It is surprising how many strokes can be made with this dry-brush technique.

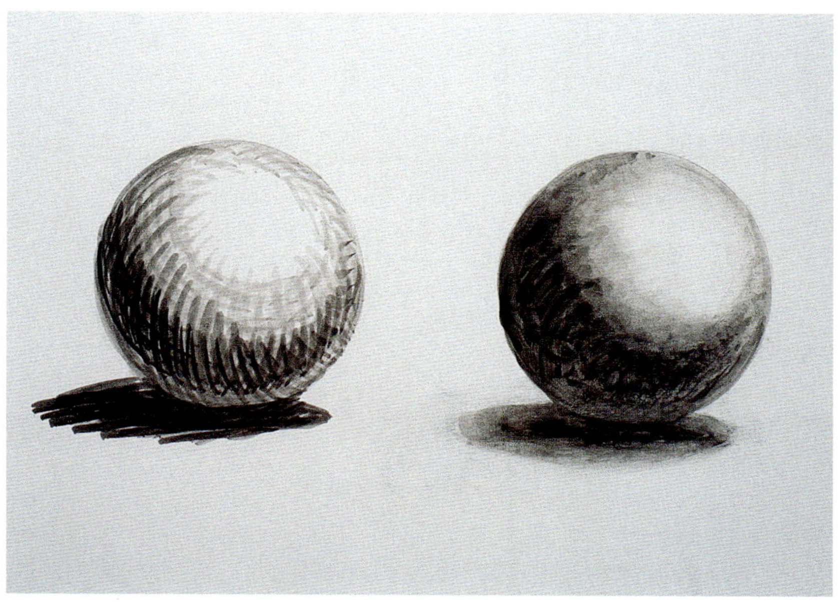

Examples of different ways of using ink. On the left, bold strokes of the brush, on the right the tones are created by washes.

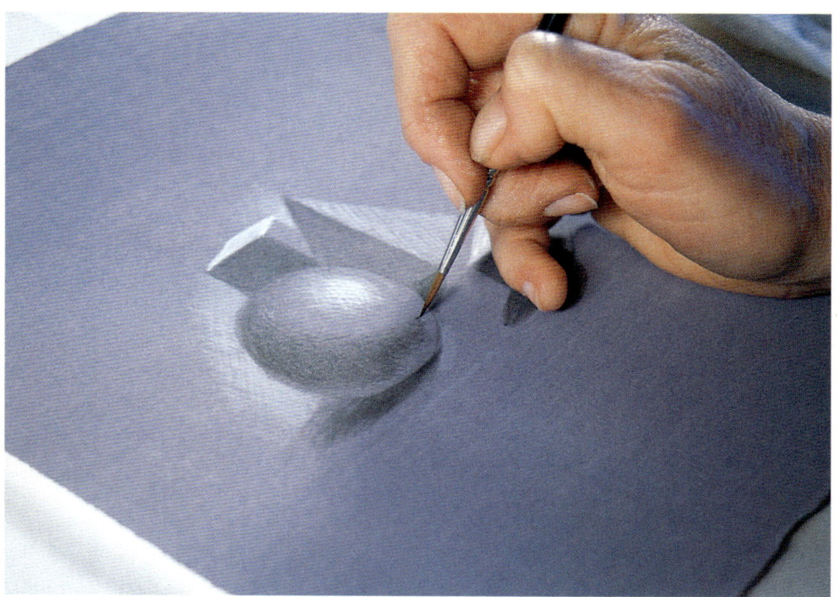

Crosshatching with the point of an almost dry brush.

Begin your drawing with a very light value of ink to establish basic form and composition. Starting with a light value ensures that any mistakes will disappear with the further development of the drawing. It also enables you to make very subtle tonal transitions. Work with this value, crosshatching in different directions, layering more densely where the darkest values will be. When you have developed the form as far as you can with this value of ink, begin using a slightly darker value; continue layering the ink in the same way, your brush skipping across the surface, using the direction of the brush strokes to help define the form. When I am doing a landscape drawing, I use five or six values of ink, from very light to almost pure black, but you can work with as many as suit your purposes.

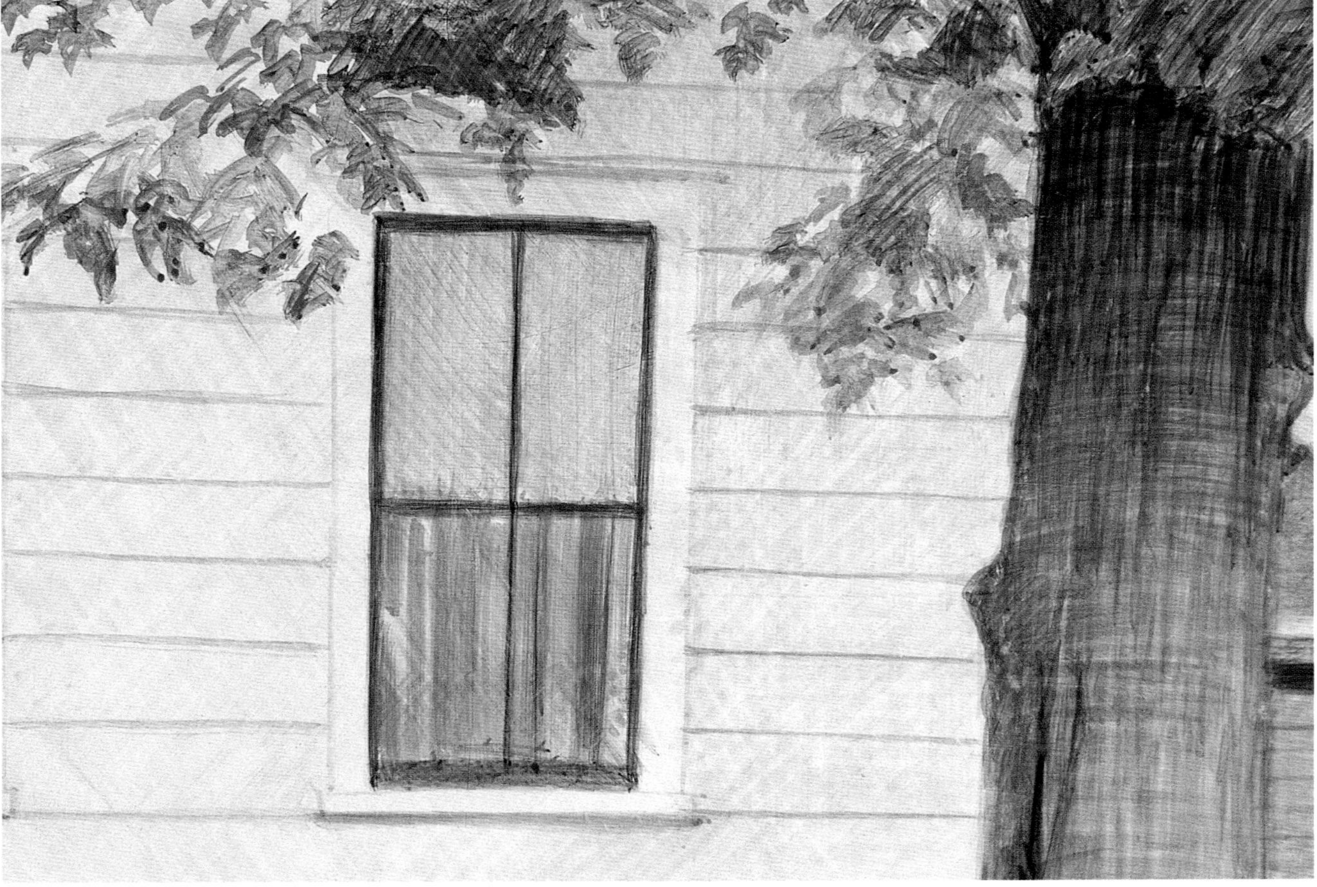

Detail of the painting *House and Tree, Pittsfield, Vermont.* In this detail, the crosshatching used to build tones is clearly visible. On the house, I used many layers of diagonal and vertical lines. The tree trunk is drawn with vertical lines and curved lines that describe volume.

For this first drawing demonstration, I have mixed three values of ink: a light value in my first palette well, a darker value in the third well, and an equal mixture of the two in my second palette well. I sit on a high stool at a table with an inclined surface. My palette and water container are at my right hand, and the small gesso panel on which I will work is propped up on whatever is handy—a roll of tape, a pencil sharpener—so that I can see it more clearly. Although I like to work the ink in a subtle and delicate way, you can use any style that feels comfortable: bold, direct strokes of the brush (or pen, a tool often used by Renaissance artists for their underdrawings); broad washes of ink similar to watercolor technique; short stippling strokes; or parallel strokes. Use the technique that works best for you.

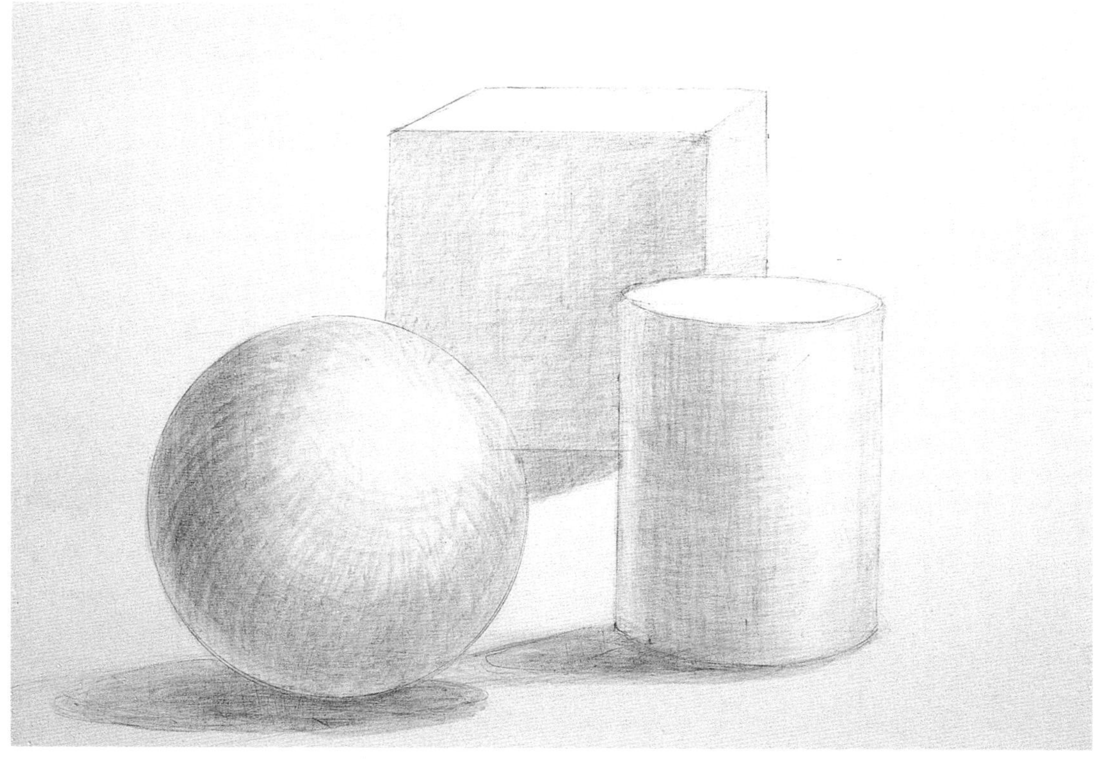

STEP 1

Since this demonstration drawing is a simple composition, I draw the outlines of the forms directly on the panel with a hard pencil, #4H. I begin by working with my lightest value of ink. First I draw the outlines of the forms over the pencil lines, then using horizontal and vertical strokes for the cube, vertical and curved strokes for the cylinder, and curved strokes for the sphere, I begin to describe their volume. I use these curved strokes to emphasize the form of the objects. On the light side of the cube, I use only two layers of ink, on the light side of the cylinder, two layers—vertical and curved. For the darker areas, I use more layers of crosshatching. The shadows are laid in with strokes that echo the plane of the table. Although my brush moves quickly across the surface of the panel, by working with this light tone my work can develop very gradually, and be very subtle. It is easier to build a tone that looks continuous using many thin layers of a light value than with one layer of a middle value.

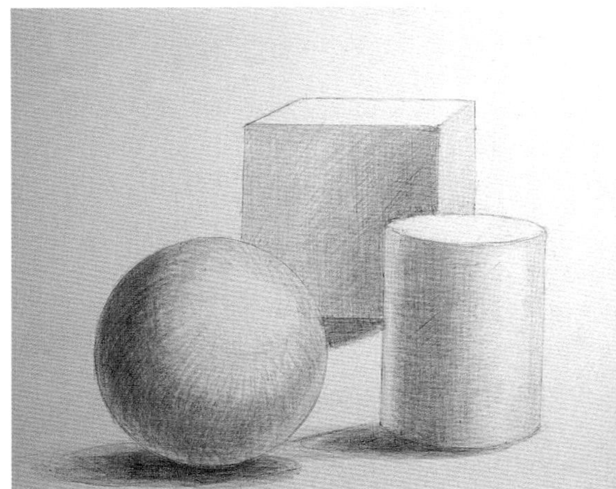

STEP 2

With a slightly darker value of ink, I go over the darker areas
of the forms and the shadows. I use fewer layers of ink in the
middle tones, to facilitate a smooth transition of value. I don't
add any of this middle tone to the left-hand side of the cylinder or the bottom and left of the sphere in order to show the
reflected light.

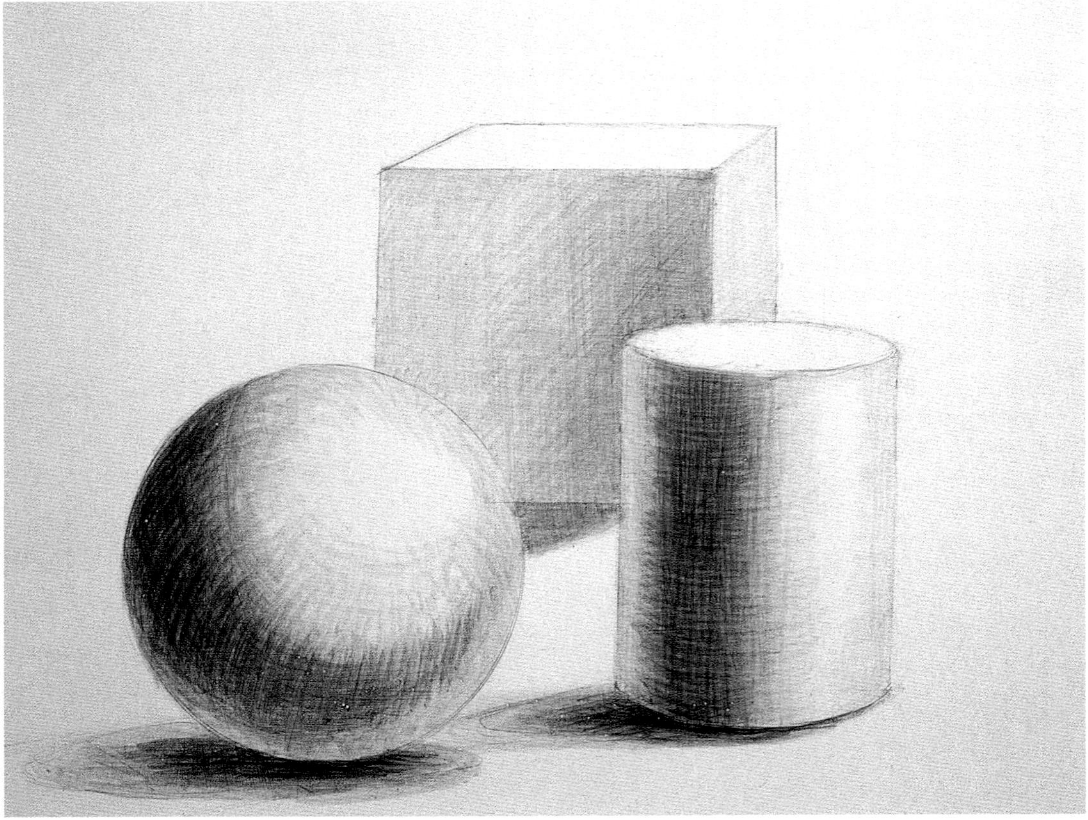

STEP 3

To make the forms more volumetric, I enhance the darks in the cylinder and sphere with my darkest value of ink.
Using the lightest value, I make the reflected light on the cylinder a bit darker. I make the shadows under the cylinder
and sphere more dramatic, and this strong contrast heightens the illusion of space, pushing the sphere and cylinder
forward and the cube back.

# Preparing Toned Paper

A toned paper that you prepare yourself is a beautiful surface on which to work. The gelatin that is mixed with pigment sizes the paper, while the color presents a wonderful middle tone. Hand-toned paper has slight irregularities such as brush marks and tonal variations that add to its character. During the Renaissance, drawings were often made on toned paper with ink or chalk and heightened with white chalk.

The paper that I prefer to use for tonal drawing is a handmade, cold-pressed watercolor paper, 140 lb or heavier. I like the character of the handmade paper, as opposed to the evenness of a mouldmade sheet, but any good watercolor paper is suitable. Place the paper on a sheet of plastic, or surface that you don't mind having to wipe clean of paint. The paper doesn't have to be taped down, because the gelatin solution will not cause it to curl. I have prepared sheets of paper up to 15 × 22 inches with no problems. Without using tape, you can brush the color over the edges of the paper, which enhances the beauty of paper with deckle edges.

Mix a color for the paper in a small bowl using your pigments that have been ground with water. Colors often used for papers are grayed blues or greens, or pale ochres or browns. You can mix a very light color, using a good deal of white, or a middle tone. More dramatic colors are fun to work on, too—reds, oranges, strong blues. The color that you mix should be lighter than the color you want on the finished paper—painting several thin coats gives a better, more even result than one thick coat.

Prepare the size by dissolving half an ounce (15 grams) of gelatin in 18 ounces (520 milliliters) of water. Add enough of this solution to the color that you have mixed to make it quite liquid. Using a 2- or 3-inch-wide bristle brush, paint the color thinly on the paper, using horizontal or vertical strokes. To get an even, smooth tone, lay down several coats of thin color, applying each layer in an opposite direction. Let the paper dry between each new layer of color. If you are not happy with the color as you apply it, you can adjust it on the next layer.

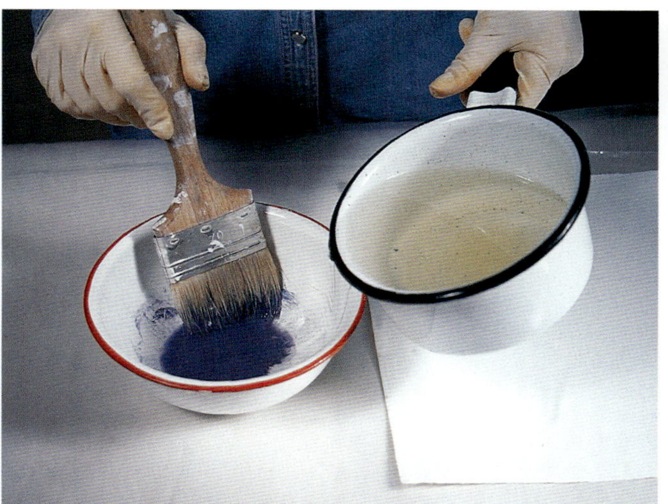

Mixing gelatin solution or size with pigment.

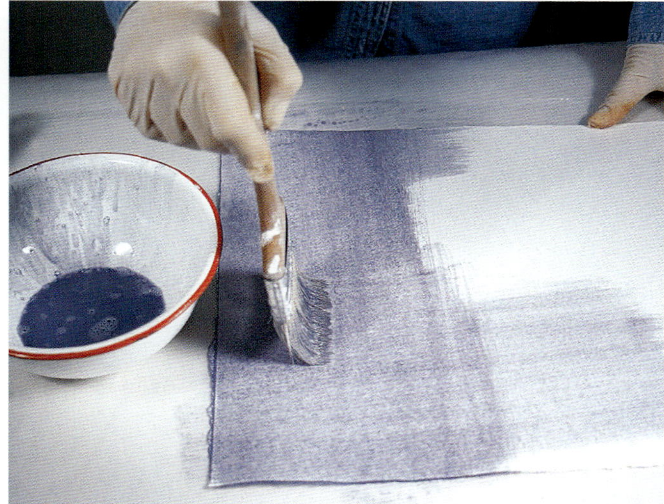

Brushing color on the paper.

After applying a few coats of color, you will have a toned paper with individual character that makes an attractive background for drawing. To make a drawing on this paper, mix several values of ink for the darks, and for the lightest values use Chinese white, or white gouache. The tone of the paper becomes the middle value. You can also use pigments tempered with egg yolk for drawing on toned papers and you don't need to confine yourself to black and white—you can work freely with color on these hand-colored papers.

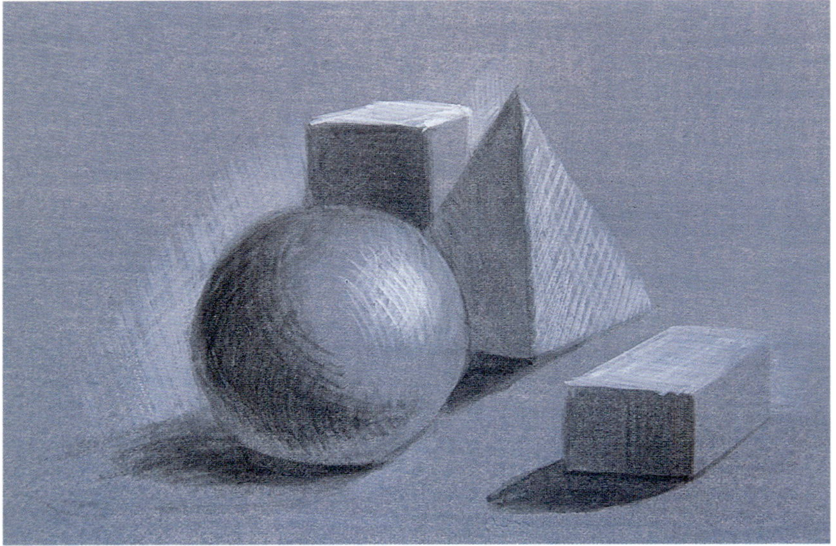

For this drawing, I prepared a grayish blue paper. For the darks, I used three tones of black ink, working up the values gradually as described in the demonstration of drawing simple forms. The lights were added gradually using gouache, leaving the paper as the middle tone.

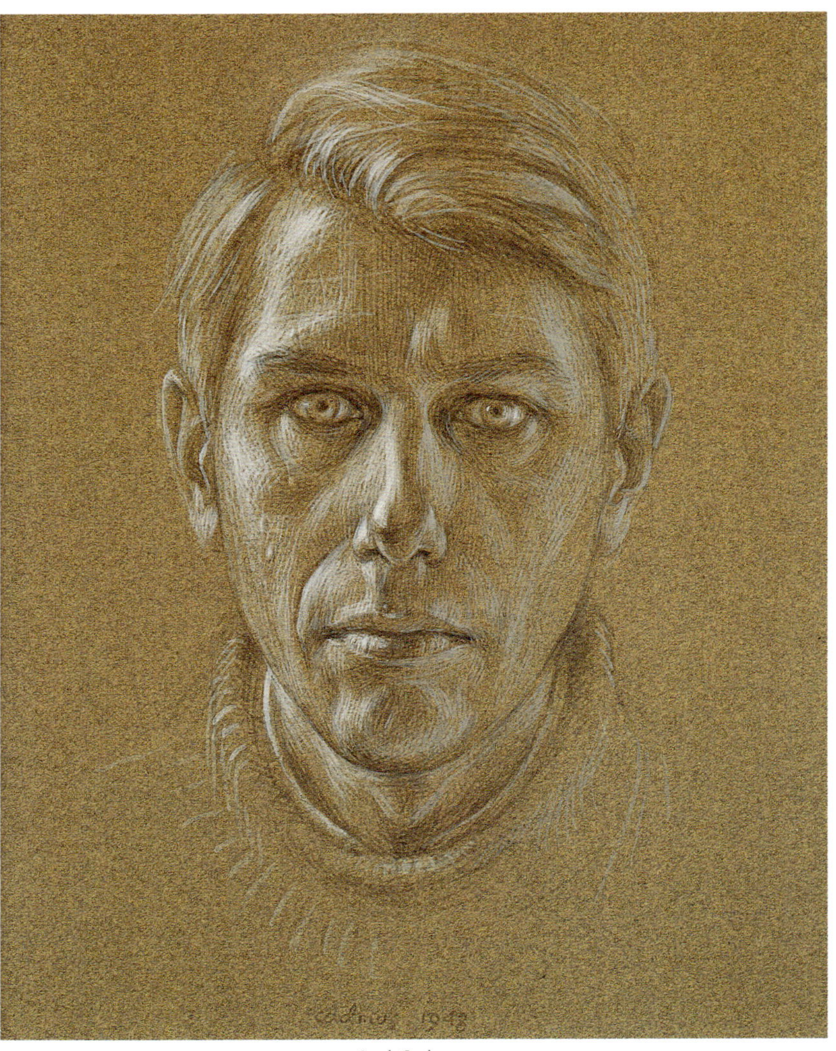

Paul Cadmus
SELF PORTRAIT
1948

We are confronted by the direct gaze of the artist in this drawing that vigorously models form in light and dark on a mid-toned ground.

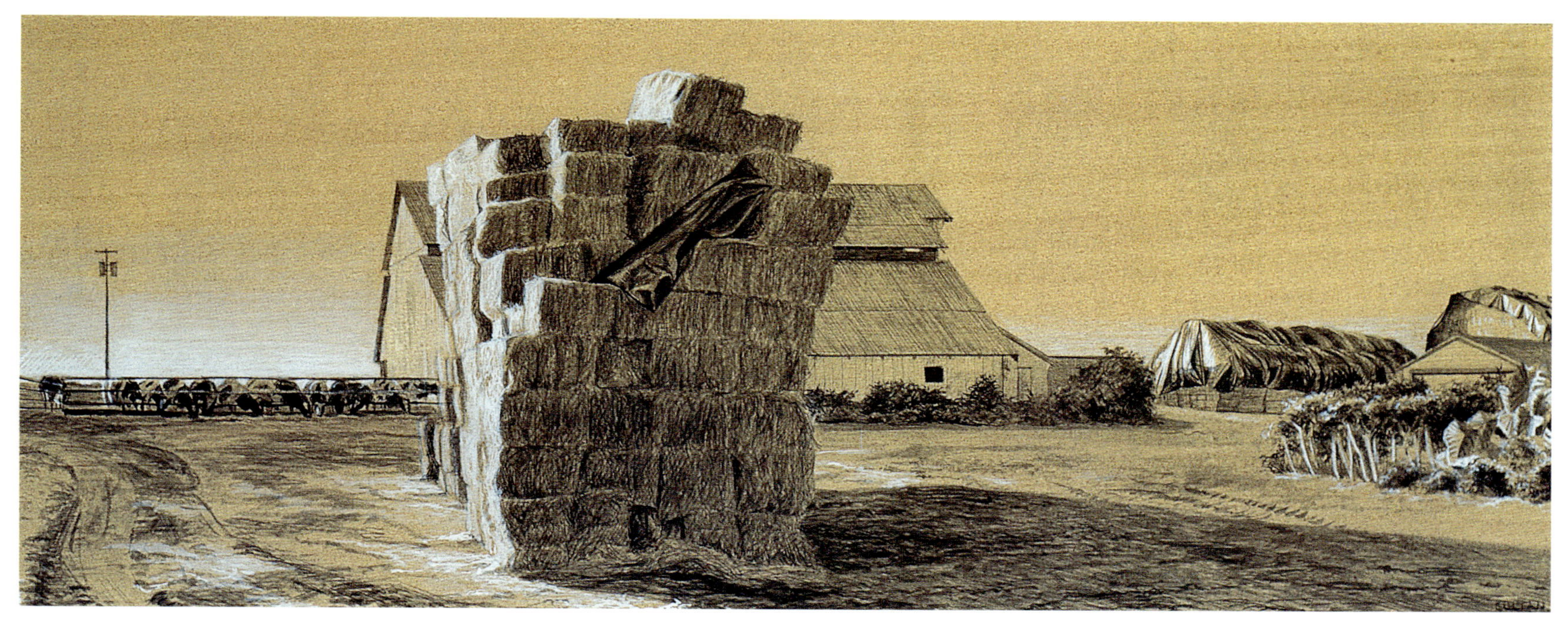



I used varied strokes of the brush to invoke the texture of hay piled up on a California farm. I chose a yellow color for the paper, the color of hay.

While looking for a motif for this drawing *Corn and Empty Ag-Bag, Waterford, Vermont*, I drove up to beautiful high pastures interspersed with cornfields. At the edge of one field were some brilliant white long plastic bags filled with hay. I chose to depict the wonderful circular form of the empty bag stretched over a metal hoop—it added a sparkling geometry in contrast to the natural forms of corn and hills. For this $9 \times 12^{1}/_2$ drawing, I prepared a sheet of handmade watercolor paper with a green tone mixed with titanium white, chrome oxide green, and raw sienna. I mixed five values of black India ink for the dark tones, and for the lights I use diluted gouache titanium white.

### STEP 1

I complete a careful line drawing on paper of the motif, including the cloud formations and the young corn in the foreground. Then I trace this drawing with a hard pencil, #4H, onto a sheet of tracing paper.

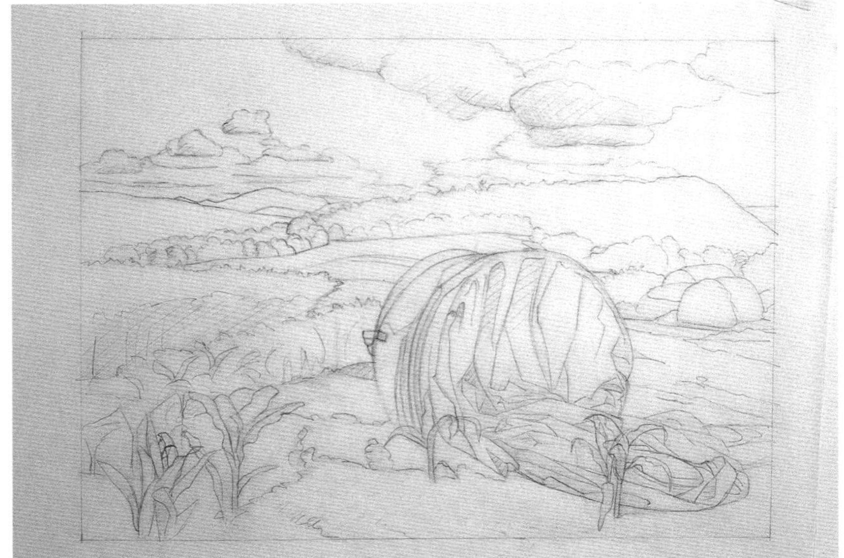

### STEP 2

I make a "carbon paper" by rubbing a thin sheet of paper with soft vine charcoal, and then wiping off the excess charcoal with a paper towel or a chamois. (This paper can be reused many times).

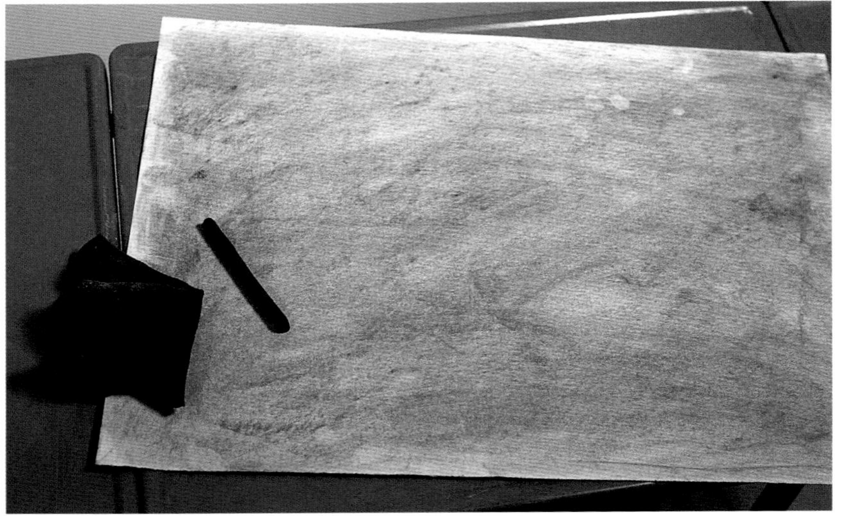

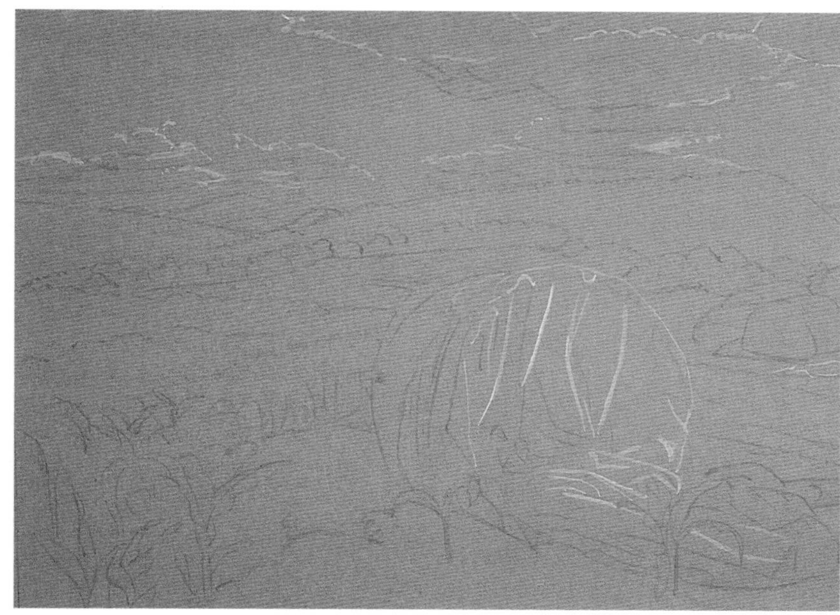



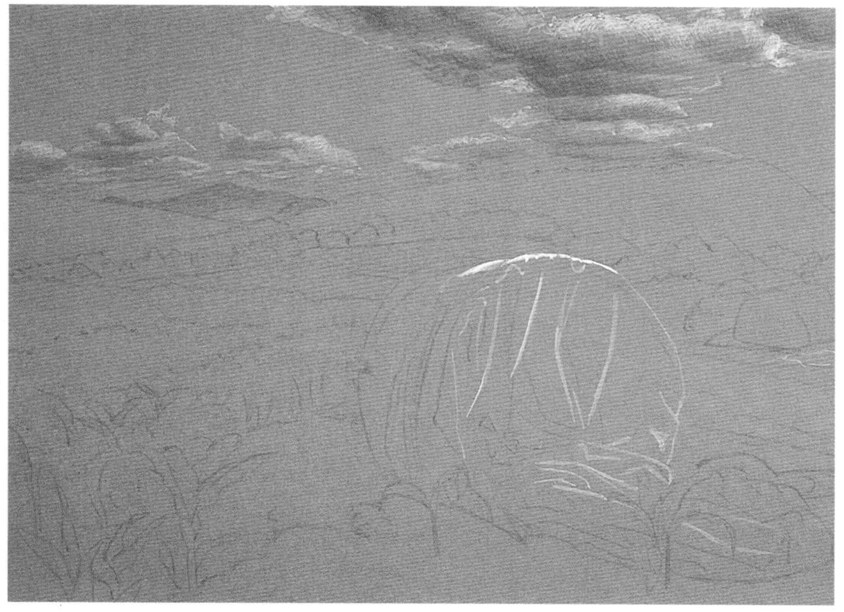



I place the "carbon" paper face down on my toned paper, then put the tracing of the drawing on top of it. Using a hard #6H or #8H pencil, I trace the lines of the drawing onto the paper. I check the tracing as I work to be sure that there is enough charcoal to leave a clear impression, but not so much as to make dark and fuzzy lines. Using a very light value of black ink, I go over the charcoal lines on the paper. For areas that will be light, I go over the charcoal lines with diluted white gouache.

When I work with ink, tempera, or gouache, I paint from "back" to "front" spatially—the sky first, then distant hills, middle ground, and finally the foreground. Because I don't build tones over the whole image at once, I must be constantly aware of value relationships with items not yet drawn or painted. I begin by using many layers of very light ink to draw the clouds and the most distant mountain. Using many layers of the lightest value of ink assures a good degree of control. There are more layers of ink in the clouds that are closer. I put some strong white on the circular form in the foreground in order to establish a value relationship with the white in the more distant clouds—a more intense white pulls forward visually.

Working on the tree-covered hills, I use two values of ink in many layers, building darker tones as the trees come forward in space, which emphasizes the atmospheric perspective. For the highlights in the trees, the most distant have a thin layer of light ink, the mid-range use the value of the paper, and the closest are painted with a thin layer of white. I draw strong darks in the foreground to indicate a contrast with the mid-tones of the distance, which create the illusion of space.

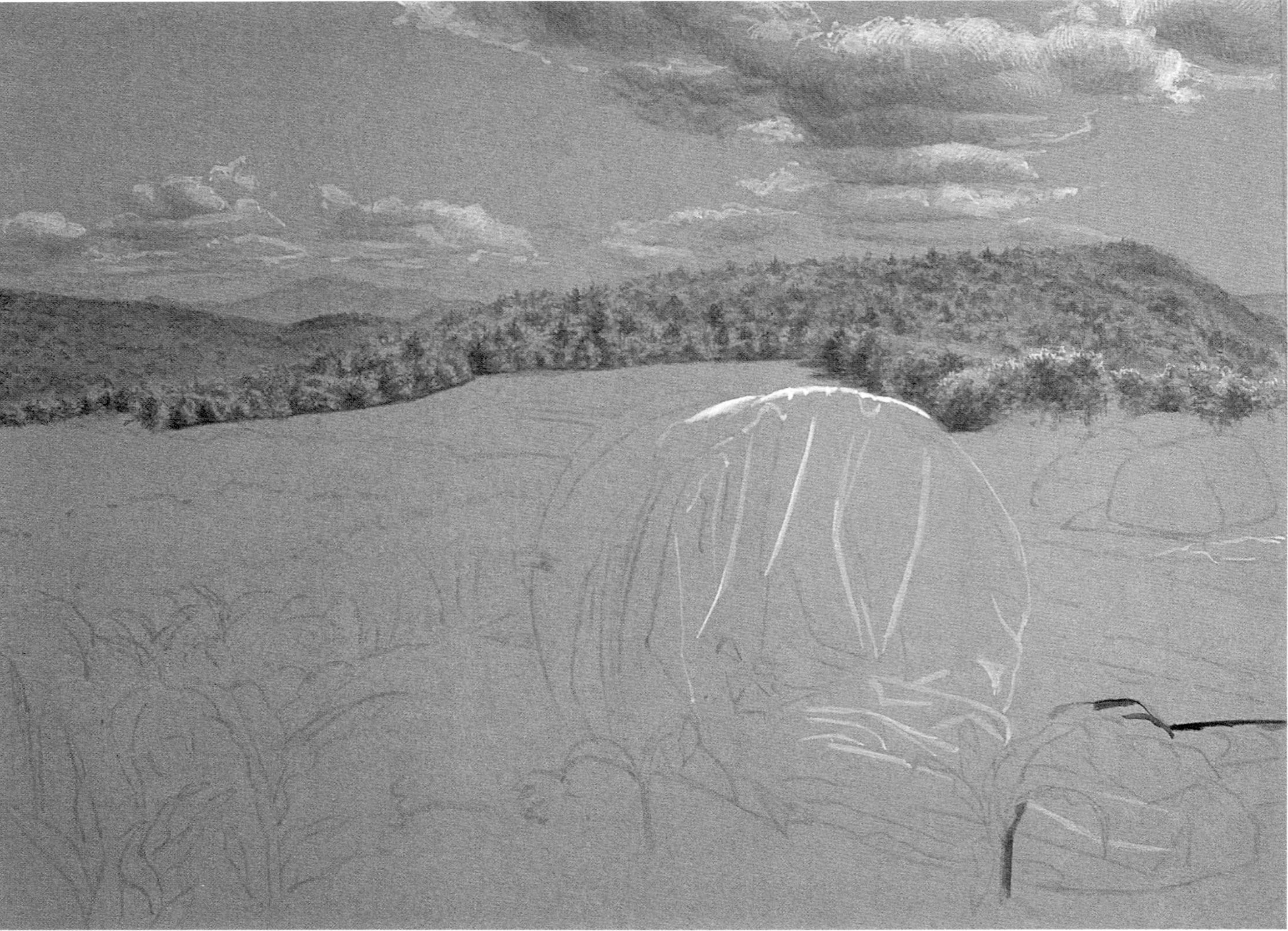

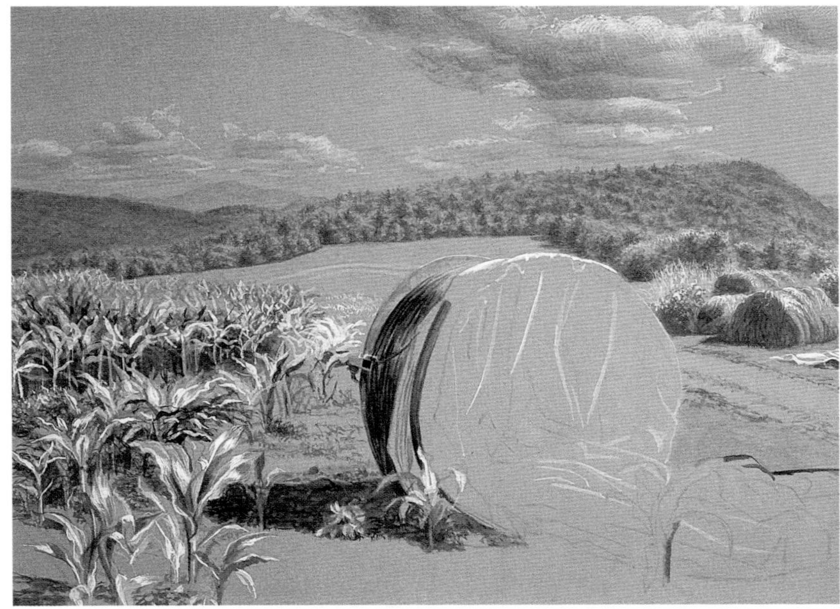



Drawing the hay bales on the right, I make their darks stronger than those of the trees, and the lights brighter; this brings the bales forward spatially. I use strokes of the brush to express the texture of hay, and different gestural strokes to describe the leaves of the corn plants. There is a progressive darkening of the spaces between the corn stalks to bring them forward. I draw very strong darks on the shadow and on the black plastic wrapped around the hoop. As these strong darks are established, the spatial illusion of the drawing is heightened.

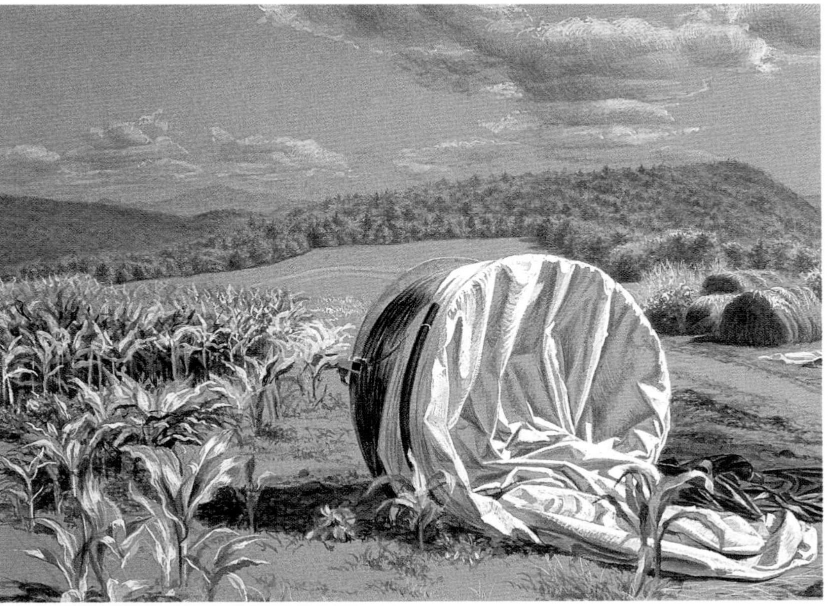



I draw the white plastic of the ag-bag, using the green tone of the paper for the middle values. Because it is such a bright object, I use ink for only its darkest shadows. I use light and middle values of ink to complete the foreground, drawing some clumps of grass and the remaining corn. I leave much of the middle tone of the paper for the ground plane.

After completing the drawing, I see that the hills and clouds are too light in value for the balance of the drawing. After darkening them, the drawing is now complete.

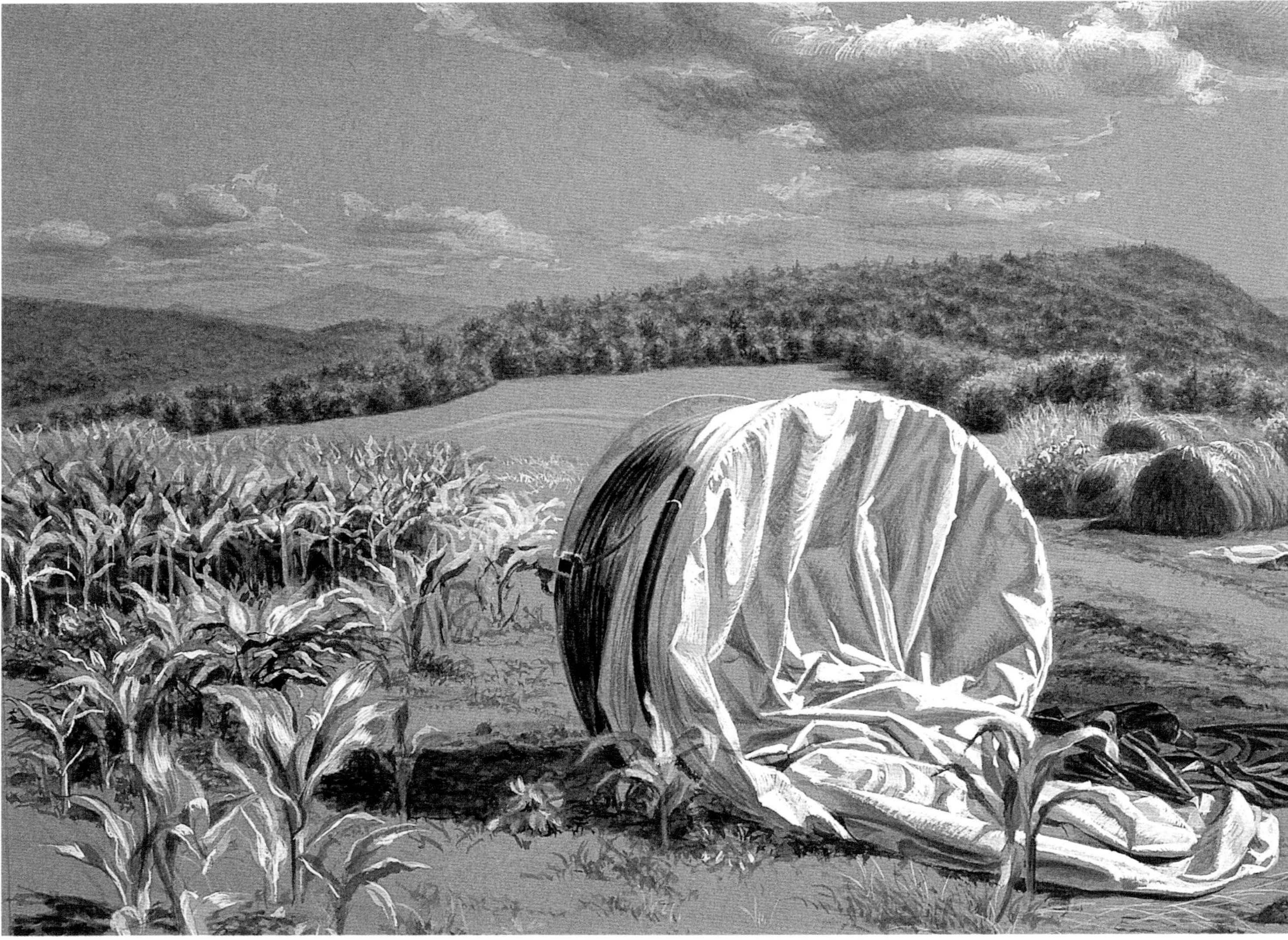

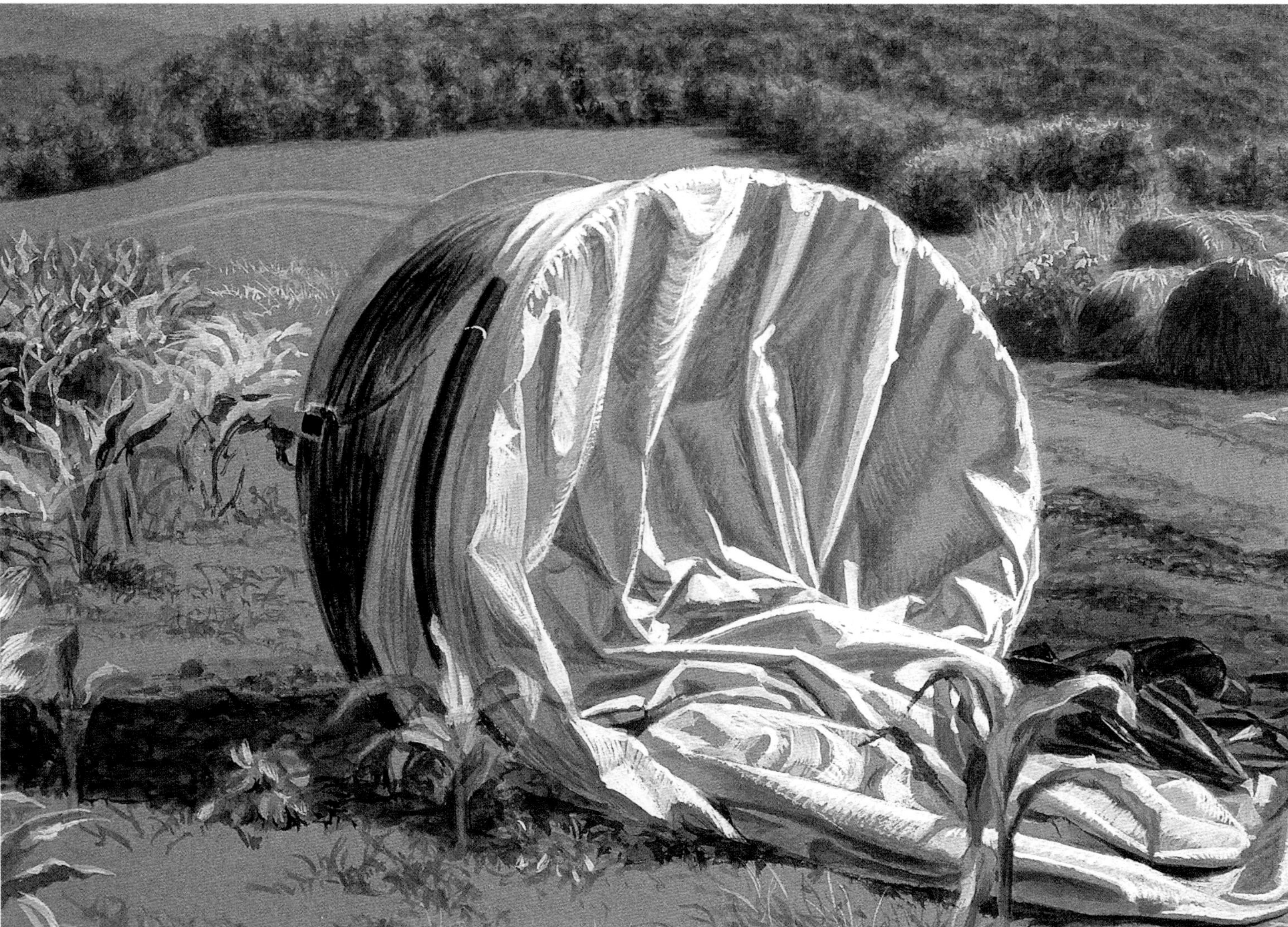



I use the white gouache quite opaquely to paint the bright highlights of the white plastic. This strong contrast allows me to use the midtones of the paper as the shadow.

# The Underdrawing for the Egg Tempera Painting

In the traditional technique of egg tempera painting as described in Cennini's *The Craftsman's Handbook,* a monochrome underdrawing in ink is completed before painting in color begins. In practice, many artists did only a summary sketch in ink using a brush or a pen. With infrared photography, we can see how different artists handled the underdrawings. Sometimes the finished painting differs slightly from the underdrawing, indicating that tempera is a medium that was used much more flexibly than many people have thought. And it can be used flexibly today. Although I develop a fairly detailed underdrawing, you may find that you wish to draw only the outline of your composition, or apply the tones loosely using a broad brush. You may also choose not to use an underdrawing at all (see "Other Approaches").

I find the clarity and organization of the step-by-step process—underdrawing, then color—very helpful. During the first step I concentrate on composition, form, space, and light as described by line and by value. I work up the underdrawing carefully because the translucence of the egg tempera makes it difficult to make dramatic changes in the painting's composition. After these essential structural elements are complete, I can then move easily to color.

Tempera is a translucent paint, so the underdrawing will have a strong effect on the succeeding paint layers. This is especially evident with darker values. A strong dark in the underdrawing makes it easier to paint darks using translucent color. Working with an underdrawing helps me to utilize the rich effects of glazes.

Whether you are a representational or abstract painter working in a subtle or aggressive style, your underdrawing should have the composition and value structure of the finished painting. The medium for your underdrawing can be India ink of any color, or even pigment that has been tempered with the egg yolk medium. You may enjoy experimenting with different colors for the underdrawing to see the effects on the finished painting. I find that black India ink works well for me, so I have used it for my demonstrations. My descriptions of the use of brush and black ink apply equally to other colored inks or egg tempera paint.

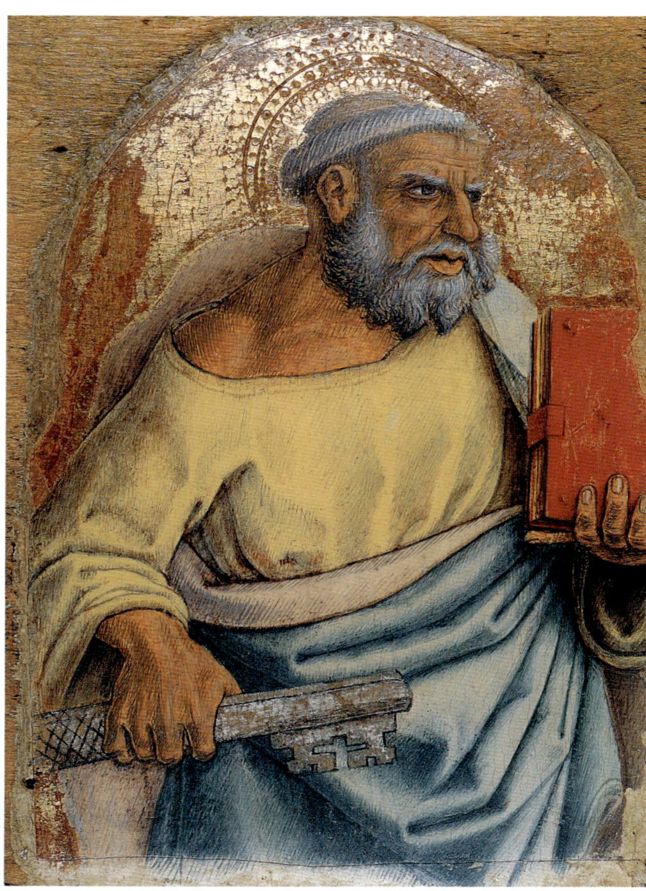

Carlo Crivelli
SAINT
PETER
circa 1470

The paint has worn away on this small panel, allowing us to see the strong ink underdrawing.

When I go outside to paint studies for landscape paintings like *Hay Bales, Hazy Day, Ryegate, Vermont,* I take my portable easel filled with gouaches and large watercolor brushes, several sheets of watercolor paper tacked to boards, and my camera filled with black-and-white film. I paint a color study on location that gives me a sense of the light, color, and atmosphere of the subject. I also use black-and-white photographs shot with a 35mm camera with a 50mm lens for notation of form and detail. I use black-and-white rather than color film because I want my own color memory to take precedence over the chemical color of photographs. Back in the studio, my memory, the color study, and 8 × 10 enlargements of the black-and-white photos are the sources for my paintings.

I always look for strong foreground elements in the landscape; they engage my interest, and create a dynamic space. The round hay bales in this image have a natural, soft geometry and create a dynamic tension in their placement across the field. I chose to paint this scene in hazy light because it created beautifully clear differentiation of the distant planes of trees and hills.

### STEP 1

I prepare a line drawing on 10$^1$/$_2$ × 19$^1$/$_2$ paper using a moderately hard HB pencil. Because the forms of the hay bales are soft, the drawing doesn't have to be very precise. I then transfer this drawing to the gesso panel in the same way I transfer a drawing to toned paper, as described above.

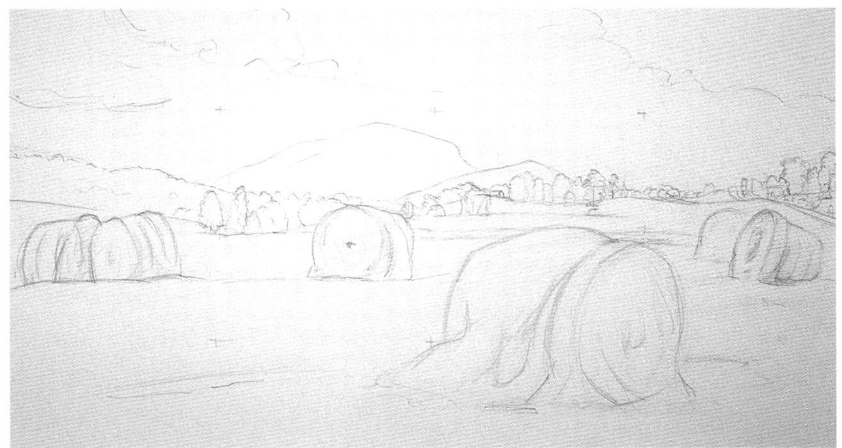

### STEP 2

I mix five values of ink in my palette wells, from very light to very dark. I will use these values in thin layers, occasionally mixing an intermediate value on the flat area of the palette. With #1 and #2 round watercolor brushes, I first draw the sky and the most distant hills using the two lightest values of ink. I indicate dark tones in the foreground to get a sense of the value contrasts needed to give the illusion of deep space.

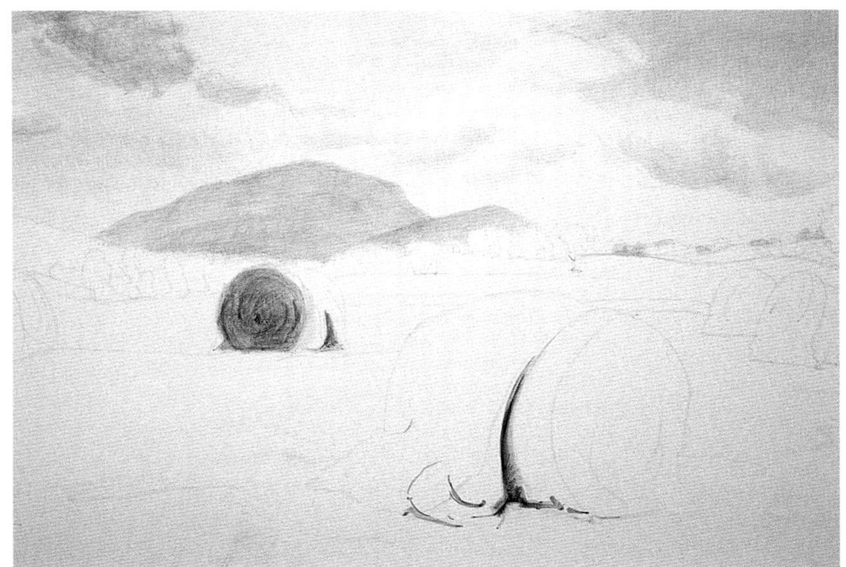

Using the three lightest values of ink, with some intermixing, I draw the varied layers of trees. I try to get the effect of receding planes by darkening the values as the trees come forward in space. As I am drawing the trees, I notice that the hay bale in the middle distance is too light, so I darken it. I use my brush loosely: not only in parallel or hatched lines, but also in varied broad strokes. If my gesso ground is not perfectly smooth, tiny scratches may show up in the underdrawing. I do not worry about this, however, because these scratches will be hidden by further layers of paint.

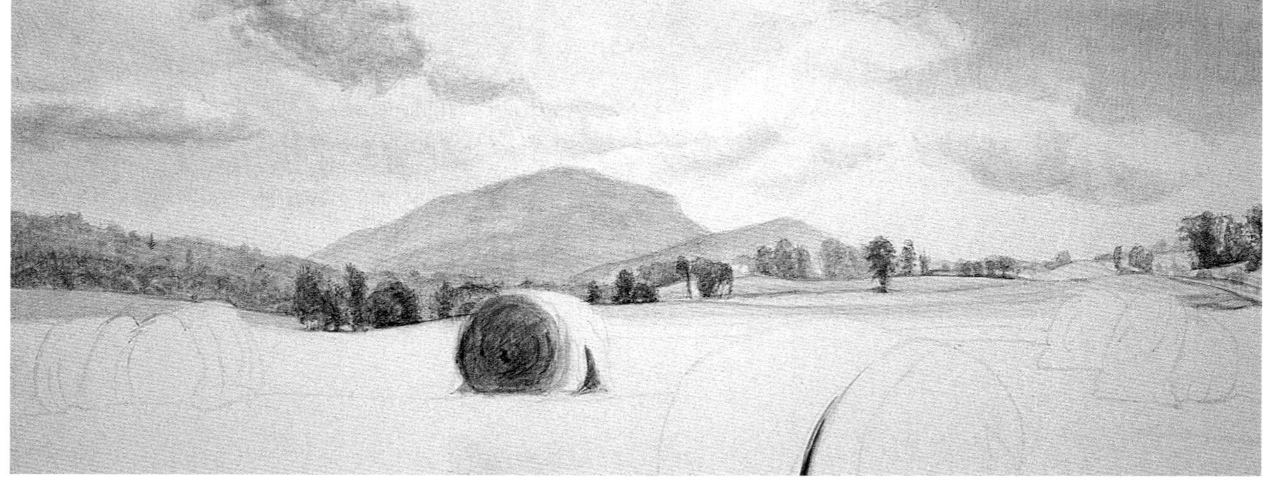



I make the tree-covered hill on the left darker in order to clarify the space. I continue working forward spatially by drawing the hay bales in the middle distance. I am not concerned with detail at this point, only with accurately portraying the values and form.

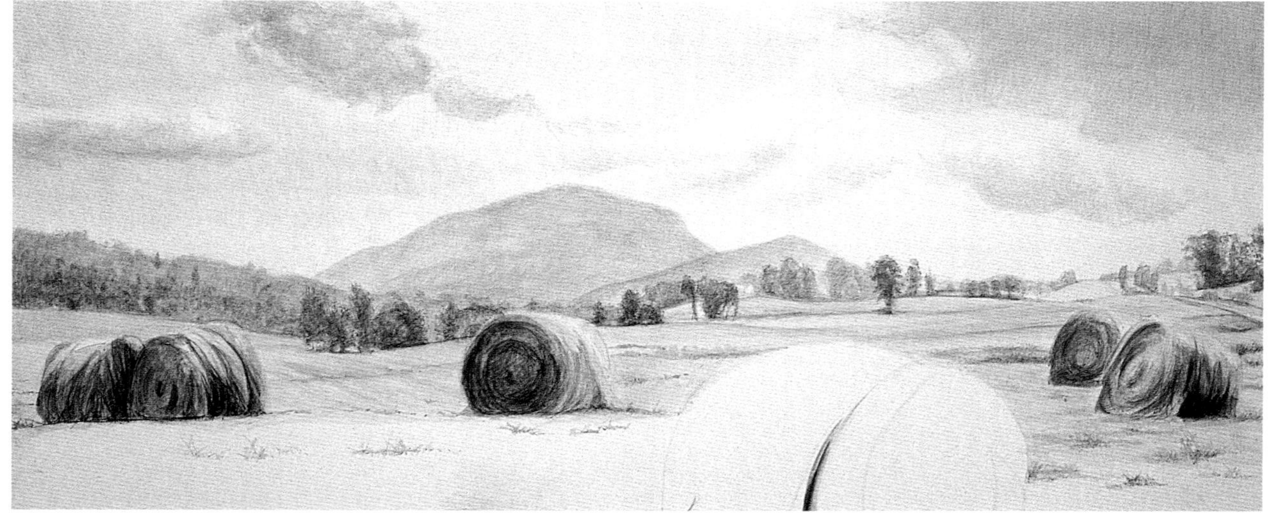

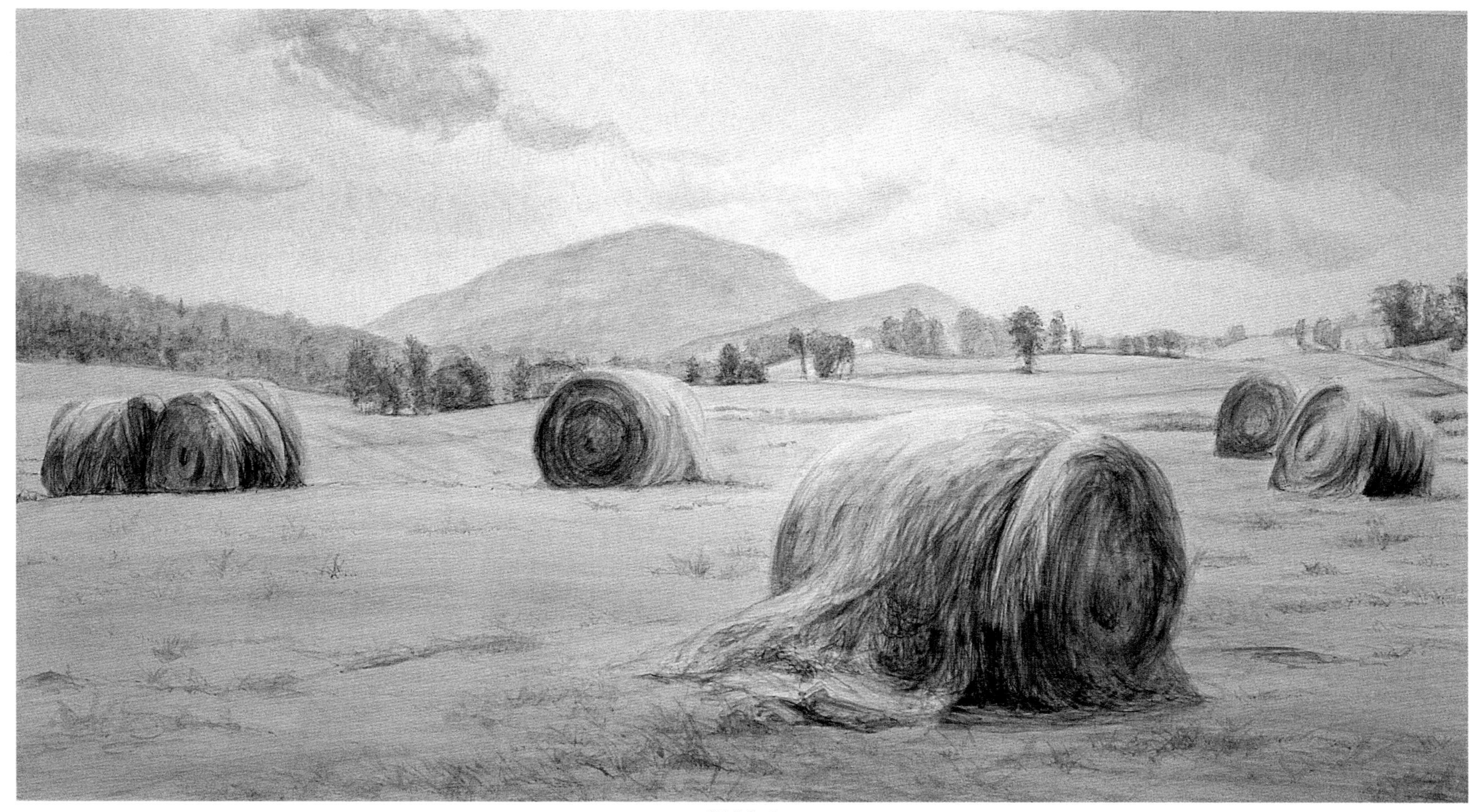



I broadly lay in the tone of the ground using a wide $3/4$-inch flat brush in a dry-brush manner, drawing several layers of a very light value of ink. I add the details of the grasses on top of this tone. As I work on the hay bale in the foreground, I find that my drawing is inaccurate, so I wipe away the ink on the light areas of the bale with a damp paper towel. I then work back into the drawing. I do this until the form is articulated to my satisfaction. The underdrawing is now complete and ready for painting.

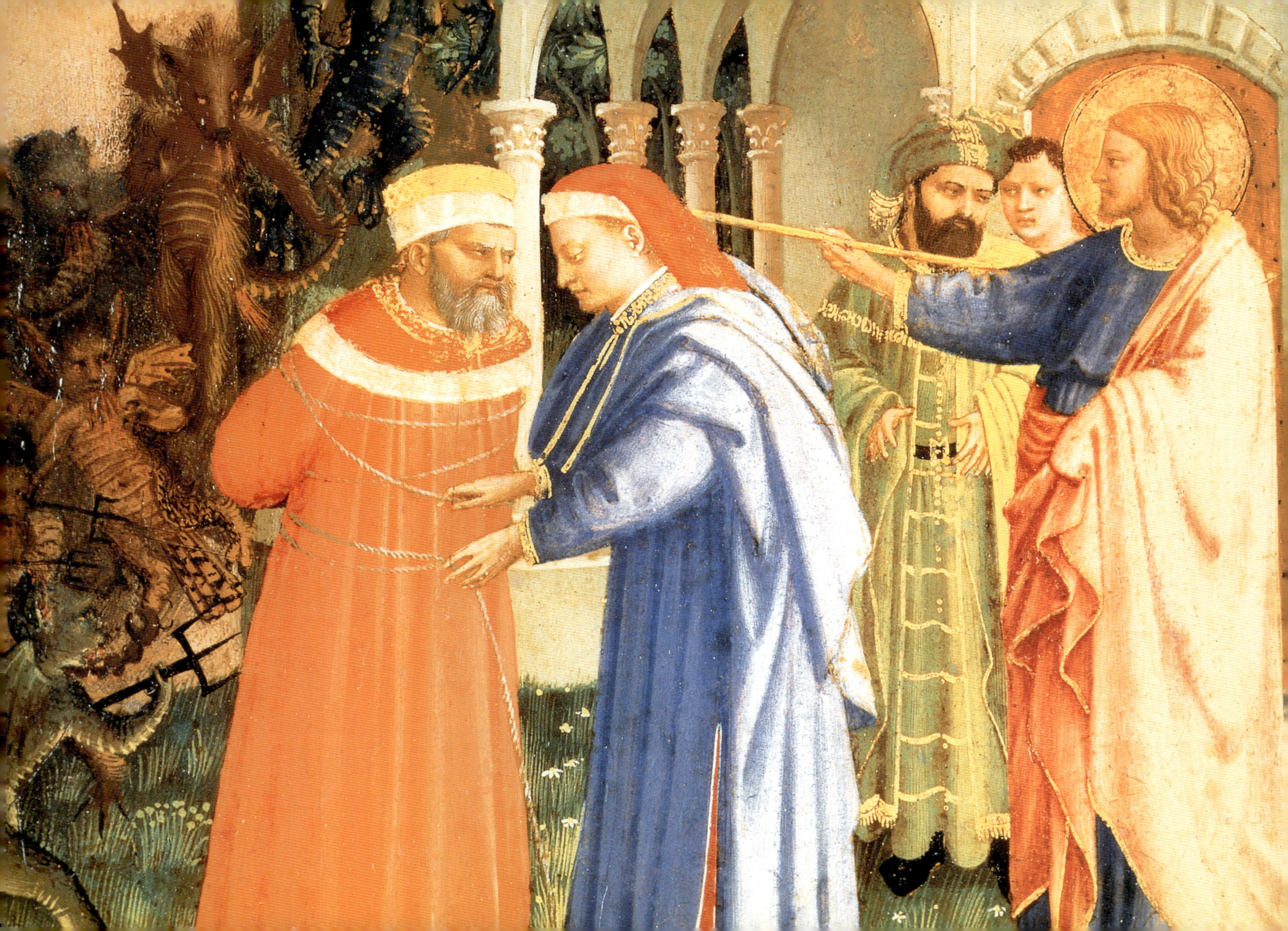

# WORKING WITH COLOR

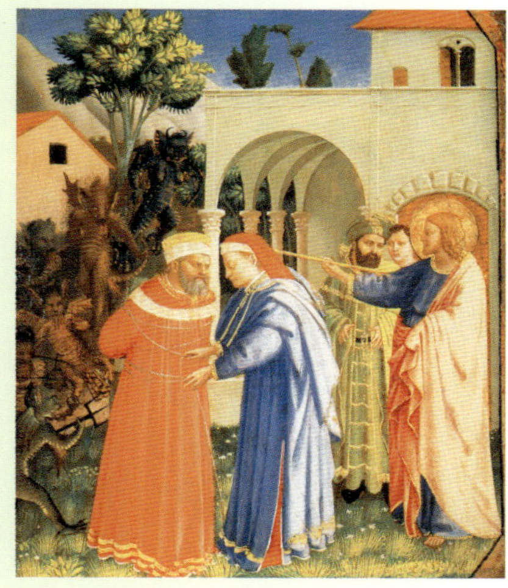



In this beautiful small panel, Fra Angelico uses the brilliant jewel-like color effects of tempera painting to their fullest extent. He also takes advantage of the precision and clarity of the medium—the delicacy and refinement of the portrait details are very affecting.

Color is at the heart of tempera painting. "Jewel-like" is often used to describe the color in Italian panel paintings; like fine-cut jewels, tempera color glows with depth and clarity. One reason for this quality of tempera is the egg yolk medium itself. Powdered pigments darken with the addition of a medium because the amount of light reflected from the pigment particles changes. For a simple illustration, think of the color of dry dirt as it darkens when moistened by rain. Every medium affects pigments differently—pigment particles surrounded by oil will have a dark, saturated appearance because the oil absorbs light. Gouache has a very light, matte appearance because there is only a small amount of the binding medium, gum arabic, so light is reflected from the surface. The egg yolk medium has an effect between that of oil and gouache: the medium absorbs less light than oil, so the pigment appears closer to its original color, but the color is more saturated than it appears in gouache.

Whether the color is used in a naturalistic, descriptive, or symbolic manner, the technique of tempera painting—the layering of translucent paint—creates beautiful and luminous color effects as light passes through the layers of color. The underlayers of color, or the layers of paint beneath the final paint layer, are referred to as the underpainting. As with the underdrawing, the underpainting has a strong effect on the finished painting. During the Renaissance, artists underpainted flesh with green earth, which would give the effect of cool tones in the middle values. On some panel paintings, you can see underpainting of a different color on drapery or architecture, enlivening the tonal modeling.

When I began to work with tempera, a painter friend visited my studio and remarked of my tempera paintings "The color is so different!" Yes, it is different—the luminosity and depth of egg tempera color cannot be matched by alla prima oil painting, making the demands of the medium worth the effort.

# The Translucence of Tempera: Effects of the Underpainting

When painting with tempera, we should keep in mind its distinctive quality—that of translucence. Watercolor is a transparent medium and achieves its
brilliance from the flow of color over white paper. Gouache is opaque and
yields beautiful milky tones. Egg tempera, because of its translucence, has a
wonderful flexibility. You can build many layers of the same color to create
an opacity of great depth. Or, in painting a light tone over a darker one,
which is called scumbling, you can achieve a cool, opalescent effect. By glazing—painting a thin layer of transparent color over another color—a warm
color results. It is very easy to adjust a color by glazing another color over it.
To warm a green hue, glaze a thin layer of red or black or yellow. You can
play back and forth between these effects until you get the one desired.
You can create optical mixtures of color by layering hues. For instance,
painting layers of yellow and blue will result in a green. There is a sense of
magic layering color—so much can happen with a thin glaze or scumble.

I generally paint the underlayers with crosshatching, but at times I
prefer to be a bit looser with the first layer of underpainting, so I apply
a wash with a ³/₄-inch flat watercolor brush (See demonstrations).

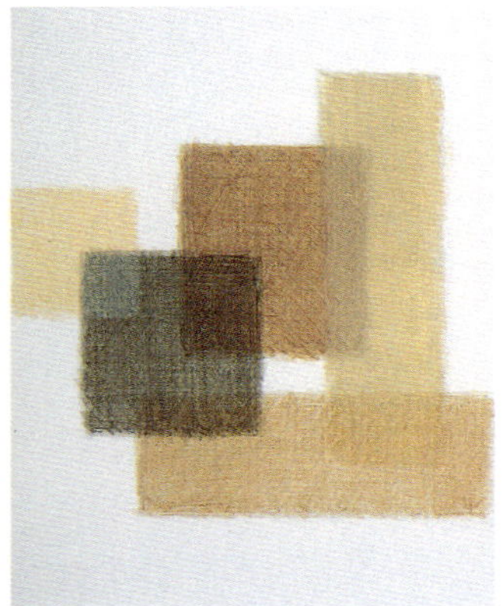

Here, you can clearly see the effect that colors have upon each other. The yellow bar on the right, passing over the light brown square, makes a cool hue. Under the bar on the bottom, it warms the color. The dark green square creates different colors, depending on the underpainted color.

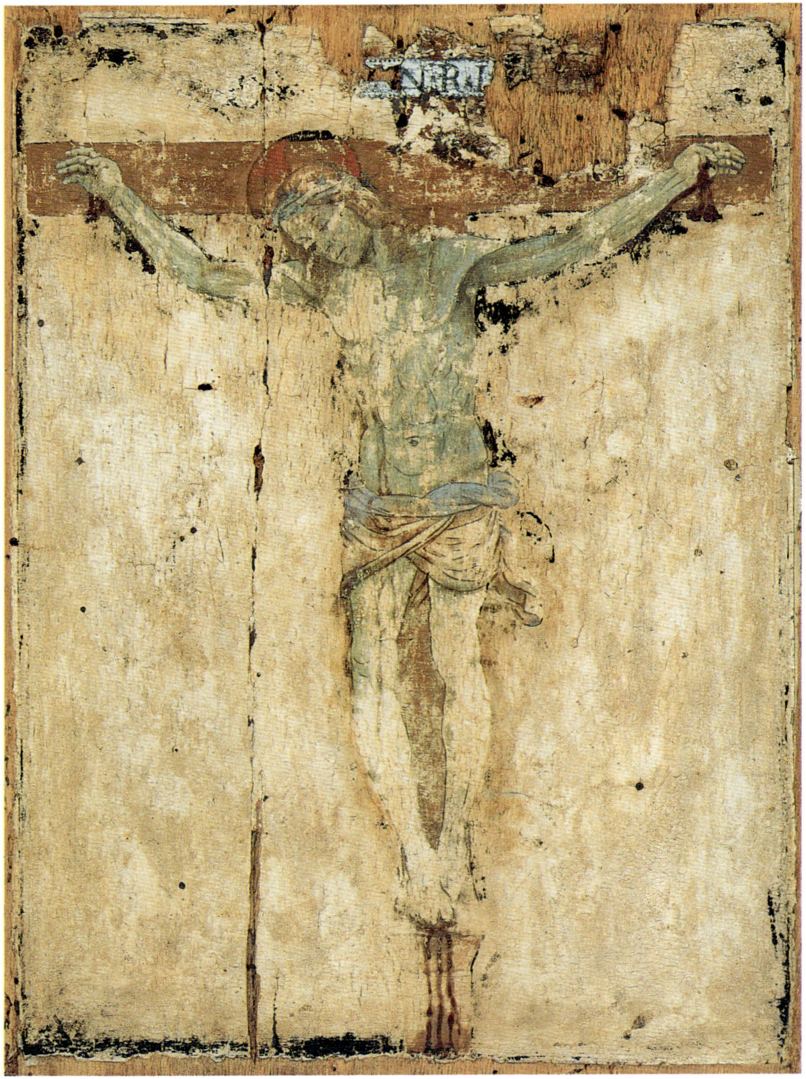

Filippino Lippi
CHRIST ON
THE CROSS
circa 1495

We can see the delicate lines of the underdrawing on this panel, outlining the form and the muscle groups. The transparent green earth underpainting is also clearly visible. This green would have affect-ed the warm colors laid on top of it, imitating the cool undertones of flesh.

# Tempering the Pigment

When your ink drawing on the gesso panel is complete, you are ready to begin using color. The pigments, which have been ground with water, must be mixed with the egg yolk medium to temper them. The preparation of this medium is described on page 31. Now you can place your colors on your palette. Use only the colors that you think you will need in this session of work, because tempered pigments last only one day. On some days when I know that I will only be working on a sky I put three blues, a red, an ochre, and a white on my palette. On other days a full array of color is necessary. Reach into the pigment jar with a palette knife, remove a small amount of pigment paste, and place it in a palette well. You don't need much pigment because it will be considerably thinned out with water for use. You'll need a larger amount of white pigment. To each mass of pigment, add an equal amount of egg yolk. Each pigment needs a bit more or less of the yolk, and you'll soon figure out the proper amount by the look of the brushed out color. For instance, earth colors and black seem to need more medium. With a wet brush, mix pigment and yolk together. You'll notice that the white pigment looks yellowish with the yolk added, as do cobalt and cerulean blue. The yellow tint on your painting will bleach out in a couple of days.

As you work over the course of the day, you will see the egg yolk separating from the pigment, floating to the top of the palette well. Be sure to keep mixing the paint to assure the correct tempering of the pigment. If you are working on a large panel, you may want to mix your colors in small jars *before* tempering them. In that way, you can temper only as much color as you will need in one day. Small plastic or porcelain saucers are useful for mixing large amounts of color.

You'll need a small gessoed panel for testing the tempering. Make a stroke of the tempered color on the panel. Let it dry for a minute or two and look at it at an angle to the light. If the surface appears dry, add more egg to the mixture. With insufficient yolk acting as a binder the pigment will fall off the surface of the panel. If the stroke of color has a low gloss, it is just right. If it is very shiny and dries very slowly, it means that there is too much egg yolk, so you should add more pigment. You'll be able to see a low gloss on your painting after you've built up several layers of paint. If the painting looks matte, add more yolk to the pigment. Another way of testing the tempering is to brush some paint onto a piece of plate glass. Let it dry for a few moments and then scrape it up with a palette knife. If it curls up, it is sufficiently tempered; if it crumbles, there is not enough egg yolk in the paint.

While you'll need to test your tempering when you first begin working with egg tempera, after a while you'll gain a feel for the correct amount of egg yolk. I find that I prefer to have a bit too much egg rather than too little, to be sure of sufficient tempering.

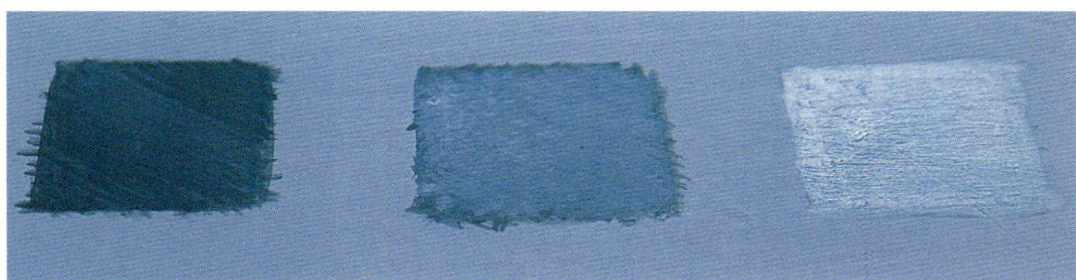

Different amounts of the egg yolk medium were added to chrome oxide green pigment. On the left, the paint looks dull, so there is not enough egg yolk; the middle sample has a low sheen that shows that it is tempered correctly; the right sample is very glossy, which indicates too much egg yolk medium.

# Paint Handling

In order to work with the tempered color so that it flows freely from a dry brush, it must be thinned with water. So, add some water to each palette well. (You will find that as the day progresses, you may need to replace water that has evaporated.) I generally like to use my paint very thinly, about the consistency of India ink, in order to make continuous

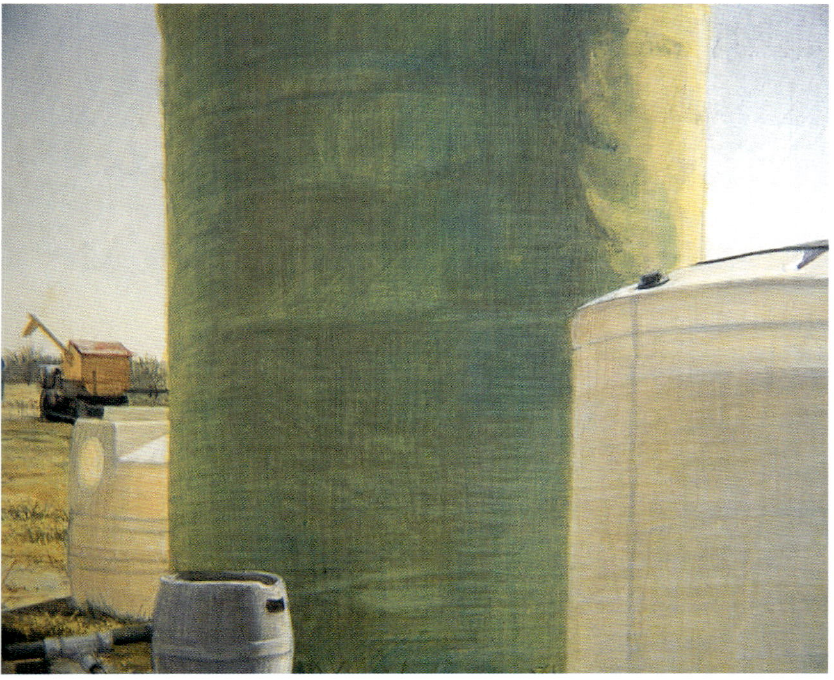



In this detail, you can see the discrete hatched strokes of paint. I apply them following the form of the tanks so as to enhance the illusion of volume.

tones, but some artists prefer the paint a bit creamier to make more distinct strokes. I use a creamier paint, about the consistency of heavy cream, when painting highlights and some textures. Whichever way you prefer to work, using the paint fairly thinly, in many layers, enables you to utilize the translucence of tempera.

You handle the brush with color in the same way that you did with ink. The brush is dipped into the pigment, wiped off on the side of the palette well, and then wiped on a paper towel until nearly dry. In this way, you will be able to paint several strokes without drops of color at the end of each mark. When used in this dry-brush, pencil-like manner, the paint dries almost immediately, allowing for rapid crosshatching and building of tones. If you try to take shortcuts by using thick paint other than for highlights, you run the risk of making white spots—when the layers of paint lift off down to the gesso, as a new layer of paint lifts off a still damp underlayer. If you have the problem of underlayers lifting, then your paint is too thick, or it has too much egg yolk medium, or you have not wiped your brush dry enough.

If you want to paint an even tone, you can do this quite easily by painting many thin layers of the same color brushed on in different directions. It is easiest to get a smooth tone when using a color mixed with white paint that is lighter than the underpainting (a scumble). This may seem tedious, but the process of working with hatched lines and developing the color slowly, is actually calming, almost meditative.

My palette has separate wells in which I place the pigments that I will need that day. I add egg yolk medium to the pigments before I begin working. I use a palette well to mix a color when I will need a lot of it— when I am painting a sky for instance. Since I paint small pictures, the palette wells are large enough for me; if you want to mix large amounts of color, plastic or porcelain saucers are useful. If I need a small amount of a mixed color, I use the flat area of the palette, occasionally wiping it with a damp paper towel to keep it clean.

I paint sitting at a table with a slightly tilted surface and keep my palette on my right side (I am right-handed), along with a quart of water and a paper towel for wiping excess paint from the brush. Brushes and pigments are within easy reach to my left. I prop up the painting panel with an object an inch or two thick. Although I work sitting down because my paintings are fairly small, I often get up to look at the work from a distance. It is important not to get entranced by details and lose sight of the whole effect of the painting.

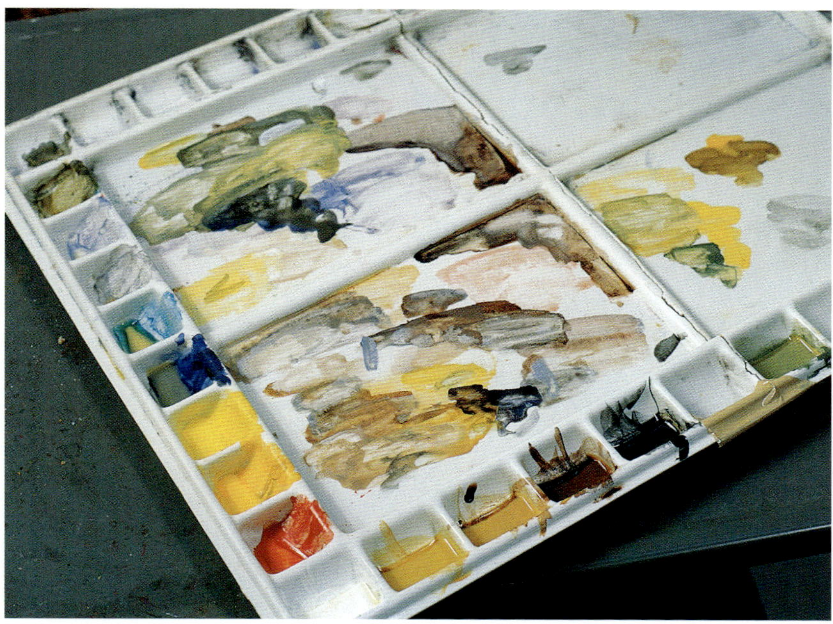

My palette for *House and Tree, Pittsfield, Vermont* (see "How Do I Paint...?"). I placed 11 pigment pastes in palette wells and tempered them. On the upper left are two values of violet for the house and a green mixed in the palette wells. I mixed many individual hues on the central area.

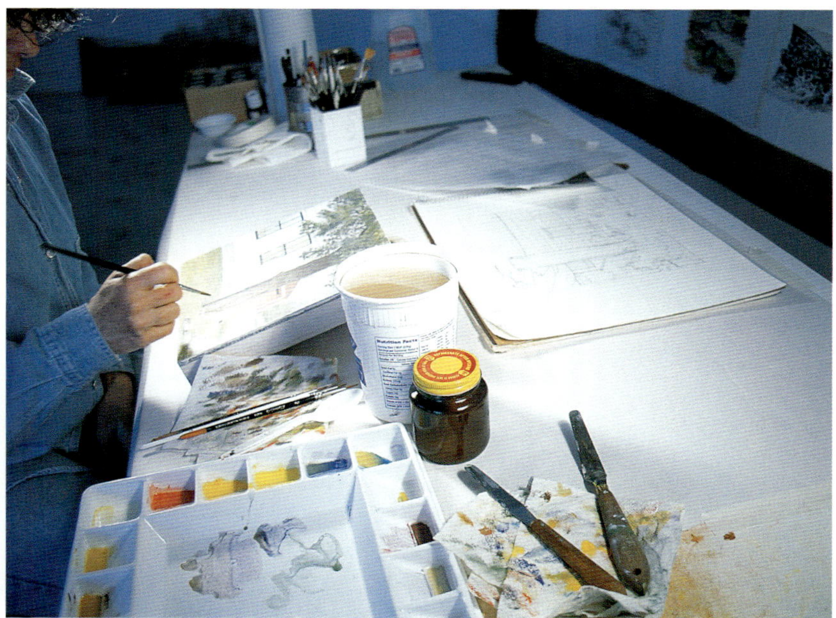

On my right at my work table are my palette, palette knives, a small jar of egg yolk medium, and a large container of water. In front of the water is a paper towel that I use to wipe my brushes dry. My painting is propped up on a roll of masking tape. On the table in front of me is the line drawing for the painting and I hang the color study on the wall to see it clearly.

# Methods of Color Mixing

The flexibility of the egg tempera technique makes color mixing an easy process. Not only can we mix color on our palettes, but because the paint dries almost immediately and is translucent, it allows us to mix color directly on our paintings. With fast drying tempera, we have none of the blurring and bleeding problems that plague the impatient user of watercolor.

## THE CHARACTERISTICS OF COLOR

In order to describe a color, we talk about its three characteristics— hue, value, and intensity. The hue is the color name of the substance, such as red, green, or violet. The warmth or coolness of a color is a function of its hue. Red, yellow, and orange are warm colors, while blue, green, and violet are cool. Within each of these colors there are warm and cool hues— warm reds (vermilion) and cool reds (alizarin); warm blues (ultramarine) and cool blues (cerulean). Generally, warm colors move forward visually and cool colors recede.

The value is the amount of light or dark in the color, and its intensity is its brightness or saturation. For example, red is a color that is bright but dark, while yellow is bright and light. Adding white to a color lightens it but decreases its intensity. When we add white to a red pigment, it becomes pink and loses its brightness.

An understanding of value—of light and dark—is essential in making the illusion of three dimensional form on the two dimensional surface of paper or panel. The modeling of forms from light to dark—whether of still-life objects, the figure, or the landscape—gives them volume and places them in space. When I am out painting the landscape, I often close one eye and squint with the other so that details are eliminated and I can see the major value relationships more clearly.

While value is the underpinning of form, hue is also used for modeling form and for painting light. Direct light is warm and is painted with warm colors, while shadows are cool. Think of the blue or violet shadows

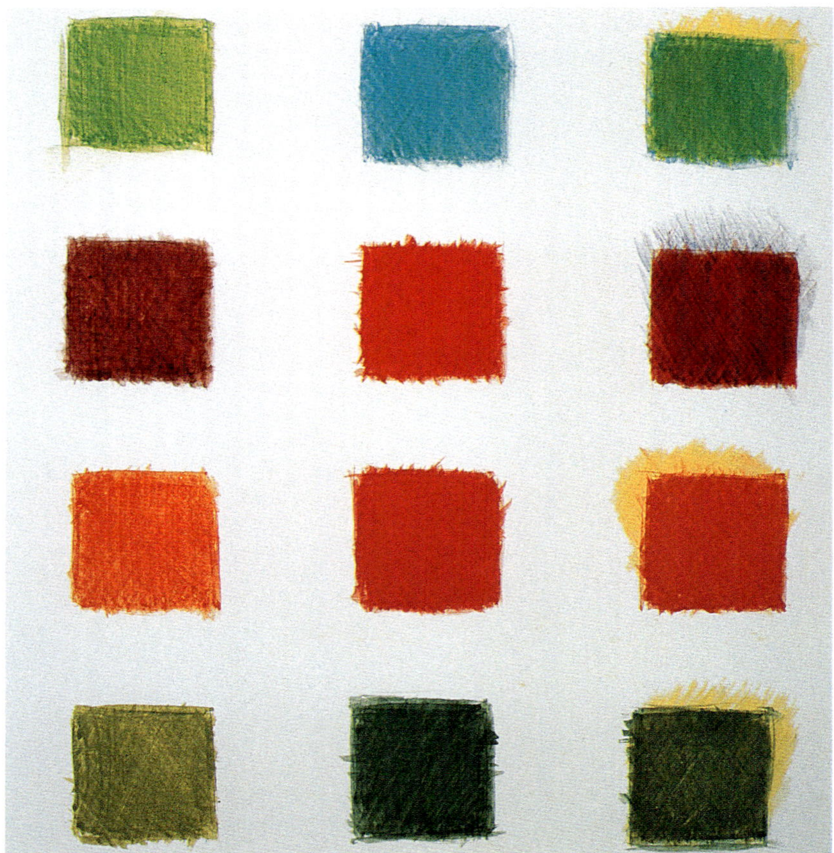

The central column shows unmixed hues, on the left they are mixed with another hue on the palette and then painted on the panel, on the right the second hue is glazed on top of the hue shown in the center. The color glows a bit more when glazing is used.

The first row has manganese blue in the center. It is mixed with cadmium yellow light on the left, and glazed with the same yellow on the right. In the second row, cadmium red light is mixed and glazed with ultramarine blue. The third row has the same cadmium red light mixed and glazed with cadmium yellow medium. In the last row, chrome oxide green is mixed with cadmium yellow light on the left and glazed on the right.

cast on snow. An object painted with warm and cool color variations as well as different values will have a livelier and more naturalistic appearance. It is very helpful to study impressionist paintings to see how light can be pictured using warm and cool colors.

The intensity of a color can be used to create the illusion of space, since an intense color will pop forward visually. Intensity diminishes as space recedes. Sometimes a painting will be brought to life by the addition of a bright color.

Various hues of translucent egg tempera paint can be layered to make new hues—red and yellow to make orange, red and blue to make violet. The color of the underpainting can have a subtle or bold effect depending on how opaque or translucent the final paint layers are.

## MIXING CONTINUOUS COLORS

In the traditional color mixing of the early Renaissance as described by Cennini, the artist worked with three or more values of each color to model form. A small dish held a color with some white added, a second had the color with more white. A third value was created by mixing equal amounts of these two values. The darkest values were painted with a glaze of pure color. Highlights were added with a color close to pure white. To paint a blue robe, the artist mixed three values of blue and blended one into the next to describe the folds. The darkest areas were glazed with pure blue and highlights were added with a very light value.

You can add to the range of values by mixing equal amounts of the first and middle value and the middle and last value, giving you five values

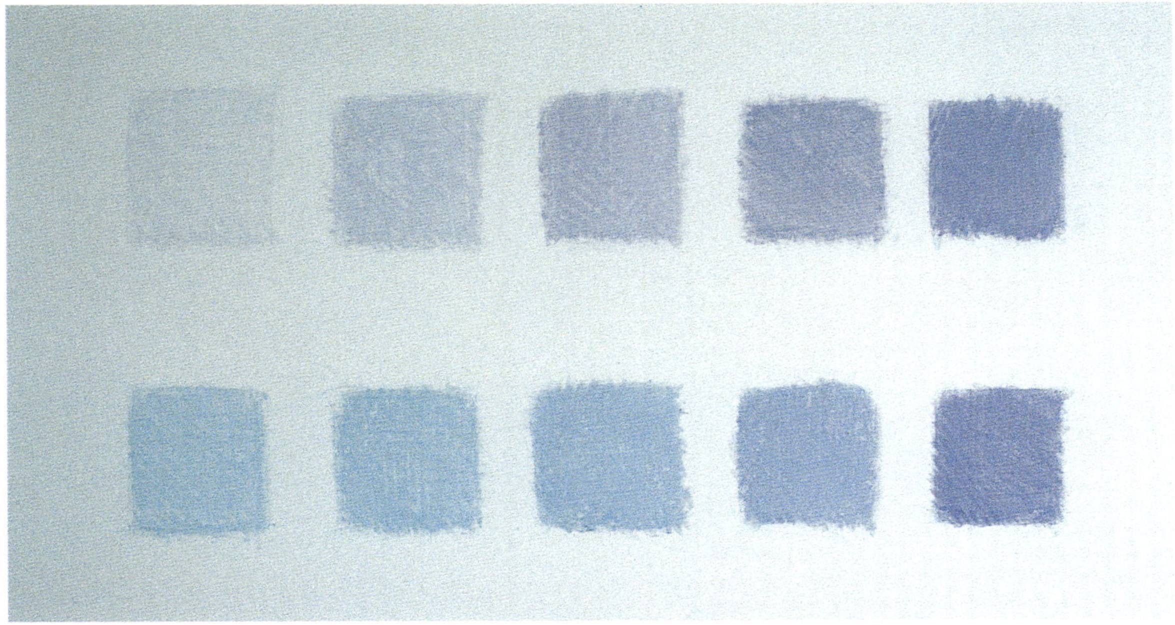

On the top row, I have mixed a range of values using cobalt blue and titanium white. The bottom row changes hue along with value. I mixed a light value of manganese blue and white (on the right) and a middle value of cobalt blue and white (on the left). The color in the center was mixed with equal amounts of those two colors; I then mixed two more colors between those three. This is generally the way I mix blues for a sky—going from a light, cool blue to a darker and warmer blue.

rather than three. This will provide a smooth transition of color for your painting as you overlap values. You can also change hues along with value, moving from a light, cool color to a warm, dark color, or from a light, warm to a cool, dark color. When painting a grassy field, you might want the distance to be cooler as well as lighter. By adding blue to the lightest value of green, and red or yellow to the darkest value, the color will make a nice transition from a warm, dark green in the foreground to a cool, light green in the distance, enhancing the illusion of space.

## GLAZING AND SCUMBLING

The translucent nature of egg tempera paint allows for the rich and varied color effects of paint layering. When a thin, transparent layer of color is painted over another color, it is called a glaze, which results in a warm hue. The glaze can be applied with hatched or parallel lines, or with a broad brush wiped nearly dry. For glazing, I often use a blunt, round watercolor brush with the bristles slightly splayed to make an even tone (wiped nearly dry, of course).

A color can be made opaque by the addition of some white paint. Overpainting a thin layer of an opaque color is called scumbling, which will result in a cool color, created by the effect of light passing through the paint. When I use a thin opaque paint, I work with the point of a brush wiped dry, and apply the paint with hatching. The scrubbing with a paintbrush in oil paint that is referred to as a scumble is not appropriate with tempera.

Glazing and scumbling can be used alternatively to create cool and warm effects. I find that I often like to layer a final glaze over underpainted scumbles so that the painting will have a warm luminosity.

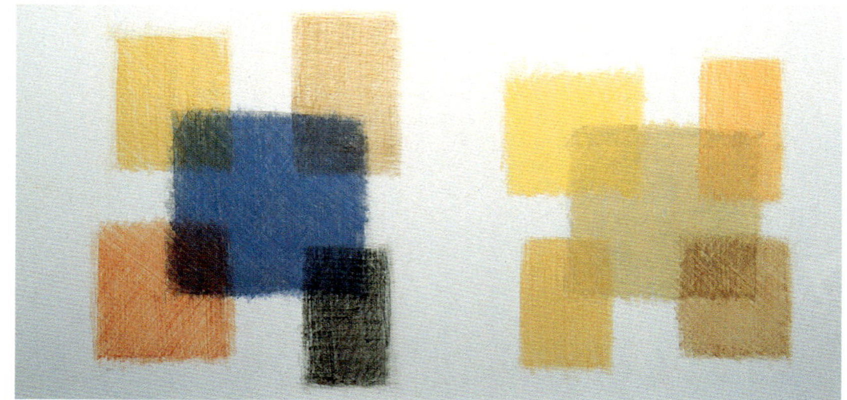

The left large square is a mixture of ultramarine blue and titanium white and glazed with (from upper left) yellow ochre, burnt umber, ivory black, and cadmium orange vermilion. The right square is a mixture of yellow ochre and white and glazed with cadmium yellow light, an orange mixed with yellow light and vermilion, burnt umber, and yellow ochre.

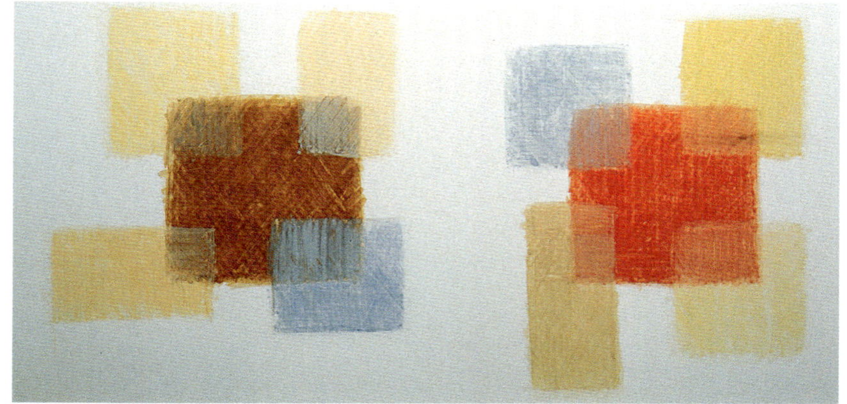

The square on the left is mixed with burnt umber and cadmium yellow light. It is scumbled with colors that are all mixed with titanium white to make them opaque. From the upper left, cadmium yellow light and white, yellow ochre and white, ultramarine blue and white, and cadmium yellow light and vermilion and white. The right square is painted with cadmium orange vermilion. It is scumbled with ultramarine blue and white, ultramarine blue and cadmium yellow light and white, cadmium yellow light and white, and burnt umber and yellow light and white.

## PAINTING LIGHT AND SPACE

Painting a landscape out-of-doors can be an exhilarating experience. While standing in the open air, looking at a light-filled sweeping view, an artist can feel a part of the world. Learning to paint the illusion of light and space is an exciting endeavor. For over twenty years I painted my landscapes on location, working on them over a period of months during spring and summer. My understanding of color has come from all those years of observing the world, and also from studying art—both contemporary art and art of the past. I no longer finish paintings on location because many of the objects that I want to paint move—machinery, animals, piles of hay. In addition, I paint either very large oil paintings, too big to fit in my car, or small egg temperas. I love working with tempera, but it is a studio medium and not well-suited for outdoors. Now I paint color studies in gouache on location to get a sense of light and air and for detail, I take black-and-white photos.

A very important concept to understand about color and its use in painting light and space is that colors exist in relationship to one another. The correct relationship of values and warm and cool hues create the illusions of light and space. As objects move towards us, their color is more intense, warmer, and darker. Farther away, they become less intense, cooler, and lighter in color. This is the effect of atmospheric perspective, in which the physical presence of the air obscures color as distance increases. On a hazy day, when the air is full of moisture, the atmospheric effect is heightened. In addition, value contrasts are greater in the foreground than in the background and details are more numerous and clear.

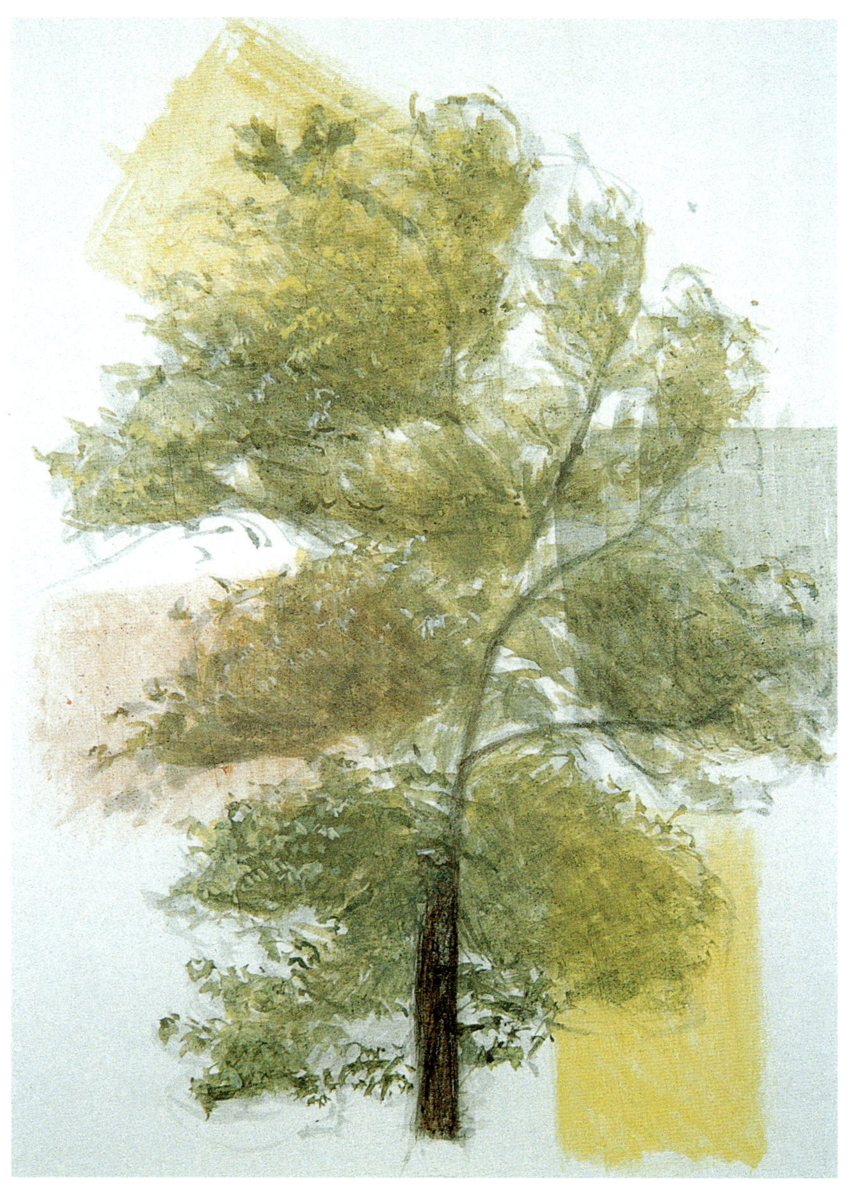

I have glazed four different colors on this study of a tree to show the different resulting colors (from middle left): cadmium red light, cadmium yellow medium, ivory black, and cadmium yellow light.

Direct sunlight is warm in color, and the shaded parts of objects are generally cool, as are cast shadows. All of these colors exist in relation to one another. There are warm greens and cool greens, and a color that appears warm in isolation may appear cool when next to a very warm hue. When mixing color, I continually ask myself, "Is this color the right hue, value, and intensity to be in a convincing relationship with other colors in the landscape? Is this green in the middle distance too yellow or too dark? Is the color of the shadow dark enough to contrast with the light, or is the contrast too strong for the illusion of distance?"

Making subtle adjustments of color is quite easy with egg tempera because of its translucence. If a color is making an object pop forward too much in space, a light scumble will cool that color and push it back. If something in the foreground is languishing in the middle ground, a glaze will bring it forward by warming the color. Making quick color shifts to keep colors in the correct relationship is almost effortless.

When I paint with tempera, I mix many of my colors on my palette, as I would with any other medium—mixing gradations of hues for large areas such as skies and ground. But then I adjust color relationships on the panel by glazing and scumbling, refining the illusion of light and space.

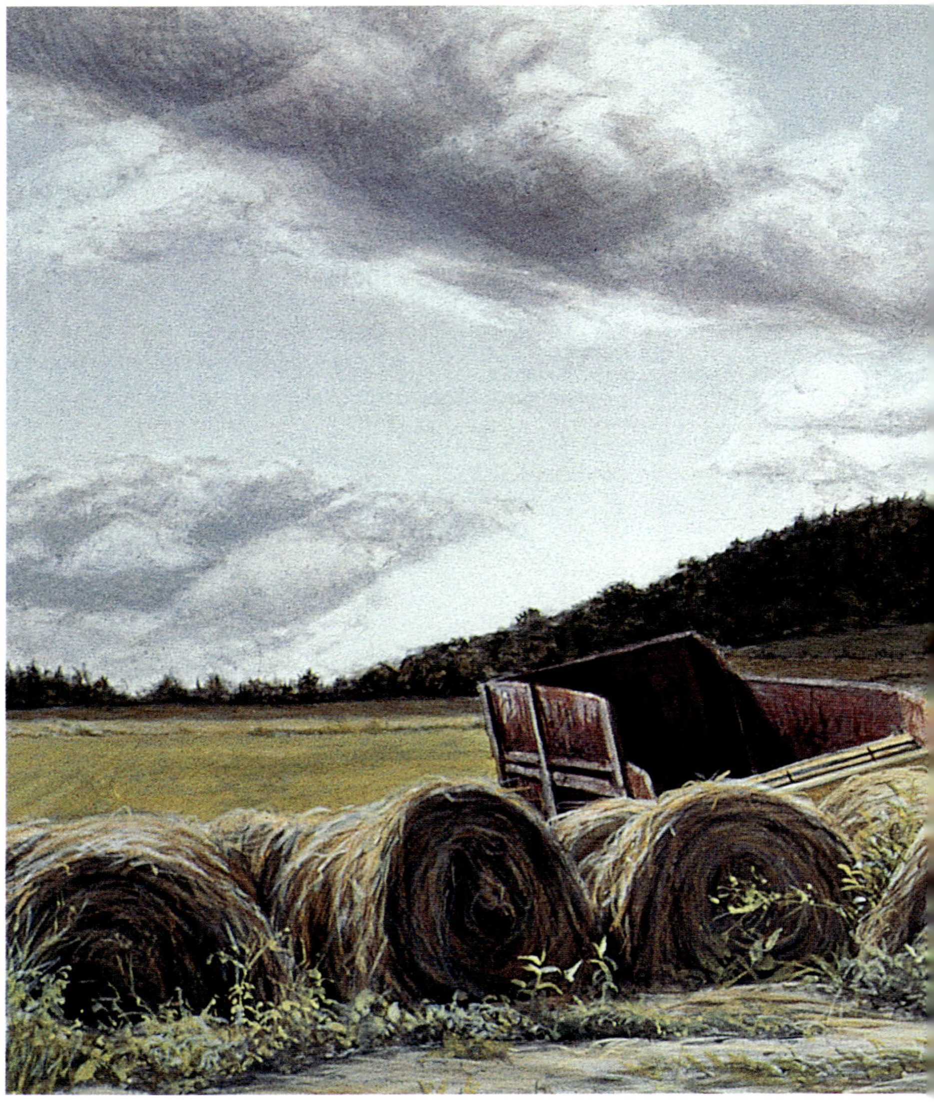

OLD BALES, GLOVER, VERMONT
7 1/2 × 19 inches

The pale blue, cloud-filled sky indicates early morning light, before the sky has turned a brighter blue. The blue in the distance is very light and cool, which I gradually darken and slightly warm at the top of the painting to bring the sky forward in space. This spatial effect is enhanced by the clouds, whose contrast increases and color gets warmer as they move closer. The warm color of the haybales, along with their strong contrast of light and shadow, brings them clearly into the foreground. The grasses and weeds in front of the haybales are bright, detailed, and sharply contrasted greens, placing then far in front of distant fields.

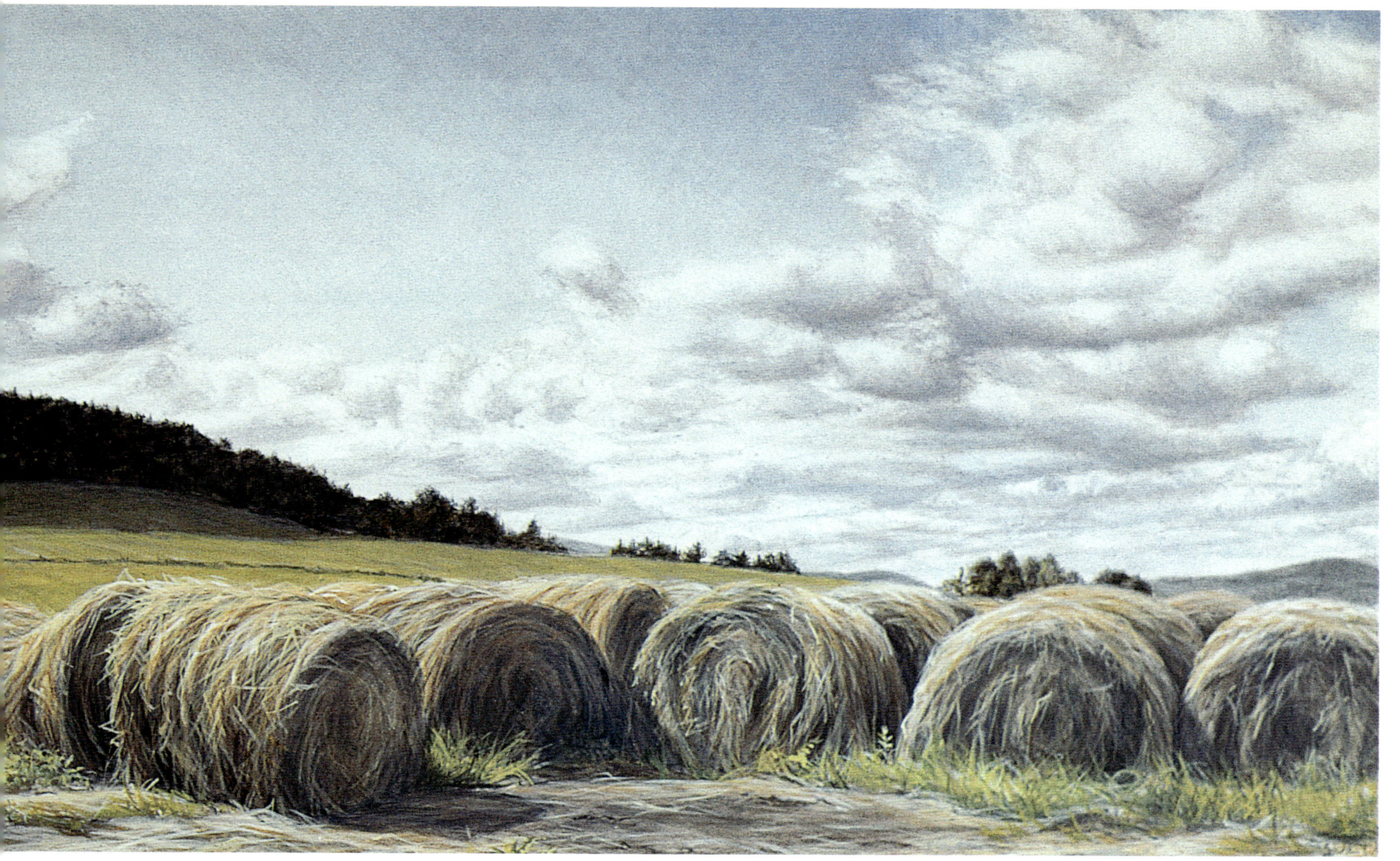

# Correcting Mistakes

If you need to correct your work at any point, a damp paper towel will lift ink or paint from the surface of the panel. If you have lifted many layers of ink or paint, you will have to repaint those layers to match the color adjacent to the correction. As I am working, I find that it is easy to remove paint by stroking it with a damp brush. This is a simple matter when paint has just been applied. I often paint over the edges of a form in the foreground and then remove the excess paint carefully with a squeezed-dry brush. In this way, I can remove only one layer of paint. Color can be removed with a damp rag or paper towel fairly easily for a few months.

If you have been working for such a long time on your painting—eight to 12 months—that the paint has begun to cure, it will not be as easy to lift with a damp brush or towel. In these instances, some artists use razor blades or sandpaper to remove paint. You must use these tools carefully so as not to mar the surface of the gesso. Since I do not spend a long time on my paintings—a small tempera typically takes no more than two weeks from drawing study to finish—I have not had to resort

to sandpaper or razor blade. I would advise using a very fine sandpaper, such as #400, to avoid making scratches on the gesso. You then have to recreate the layers of underdrawing and underpainting. This should not be too difficult, even if you don't remember the sequence of color (which I certainly wouldn't since I'm unsystematic with my color mixing). Color can be adjusted easily by the layering process. I find tempera color much easier to match than gouache, which dries so much lighter. Egg tempera paint dries right away and doesn't change color.

Another option, and the simplest one, is overpainting the mistake. Because egg tempera is a translucent paint, you will need several layers to cover a mistake. On the other hand, if you want to change a color, it is a simple matter to overpaint a different hue. I was recently working on a landscape and when the painting was nearly complete, I realized that the grassy green of the distant field was too bright, causing it to pop forward visually. I painted a very thin layer of white paint over it and the green became lighter and cooler—the effect of scumbling pushed the field back in space.

For this demonstration, I painted a perceptual study of an apple. The painting is small, $6 \times 9$ inches, but the apple depicted is larger than life size. With patience and concentration, I used a step-by-step process to layer the paint. The color emerged slowly from the underdrawing, gaining in luminosity and brilliance. The painting process is slow but not difficult, and it is very pleasurable.

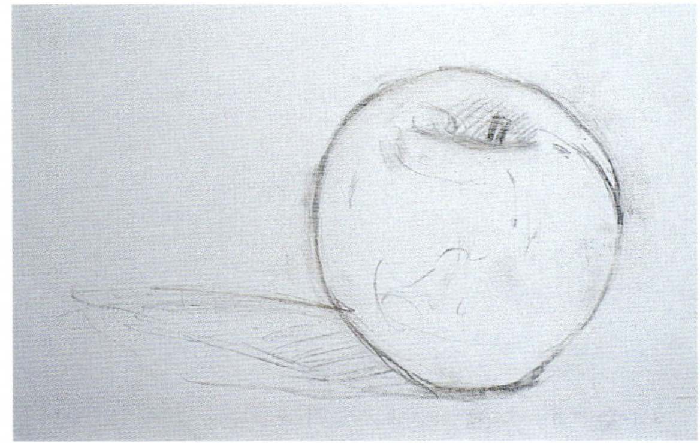

STEP 1

Since the composition and form are simple, as opposed to the complexity of my landscapes, I'm able to draw directly on the panel with soft vine charcoal. When I am satisfied with the drawing of the contours and the placement of the apple, I go over the lines with diluted India ink. I wipe off the rest of the charcoal with a paper towel.

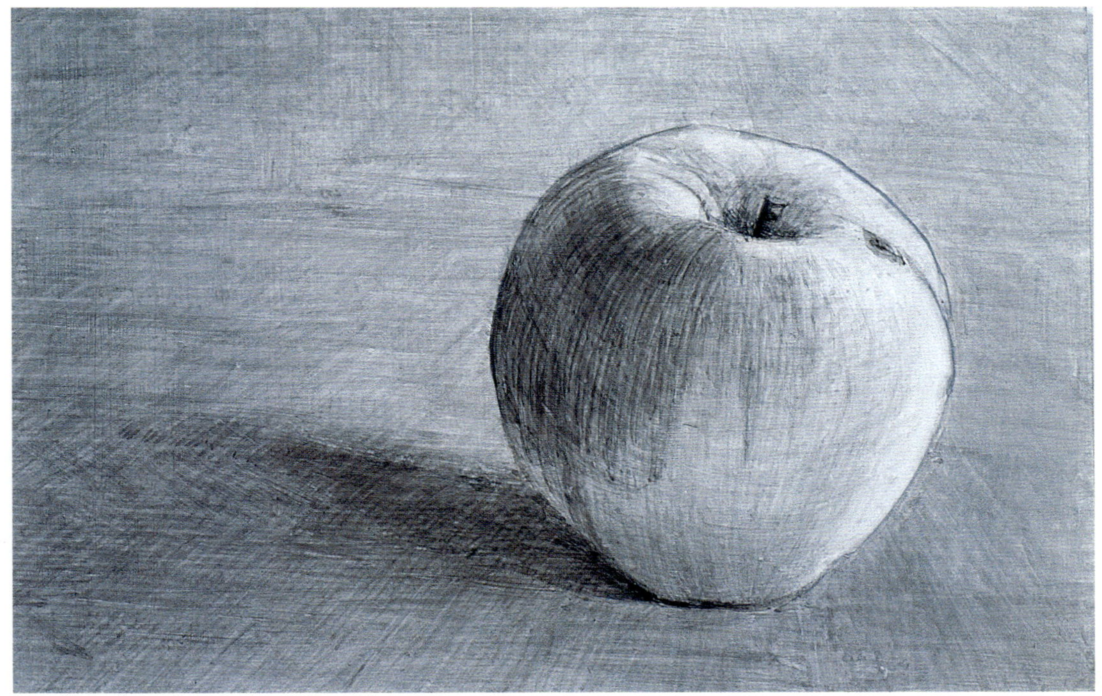

STEP 2

I complete a tonal drawing of the apple and table surface as described in "Drawing Is Your Foundation." I use five different values of India ink, from very light to very dark. With crosshatched lines, I draw the plane of the table top and the apple. My aim is to use light to describe the form of the apple.

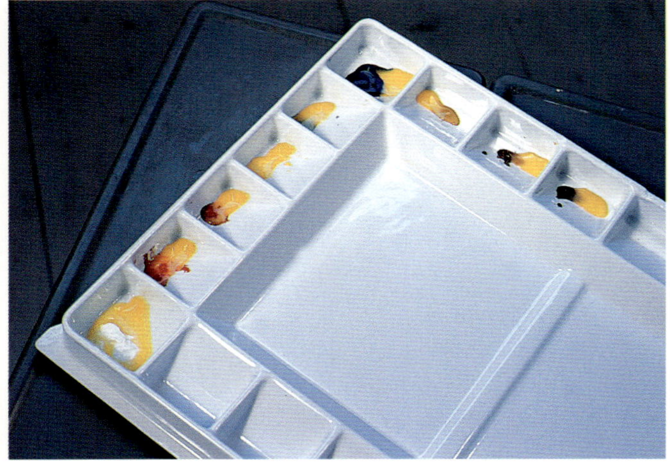



I place the colors that I will need on my palette: titanium white, cadmium orange vermilion, cadmium red deep, cadmium yellow light, cerulean blue, ultramarine blue, French ochre, burnt sienna, and burnt umber. I temper the colors, adding an equal amount of my egg yolk medium to the mass of pigment. Then I thin the colors with water. I leave some white paint unthinned, in a separate palette well, to use for highlights.

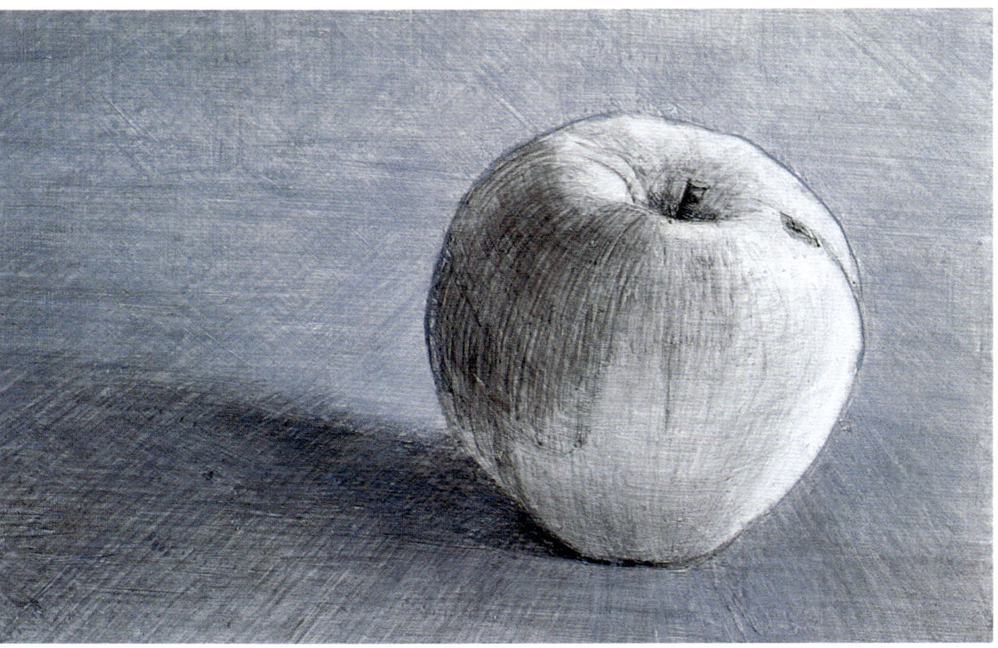



In general, when I am working with egg tempera, I like to build my colors slowly and use the warm effect of glazing. Since the underdrawing is in the correct value, if the first layers of color on the panel are lighter—scumbled—later layers can get back to the correct value by slowly layering darker tones. Scumbling these light tones also makes it easier to paint a continuous color. It would be very difficult to paint a smooth tone without white added to the color mixture—the use of white is very important in tempera painting. However, when working with dark values, it is often more effective to start with a hue having the same value as the underdrawing and then glaze a thin layer of pure color, with no white added, over it. Strong lights benefit from a thickly applied light color, even pure white, which you can then glaze thinly. This gives a sparkling look to the highlights.

I begin this painting by working on the table plane. In painting, as in drawing, working from distant planes to the foreground enables me to overlap form and detail cleanly. My first layers of color—mixed of ultramarine blue, umber, and white—are thinly applied in a lighter value than the underpainting. I have mixed three values of this color that correspond to the values in the underdrawing. The scumbling makes the color look cool, gray, and translucent. I work with a dry brush, crosshatching horizontal, diagonal, and vertical lines. Using these varying directions of brush strokes will help me to eventually get an even tone.

Then, I mix three slightly darker values, again going over and over the same areas until the color begins to emerge and the ink underdrawing disappears. As I'm doing this, I sometimes play with a lighter or darker tone. You can experiment with color a good deal in this way, pushing and pulling until it satisfies.

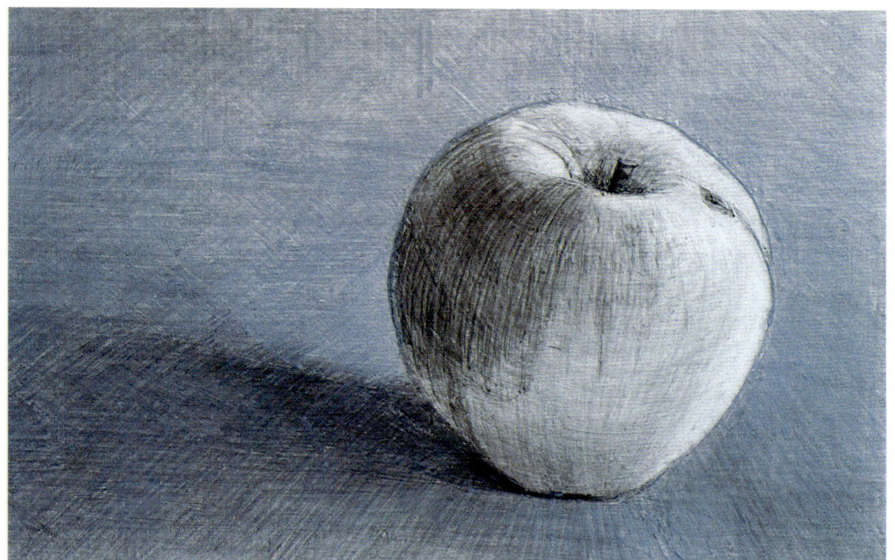



I work first on the light areas of the table plane. After the first couple of layers, I mix darker values and go over and over the surface with the thinned color, crosshatching again and again to get even tones. The pencil-like lines don't entirely disappear and I use them to enhance the illusion of form and space. On the table plane, I emphasize the horizontal, and the diagonals that describe perspective.

Spatial illusion can be pushed in other ways. I use more transparent color towards the back of the table and more opaque color, mixed with more white, towards the front. I also paint a thin layer of a light value over the darker tone in the distance (scumbling), resulting in a cooler hue. The foreground gets a thin glaze of a darker color—its darker value and warm hue (the result of glazing) pulls the plane forward.

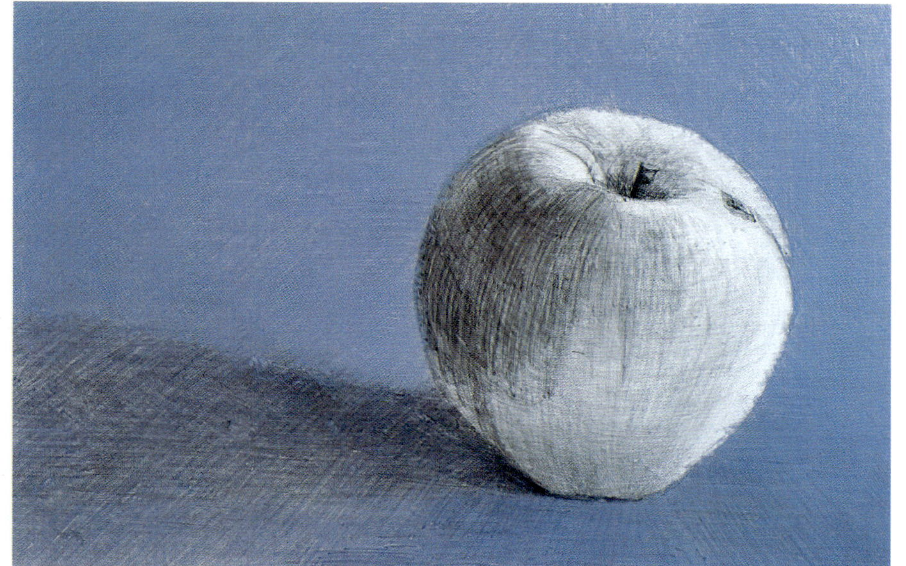

After completing the light values to my satisfaction, (they can always be adjusted later), I work on the shadow. I begin by scumbling two values in all but the darkest shadow under the apple. Then, again working with hatching many lines in different directions with an almost dry brush, I glaze somewhat darker tones. I add umber to the shadow color to make it warmer. The strongest dark is made with ultramarine blue with no added white. To get a smooth transition between the shadowed area and the lights, I have to go back and forth from light values to darker values until the transition works.

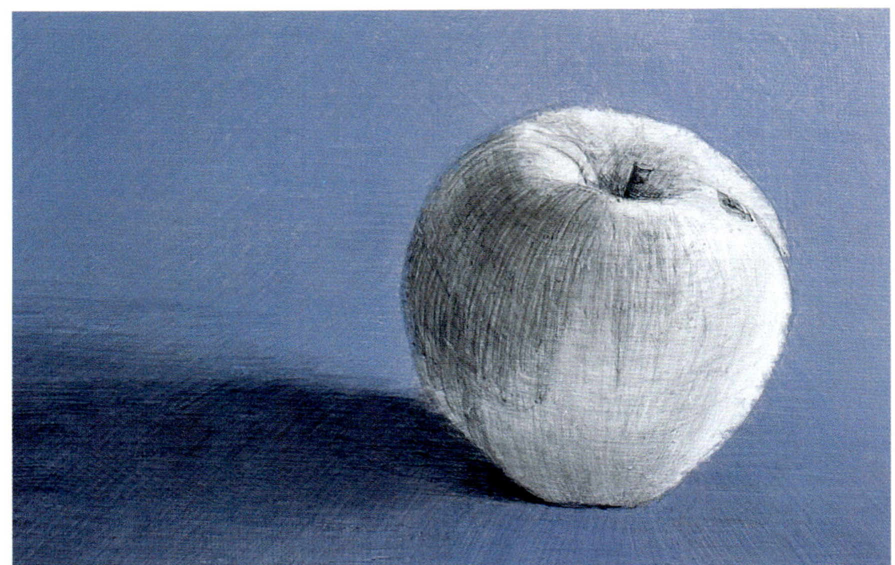



On to the apple. For both the yellows and the reds, I scumble in the half-tones with two values. The yellows are made up of yellow, sienna, ultramarine blue, and white. The reds are mixed with vermilion, red deep, ochre, and white. I paint a thicker layer of white with a touch of yellow added for the lights.

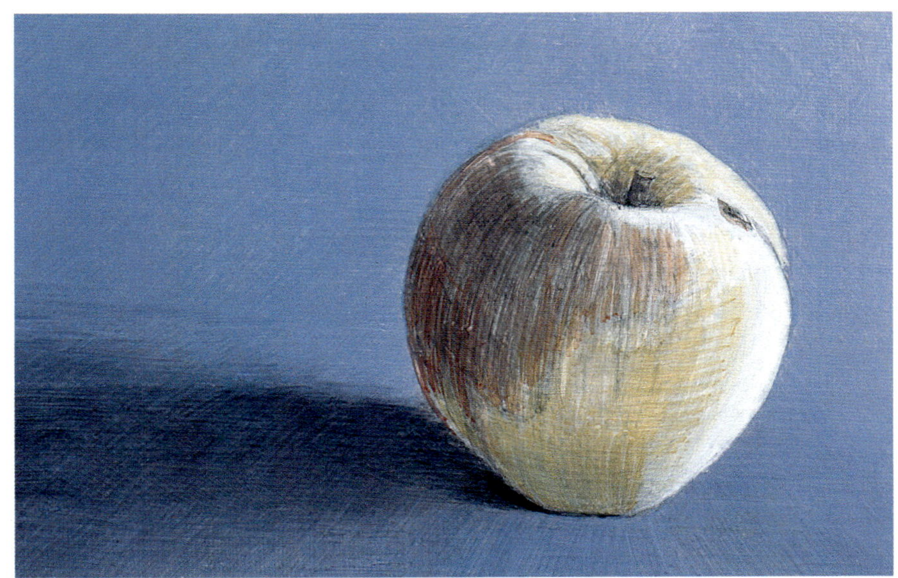

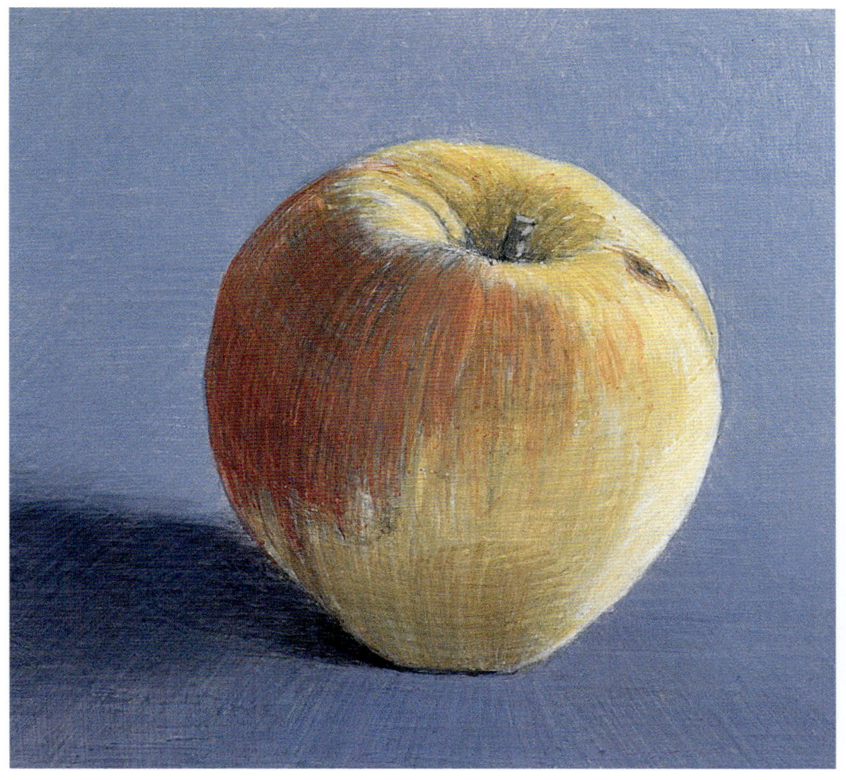

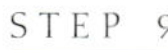



Then I begin glazing with slightly darker values. For the lights, I use a thin glaze of yellow with a bit of vermilion added to warm the yellow. This glaze has no white in it. The light value comes from the first layer of thick light paint. For the yellow middle tones, I use a different mix of colors than for the first scumble—yellow, sienna, and cerulean blue. For the darker yellow, I add umber. The reds are made up of vermilion, red, and white. The darker reds have less white paint added. The stem is umber, with a heavy white in the highlights. I use hatched lines that enhance the form by curving around its volume. The red blush of this apple has subtle vertical striping, so my brushwork repeats that pattern.

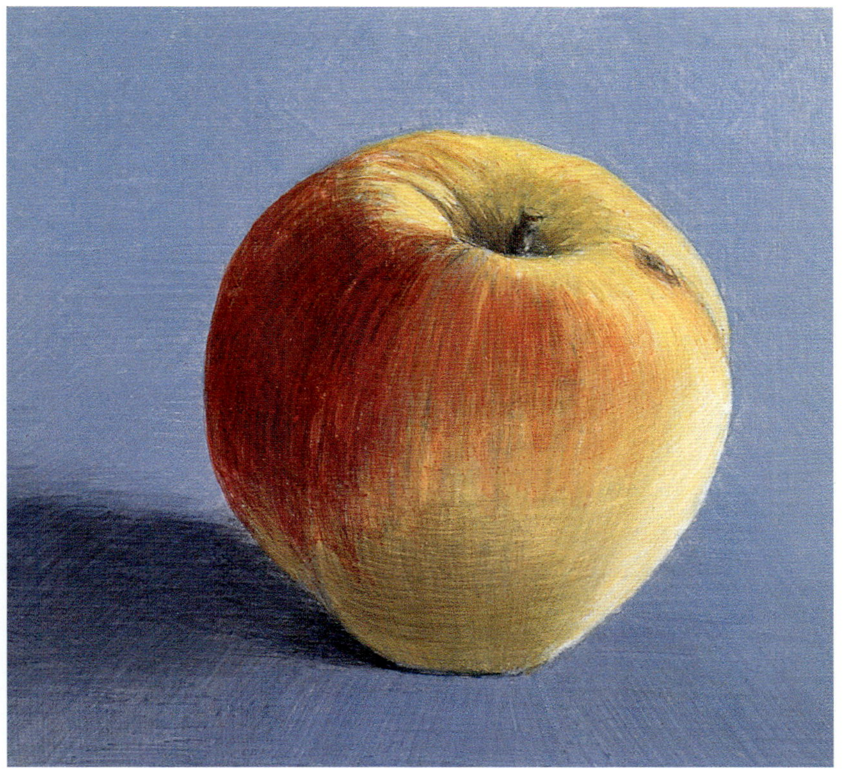



I continue to build the color and form of the apple by pushing both lights and darks. I find that the light area is not bright enough, so I repaint a thick pure white over the area. By glazing it with the same yellow and vermilion that I had used before, the effect of light is stronger. For the mid-tone yellows, I glaze yellow mixed with ochre, making them warmer and enhancing the volume. I use this same color over the dark in the stem area, which creates a cool tone. The darkest yellows get a glaze mixed with yellow ochre, sienna, and ultramarine blue. I paint the reds with darker values of red and vermilion. In the darkest area of the stem, I put a glaze of umber mixed with ultramarine blue.

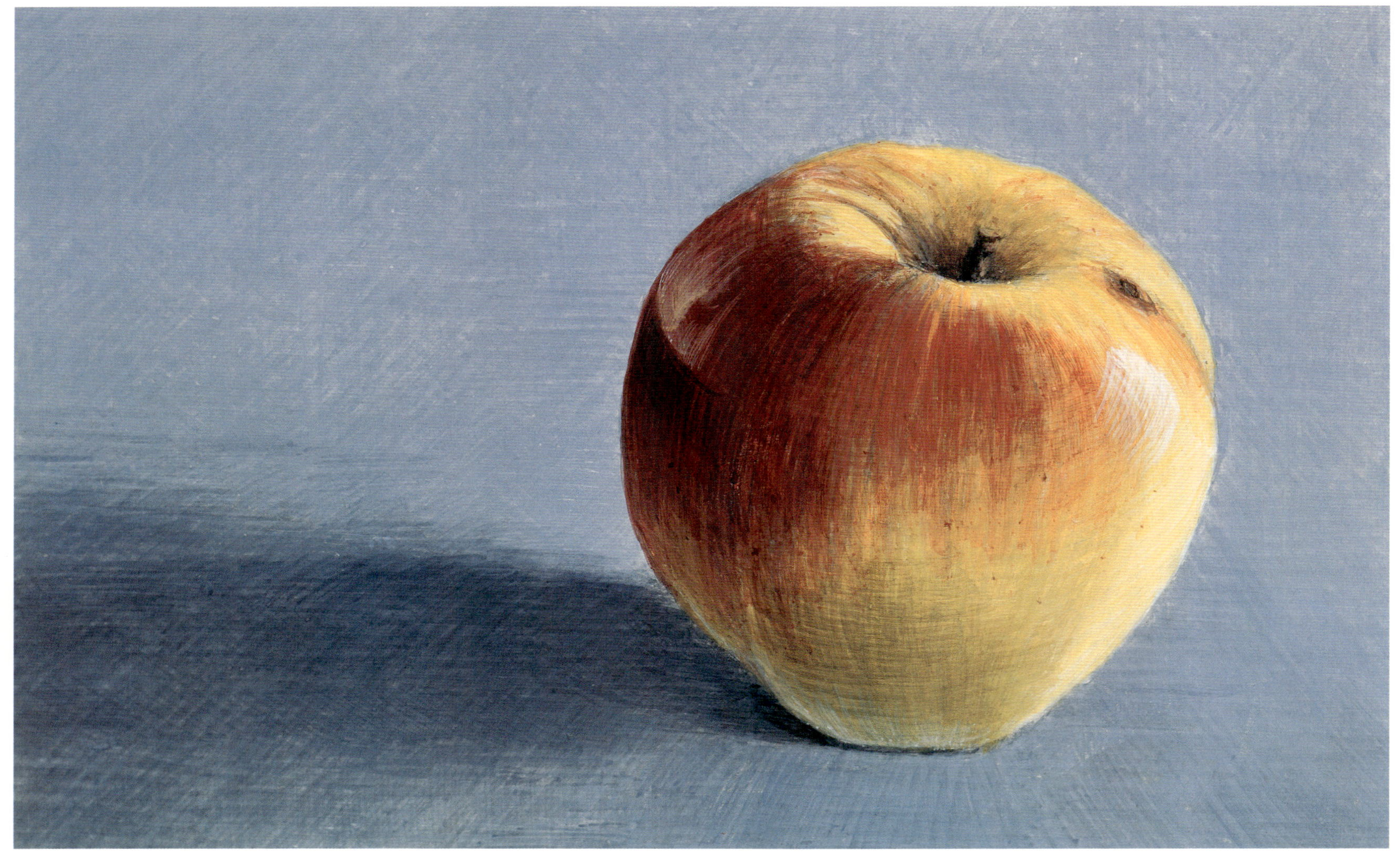

STEP 11

My final touches add reflected lights, highlights, and details. There is cool reflected light on the bottom of the apple, which I paint with a very thin scumble of white paint. I mix a somewhat thicker white with some ochre for the reflection, and use pure white for the highlight. There is a strong, dark red beneath the reflection. To paint this, I use a glaze made up of red and ultramarine blue. Finally, there are small dots of red color on the apple that I add to heighten the naturalism.

My palette for *Hay Bales, Hazy Day, Ryegate, Vermont,* consists of titanium white, cadmium orange vermilion, cadmium orange light, cadmium yellow medium, cadmium yellow light, chrome oxide green, ultramarine blue, manganese blue, yellow ochre light, raw sienna, brown ochre, burnt umber, and ivory black. I place some color paste in the wells of my palette and temper the pigment with egg yolk, then add a few drops of additional water as thinner and mix the paint with a brush. I leave some white paint unthinned for details and the strongest whites on the clouds.

When I paint a landscape, I am trying to make the objects that I see appear tactile; I'm trying to convey a sense of their presence. I feel a kinship with the artists of the early Renaissance in this, as they were calling up a tangible reality in their religious narratives. The process of painting with egg tempera enhances this kind of connection with the subject because of its slowness, clarity, and precision.

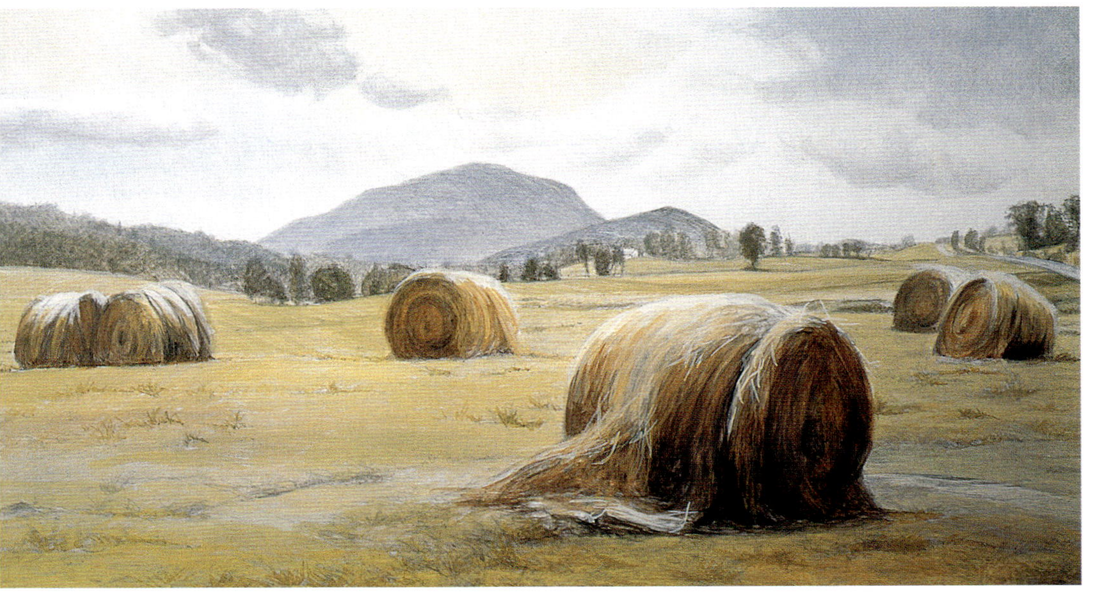

STEP 1

I begin by scumbling light veils of color over the underdrawing (see page 61), which results in cool, grayish hues as the underdrawing begins to disappear. I work broadly, not yet concerned with detail and refinement. If color mistakenly is painted onto overlapping forms, I use a damp brush to remove it.

I occasionally underpaint with a darker color than I want the final color layer to be, so that I can use the cooling and distancing effect of scumbling. I do this with the lower left area of the sky, painted with a mixture of manganese blue and white and the warm areas of the sky, painted with raw sienna and white. I paint the mountains darker than their final color will be, using ultramarine blue, black, and white.

I scumble in the greens of the trees, mixing the color warmer and darker as the groups of trees move forward in space. I underpaint the grassy ground very broadly, scumbling over the underdrawing. To heighten the spatial illusion, the paint is thicker and details are more strongly contrasted in the foreground. On the hay bales I underpaint a very warm color, mixed of orange, yellow medium, yellow ochre, and white which will influence the final paint layers on the hay.

Because I like to work from back to front spatially to overlap forms and details more easily, I work on the sky first after completing the initial underpainting layers. For the blue on the upper right, I glaze two values mixed with manganese blue and white. I paint the clouds on top of this blue, with a thicker white on the clouds that are closer.

I brush several layers, in different directions, of thinned white paint on the warm parts of the sky, making them lighter and cooler. The yellowish underpaint still shows through these final layers. I also paint thinned white on the lower left part of the sky, making it lighter and cooler and pushing it back in space.

I glaze the shadows on the clouds, using colors mixed of ultramarine blue, vermilion and white. I then scumble back into them with thinned white paint to soften them.

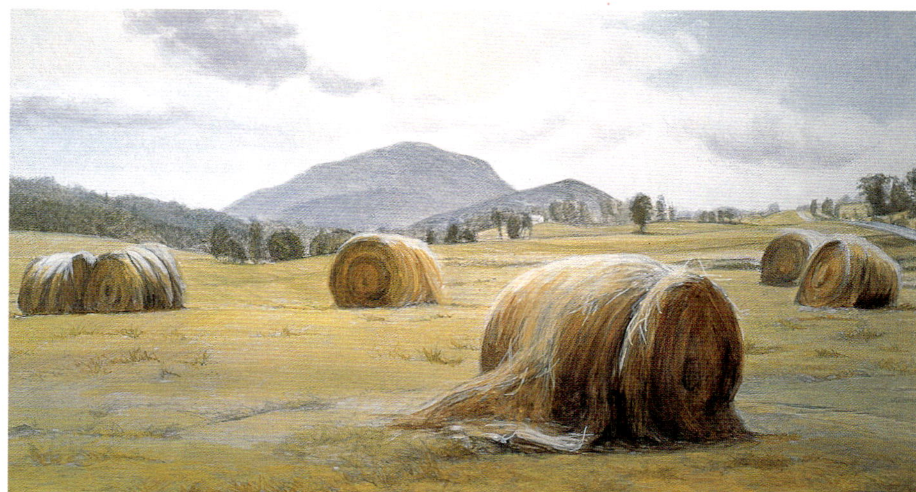



After finishing the sky, I work on the most distant hills, scumbling with thin layers of white until the value is correct. The scumbling heightens the illusion of distance and haze as the hills become lighter and cooler.

Moving forward, I paint the distant trees; for the most distant I mix a color with ultramarine blue, black, and white. I add yellow medium to warm the color for the closer trees. The closer trees also have more visible details that I paint with a light color and then glaze darker. For the tree-covered hill on the left, I paint a middle value, then add lights. I glaze these lights darker and then add additional darks.

I work on the most distant fields, glazing them with a mixture of white, yellow light, yellow ochre, and green. To create the effect of hazy distance, I then scumble a thin layer of white over this color on the farthest fields. The amount of detail that I paint on the fields, as well as their contrast, increases as they come forward spatially.

The closest trees are painted with a color mixed of varying amounts of white, ultramarine blue, yellow light, black, and vermilion. If they are too dark, I use a scumble to lighten them. I spend a good deal of time adjusting the color and value of the trees. After working on the trees, I feel that the darks on the left-hand hill are not strong enough, so I glaze them a bit darker.

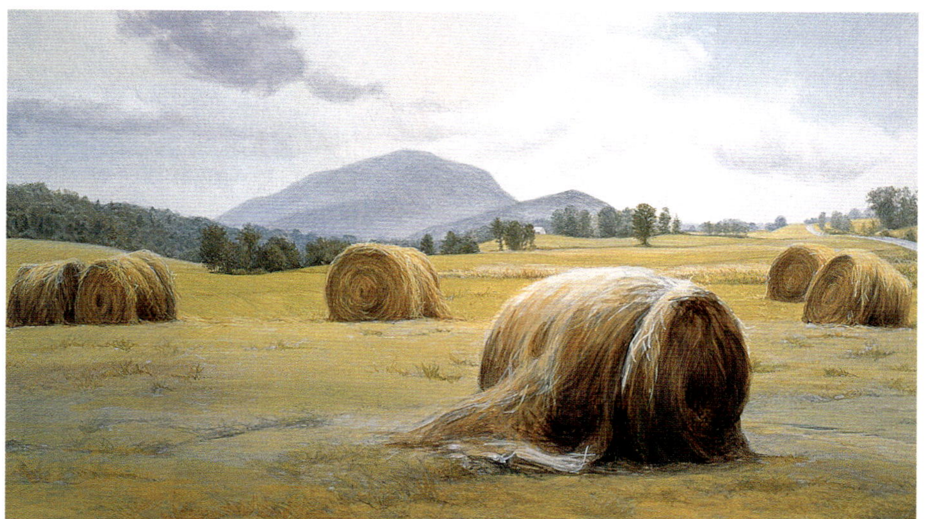

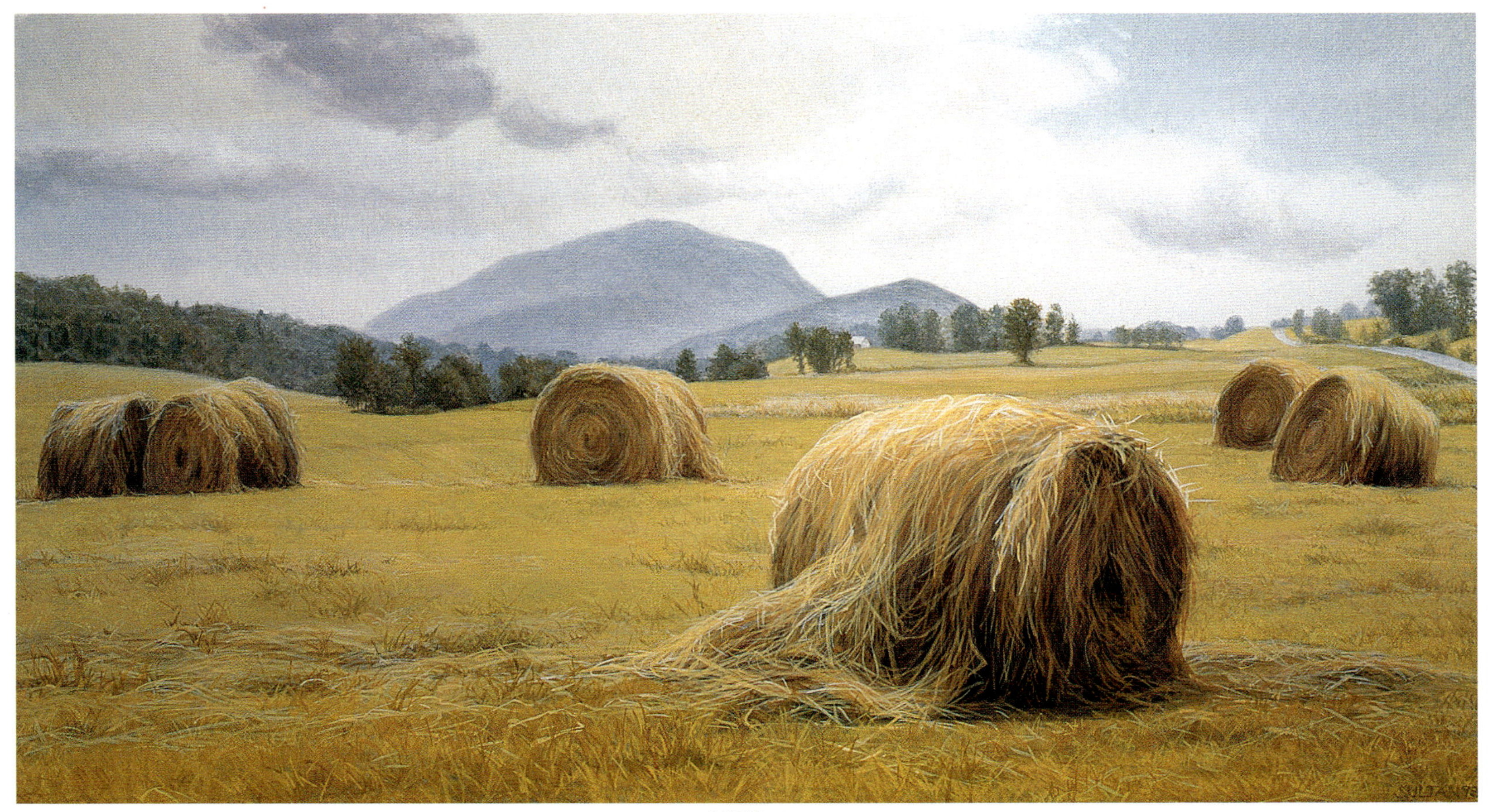

STEP 4

I paint the middle ground hay bales, using burnt umber, raw sienna, yellow ochre, black, yellow medium, and white. On the light areas of the hay bales, I first glaze yellow medium over the underpainting. Then, I add details with lighter paint on top of this glaze. After finishing the middle ground hay bales, I paint the darks on the foreground bale and add some middle values.

Before completing the foreground hay bale, I paint the grassy ground using green, yellow light and yellow medium, vermilion, and white. I paint a green that is a step darker in value than the underpainting, layering the color in different directions. I then mix an even darker green, layering it again over the underpainting. I add more yellow medium to the area of the grass in the close foreground. I add both light and dark details after painting in these general tones, for which I use thicker paint.

My final job is to complete the hay bale, which I paint using yellow ochre, brown ochre, raw sienna, burnt umber, ultramarine blue, and white; in the light areas, I use yellow medium and white. I work from dark to light because of the density of detail on the hay bale; I want the illusion of texture in the strands of hay. For the strongest lights, I use thick white paint that I glaze with a light yellow.

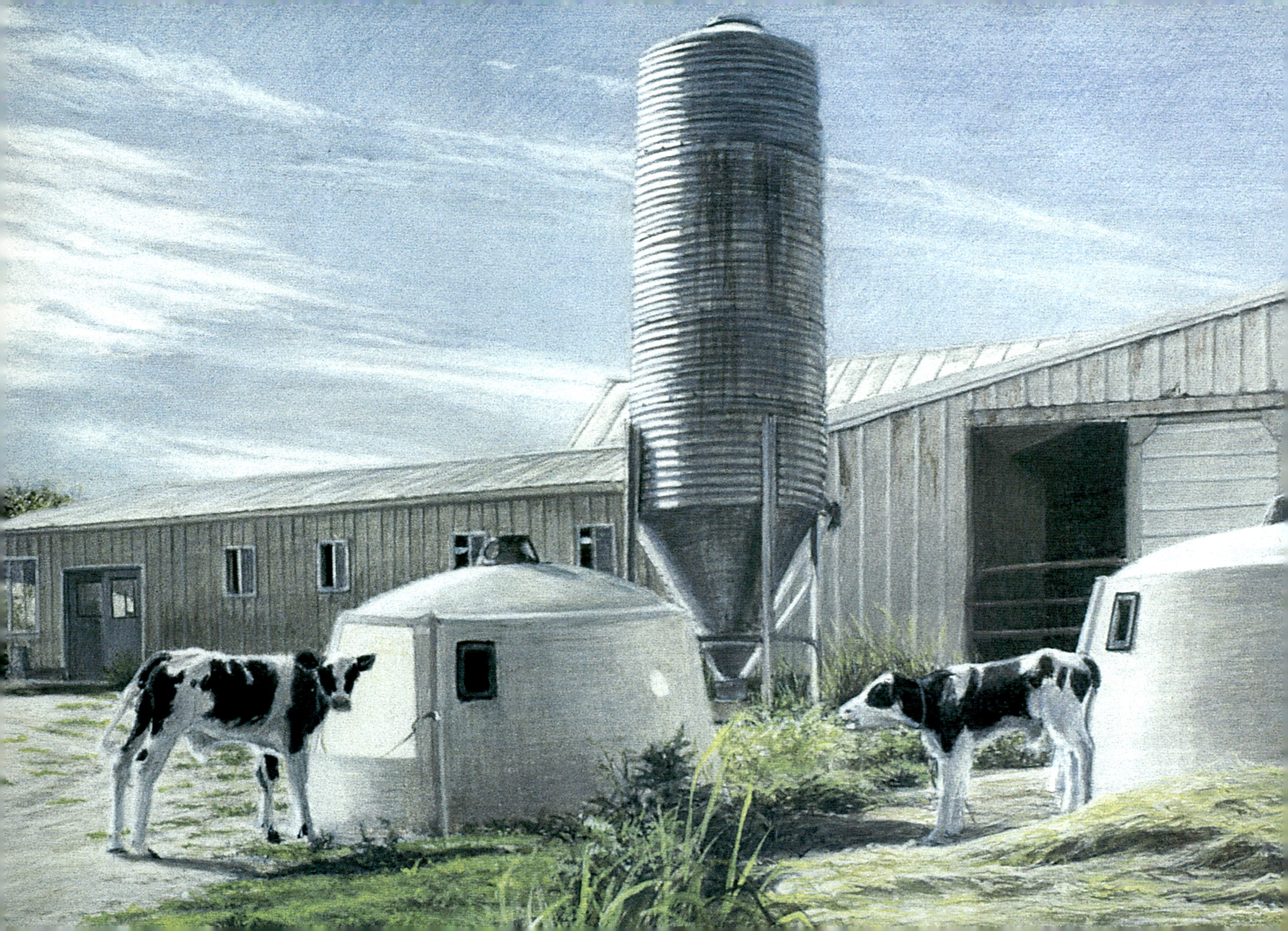

# HOW DO I PAINT...?

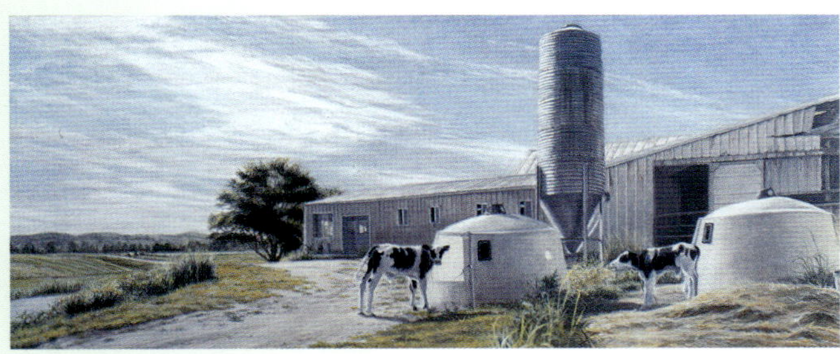

CALF HUTCHES, RYEGATE CORNER, VERMONT
8 × 20 inches

In this painting, the sky is a light value of cool manganese blue. It contrasts strongly with the darker backlit buildings, giving the painting the appearance of being light-filled. The clouds, which move from the upper left to the lower right, balance the opposite diagonal shape of the buildings.

There are two types of problems that we come across when painting with tempera: technical glitches that are unique to the egg tempera medium, and problems of rendering the image. I have discussed technical problems in previous chapters, so here I will discuss some particular issues that arise in painting the landscape. When we want to paint a cloudy sky, tall grasses, leaves, details, or textures, the tempera medium lends itself to certain solutions. Some things, such as details and textures, are actually easier to paint with tempera than with oil or watercolor because of its fast-drying, precise nature but picturing the soft edges of clouds can be a bit more difficult.

Although I am using landscape for my demonstrations, the same techniques will hold true for still-life, figurative, or abstract painting. To paint a smoothly transitioned tone on a background color, we would proceed in a similar way to painting the blues of the sky or the wall of a house. Painting texture in a landscape is akin to painting texture in a still life.

The sky establishes the quality of light in a landscape painting, so it is very important. A light cerulean blue will have a different effect from a deep cobalt blue and the nature of the light will change when different types of clouds are added. Cloudy skies can be a useful compositional device to counter-balance the shapes of landforms. For the painting, *White Hillside, Barnet, Vermont,* I use the diagonal of the clouds to balance the implied diagonal from the top of the silo to the trees on the left.

Painting the sky requires patience with layer after layer of thinned color. This translucence, once achieved, brilliantly reproduces the actual effect of light pouring through the atmosphere.

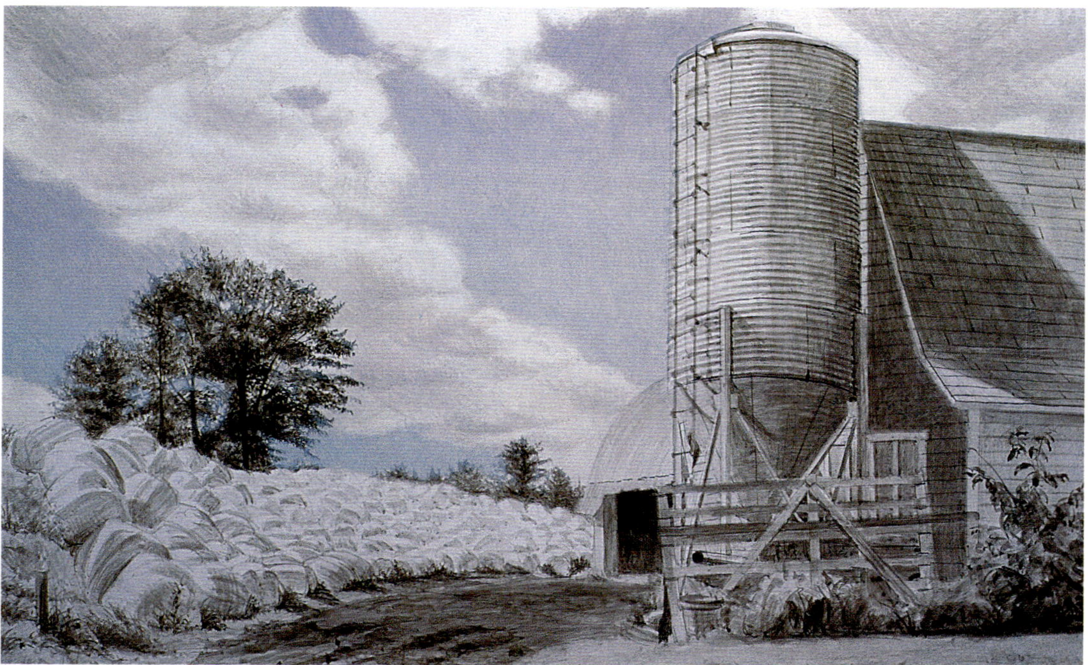

STEP 2

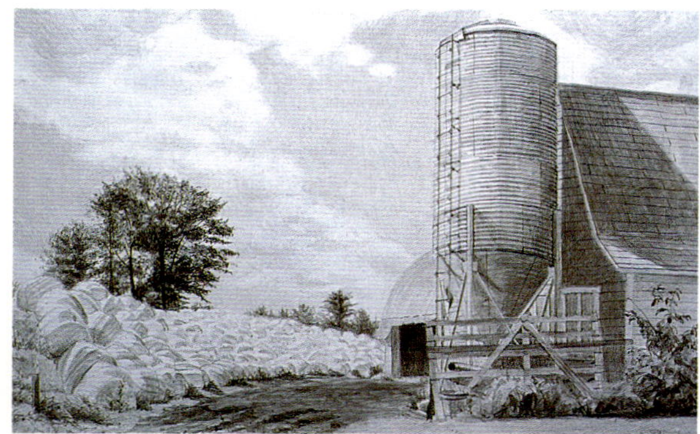

STEP 1

The underdrawing: To draw the flat part of the sky, I need a smooth transition from the light value at the horizon to the middle value at the top of the panel. I use three light values of ink in thin layers, darkening as I move from the horizon to the sky above. I use curved strokes to describe the form of the clouds.

For the first layers of color on the blue of the sky, I mix five values from a cool, light blue to a warmer, darker blue that will be lighter than the underdrawing. For the lightest value I mix cerulean blue (a cool blue) and titanium white; and for the darkest, cobalt blue and white. I mix an intermediate value from an equal amount of these two values, then two more values between those three.

Using a blunt-pointed brush slightly splayed so that my strokes will blend, I paint many thin layers with these five values, gradually blending them with horizontal, vertical, and diagonal strokes, until the underdrawing begins to disappear. I begin with the lightest value covering the lightest value of the underdrawing, painting many layers until the cool scumble begins to look opaque. I paint some of this light color over the next, slighter darker value of underdrawing. I then switch to the next blue, subtly mixing it with the lighter tone and scumbling it over the drawing. I move up the panel making the blue darker and warmer as the sky comes forward. I brush some blue over the white edges of the clouds to soften them. I paint thin layers of white on the clouds in the foreground, the white of the distant clouds has some ultramarine blue added to it. For the shadows in the clouds, I scumble a mix of ultramarine blue, cadmium red light, and white for the foreground clouds. Cooler distant clouds are painted with ultramarine blue and white.

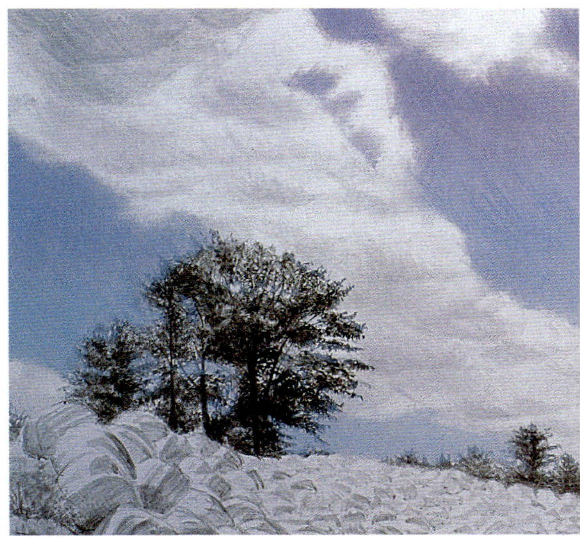

S T E P   3

For the final layers of blue, I mix slightly darker values than I used in the underpainting, but still use the color change from cerulean to cobalt blue. I use very thin crosshatched layers of color, this time as a glaze. At the top of the sky, I glaze a thin layer of pure cobalt blue. These glazes—darker color over lighter—give a deep and transparent look to the sky. While I am working near the trees, I paint over their forms and then remove excess paint with a damp pointed brush. In this way, when I later paint the trees, they will overlap the sky.

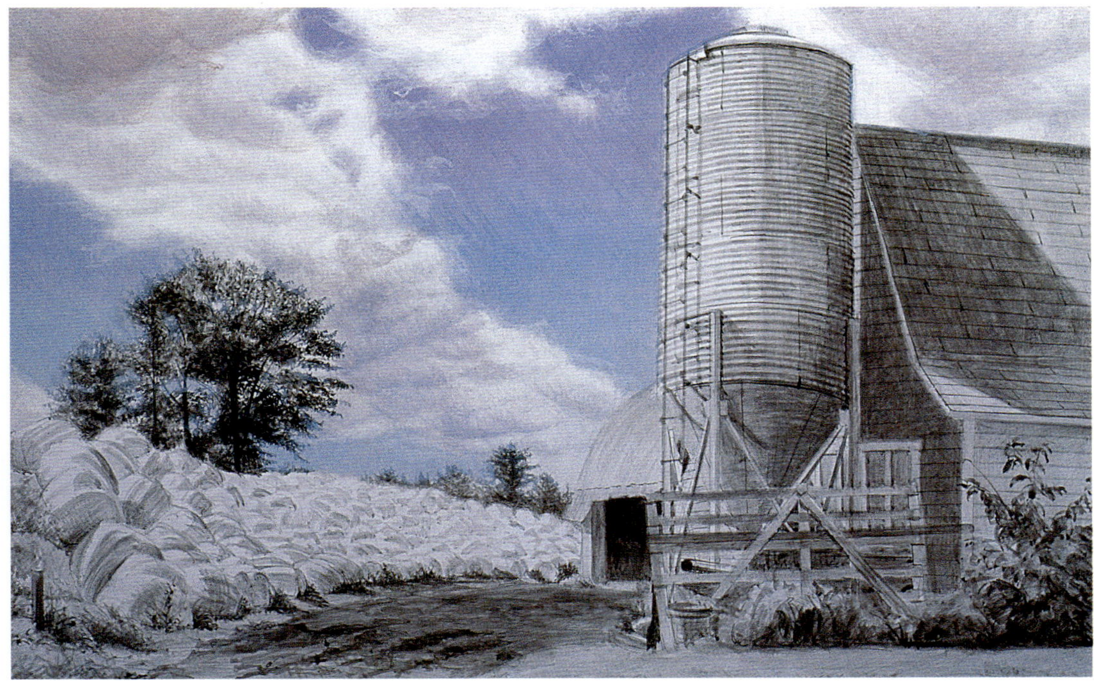

S T E P   4

I mix slightly darker values of the same hues for the final painting layer of the clouds. Starting with the distant clouds, I paint thin layers of white and the mix of ultramarine blue and white. I go back and forth between values to soften the edges between them. I darken the most distant whites with a light blue and then scumble white over them again to push them back in space. Thin layers of white soften the edges of the clouds where they meet the sky.

As the clouds move forward spatially, I use a warmer color—cadmium red light has been added to the ultramarine blue and white. Using two values of this hue, I continue to layer the color thinly, often scumbling white over forms and edges to soften them. As a final touch for the foreground cloud on the left, I glaze a very thin layer of yellow ochre, which warms the color bringing it forward in space.

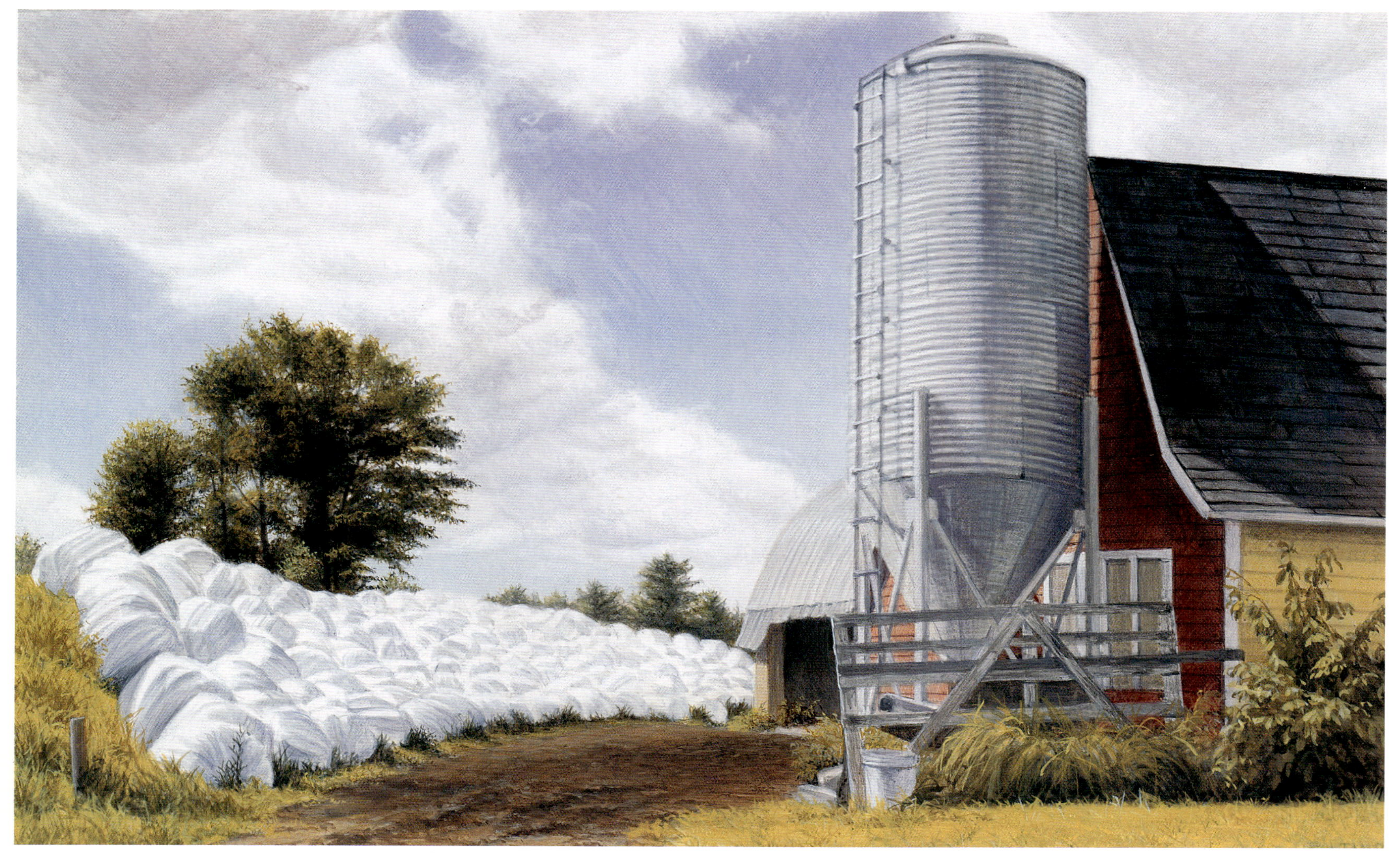

WHITE HILLSIDE, BARNET, VERMONT
9 × 14¹/₂ inches

Egg tempera is a wonderful medium for painting detail. Its fast-drying nature allows for clear and rapid painting of texture and pattern. You can lay down a complex web of brush strokes, each stroke maintaining its individual character. As we work, we must be careful to balance the larger structure of value and form with the smaller pieces of information presented by detail. Details fit inside the form, inside the lights and darks. If details threaten to overwhelm the structure of the painting, it is a simple process in tempera to correct the imbalance: a very thin layer of glaze or scumble will pull the painting together.

My palette for *Blue Bucket, Barnet, Vermont,* consists of cadmium red light, cadmium brown, cadmium yellow medium, cadmium yellow light and cadmium lemon yellow, yellow ochre light, chrome oxide green, ultramarine blue, manganese blue, brown ochre, satin ochre (a greenish brown), burnt umber, ivory black, and titanium white.

My description of my working process for painting details may sound a bit long-winded and complex. In actual practice, however, the painting goes very quickly, since the various layers of paint dry almost immediately. The clarity of the brush strokes give the details in egg tempera painting a very engaging quality.

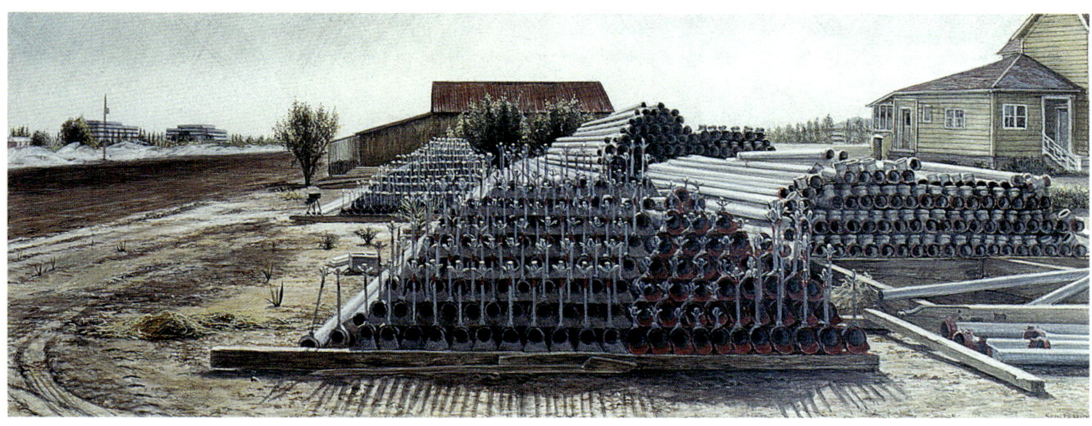

IRRIGATION PIPES, SAN JOSE, CALIFORNIA
7 1/2 × 20 inches

I was very intrigued by the irrigation pipes piled up like classic pyramids, but the thought of painting all that detail was overwhelming. Once I began working, I found that the clarity of tempera paint, along with its fast-drying quality, made the details easy to paint.

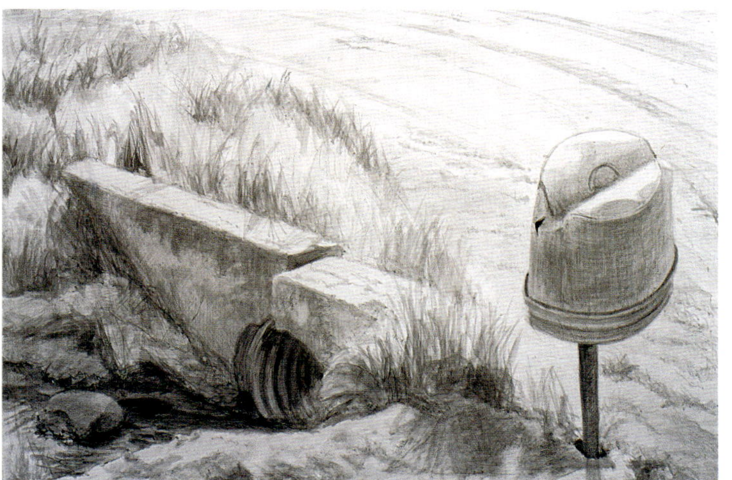

STEP 1

The underdrawing: For the foreground of this 12 × 12 painting, *Blue Bucket, Barnet, Vermont,* the underdrawing is fairly broad. I indicate the main areas of light and dark, attempting to achieve the effect of sunlight. I paint in loose indications of detail on the road and in the grass. It is not necessary to be refined in the underdrawing; it acts as a foundation for the later layers of more precise information.

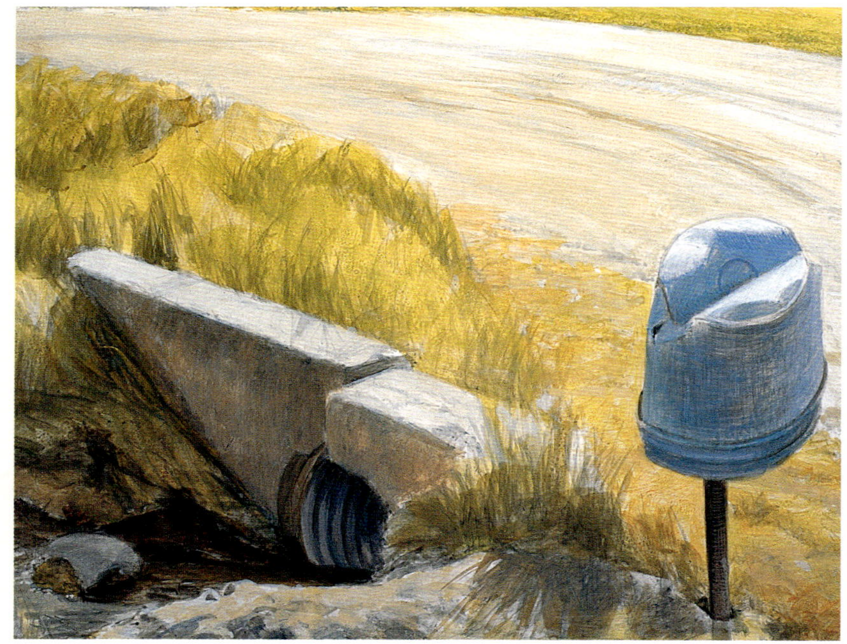

STEP 2

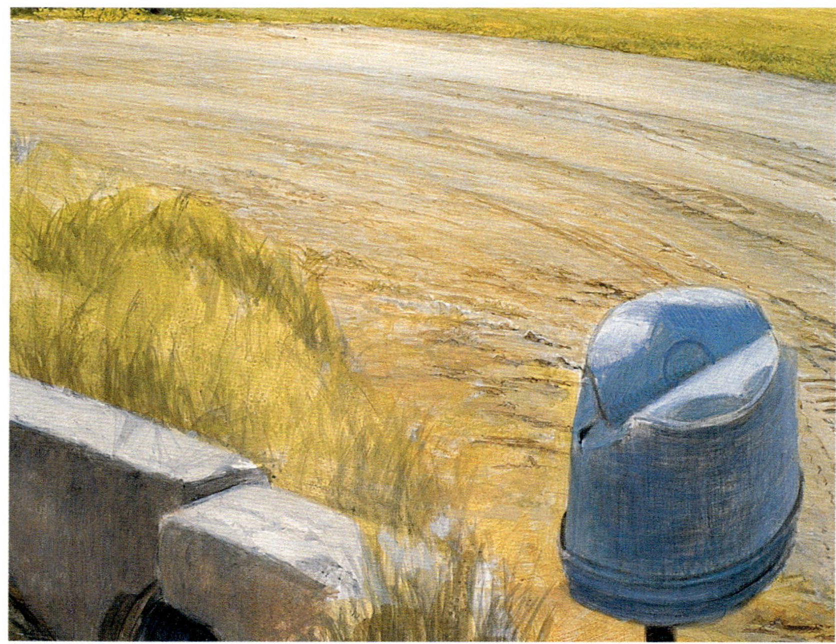

STEP 3

I begin my underpainting by laying in broad washes of color. For the road, I use a ³/₄-inch flat brush to paint a layer of white mixed with yellow ochre and then a layer of white and satin ochre. I begin to add some darker details, some mixed with satin ochre and white, some with ultramarine blue, satin ochre, and white. I add some highlights with pure white.

For the green grasses, I mix varied amounts of medium and lemon yellow, manganese blue, red, and white. I follow the underdrawing in its patterns of light and dark. I paint the cement of the culvert with a grayish red mixed with ultramarine blue, yellow ochre, red, and white. I want a reddish underpainting to add liveliness to the final paint layer showing the reflected light on the cement. The bucket is painted with ultramarine and manganese blue and white.

I now work on the road, which is the most distant part of the foreground of this painting. With the road complete, I can then easily paint details of grass over it. With layers of cross-hatching, I paint in the base colors of the road before adding details. I scumble a light color in the distance to cool the color and push the road back; I glaze a very thin layer of yellow ochre in the foreground to warm it and bring it forward. The illusion of space is also heightened by using thicker paint in the foreground. I begin to add darker details slowly, building stronger darks in the foreground. If they appear too dark, I scumble a light tone over them. For the lights in the details, I use white paint, thickest for the brightest lights. I then glaze these details with a warm color mixed with yellow ochre.

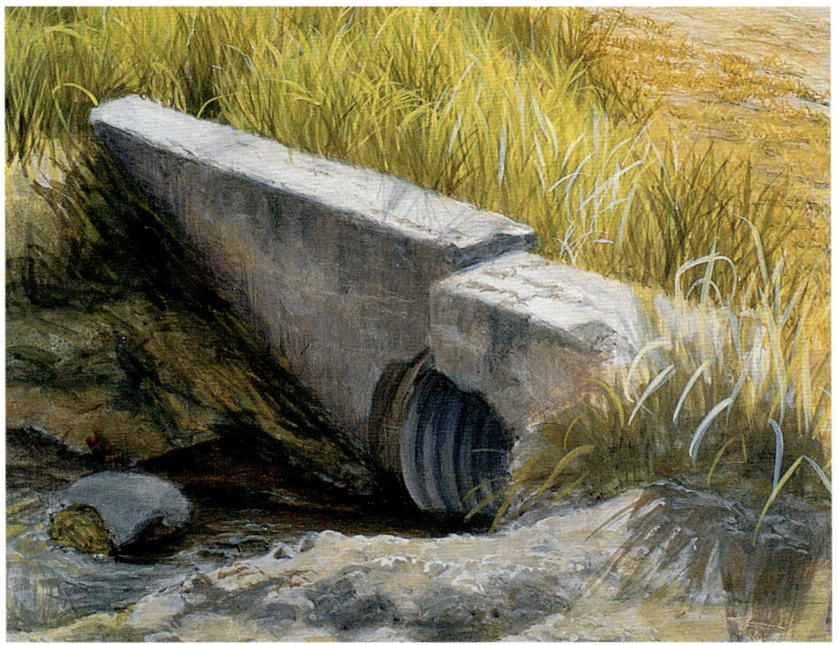



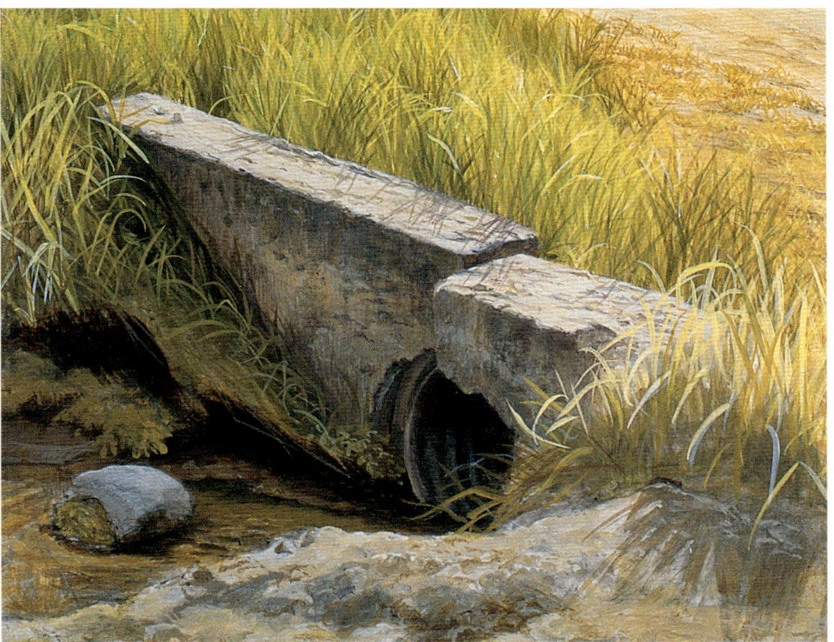



I next work on the short grass by the edge of the road. For the darks, I use a thin paint while I use a thicker paint for the lights, painted with a very light yellow which I glaze a bit darker. I paint the tall grass from back to front, to give the spatial illusion of overlapping. While I am painting the details of the blades of grass, I keep in mind the large patterns of light and dark. With fluid brush strokes that mimic the gesture of grass, I add darks to the mid-tones and then add the lights. For the lights on the grass towards the foreground, I use a thick, light paint mixed with white and lemon yellow.

On the concrete, I begin to add details of texture with transparent tones of brown ochre, which allows the underpainting to show through. On the dirt in the foreground, I start to develop the complexity of the surface texture: mid-tones of brown ochre and white are added to the darks, and lights are indicated by touches of white paint.

With a fine brush, I work to complete the concrete wall. I glaze darks mixed with ultramarine blue, brown ochre, burnt umber, and white, then add lighter colors, which I glaze darker again. I work this way until the balance of color and value is right. For the top of the wall, I paint a light color over the sketched-in details, then repaint these textured details.

I paint the grass in front of the wall with thicker, less transparent color which heightens the illusion of space. I use pure white for the highlights on the grass, glazing them with lemon yellow.

For the water, I underpaint with yellow ochre on the light areas. For the shadowed area of water, I glaze yellow ochre on top of a dark layer mixed with ultramarine blue and umber. I paint the light and dark details that indicate running water and add more texture to the dirt in the foreground.

I paint a dark glaze, again mixed with blue and umber, over the details of water. I next lay in darks and put the mid-tones on top of the darks, then go back to the lights in the grass in the foreground. I go back and forth with these values because they are rarely right the first time. I continue to layer color until I'm satisfied.

For the shadow of the grass on the ground, I first paint the texture with light and dark paint, different values of a mixture of brown ochre, yellow ochre, ultramarine blue, and white. Then I layer a bluish-violet shadow color on top of the details. I finish the dirt by directly painting in the various hues making up its texture. I then find that the light areas are too light, so I glaze them darker. After I finish getting the form of the bucket, I paint the detail of the smudges of dried dirt by thinly layering a light value mix of satin ochre, yellow ochre, and white.

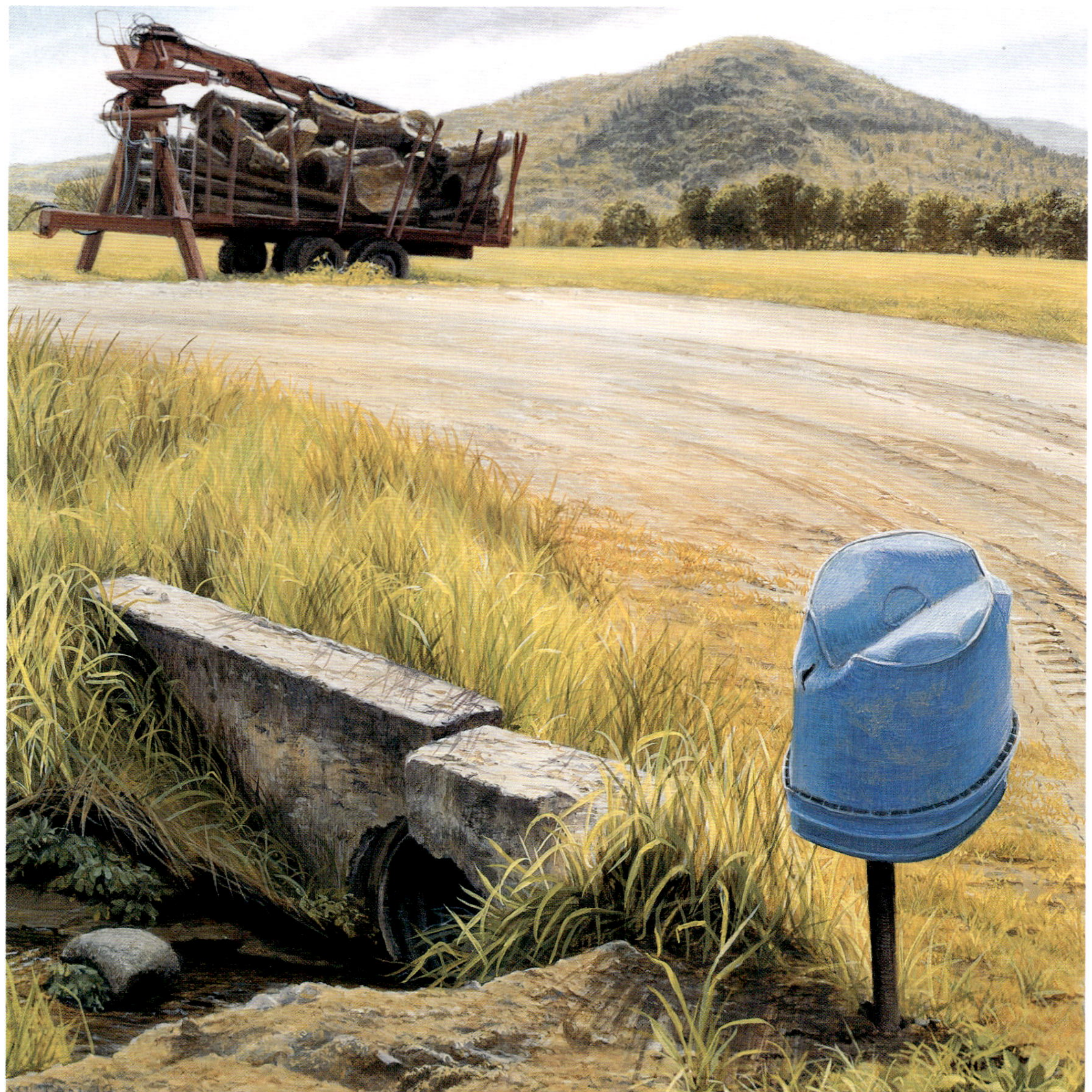

Painting foliage presents similar problems to those of painting details. It is important that the details of the foliage do not overwhelm the sense of form and light in the painting. Trees and shrubs have different shapes that can be described by value. The details of the foliage must fit into this larger pattern of light and dark—darker values of leaves in the shadows and lighter values in the light areas. When I am painting leaves or other kinds of foliage, I never draw each individual leaf, but fluidly paint a group of gestures that describe leaves. When I am working on foliage detail, I don't thin my paint too much—it is much easier to paint crisp details with slightly thicker paint. Good brushes are essential for this activity, and I find that I use differently shaped brushes for different tasks. For instance, for the needles of the yew in the foreground, I use a very thin brush; for the vine and tree in the distance, I use a small brush with a fuller belly.

My palette for *Yew and Open Doorway, Germantown, New York,* is titanium white, cadmium orange vermilion, cadmium yellow medium, cadmium yellow lemon (especially useful for backlit and highlighted leaves), ultramarine blue, cobalt blue, cerulean blue, yellow ochre light, raw sienna, French red ochre, brown ochre, burnt umber, and ivory black. I mix greens using yellows and blues or black, sometimes adding red to warm the color further. If a dark green is not warm enough, I can float a thin glaze of black, yellow, or red.

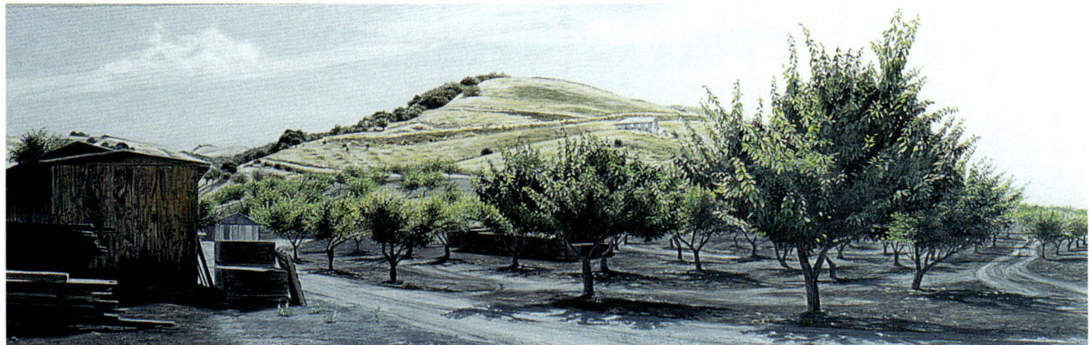

APRICOT TREES, SAN JOSE, CALIFORNIA
9 × 28½ inches

It was easy to paint the layered and overlapping leaves quickly because each layer dried right away. I used the brush in a gestural manner, making a mark that was a leaf shape. For the leaves in the foreground, I used a thicker paint than in the distance to enhance the spatial illusion.

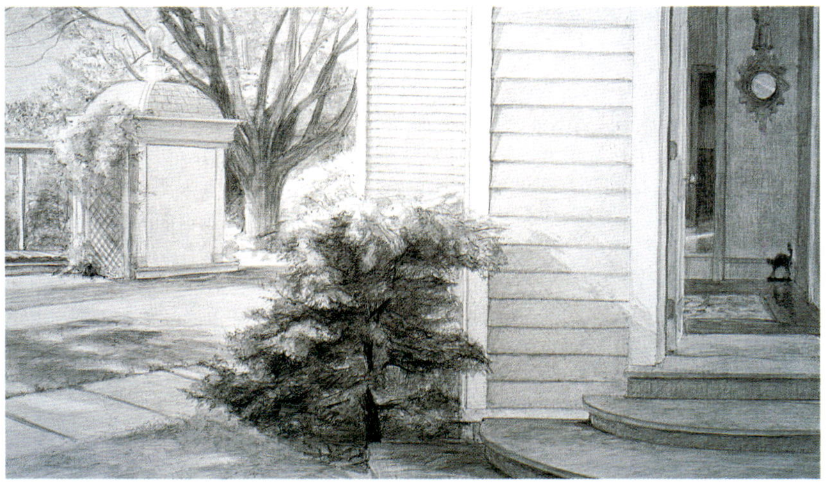

STEP 1

I first complete the underdrawing for this painting: *Yew and Open Doorway, Germantown, New York.* In the underdrawing, I am concerned with getting the form of the foliage as expressed by value. The specifics of foliage will be developed during the painting process. The yew has the strongest darks in the underdrawing, bringing it dramatically into the foreground.

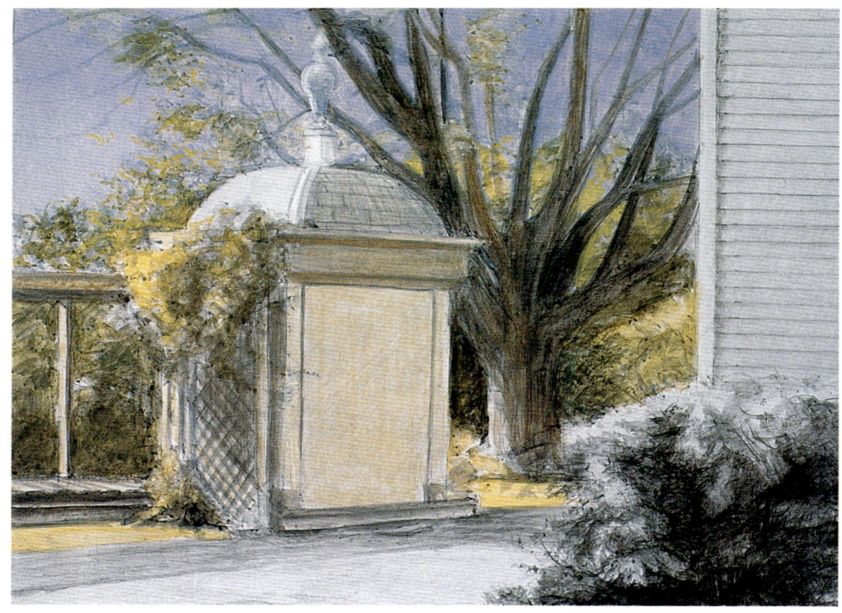



Before working on the foliage in the background, I paint the sky. In this way, I can paint the details of leaves over the sky, adding to the illusion of the painting. Then I loosely paint thin washes of color over leaves, branches, and the buildings.

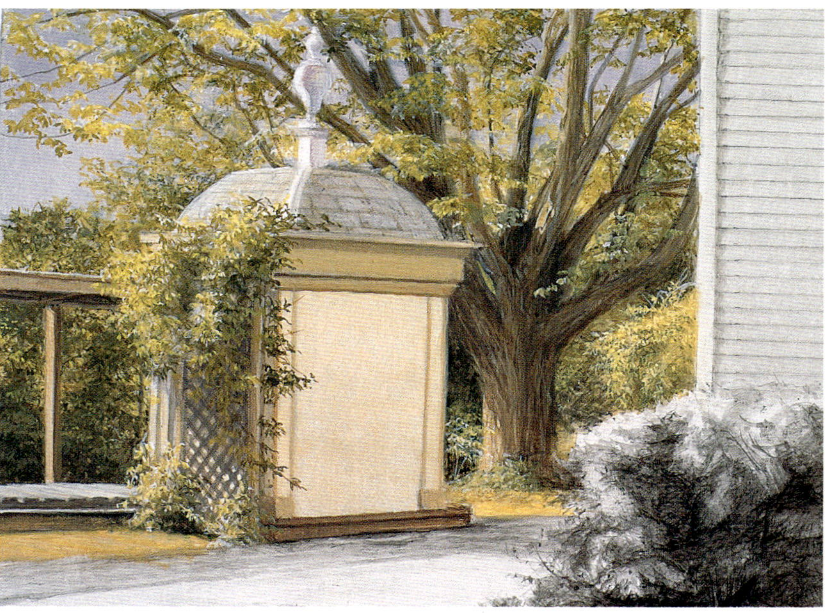



I begin to paint the details of leaves by painting distant lights with touches of white mixed with some lemon yellow. I can make this color more brilliant later, if necessary, by glazing with yellow. I then lay in darks with mid-tones on top of the darks, just as the leaves are layered. I usually have to go back and forth between light, dark, and mid-tones until I am satisfied with the result, always keeping in mind the larger structure of the foliage. To paint the light leaves in front of the tree trunk, I use a thicker white paint, and then glaze it with a thin layer of lemon yellow.

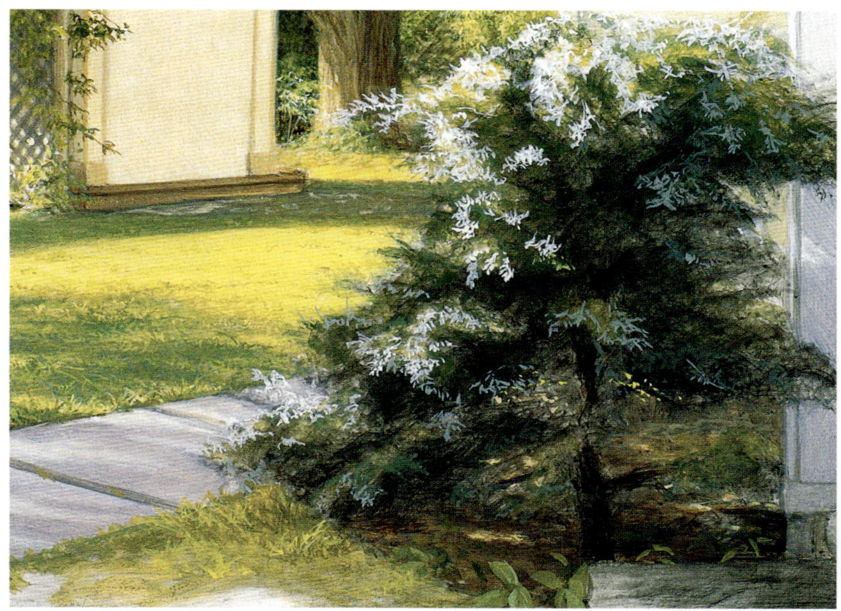



After finishing the areas of the painting that the yew will overlap—lawn, path, and house—I mix three values of a cool green with ultramarine blue, black, lemon yellow, and white for the yew. I thinly wash these three values over the corresponding values of the under-drawing. I then carefully paint mid-tones mixed of black, blue, and white over the darks. For the brightest highlights, I use a very thin brush loaded with white paint, making gestures with the brush to give the effect of needles.

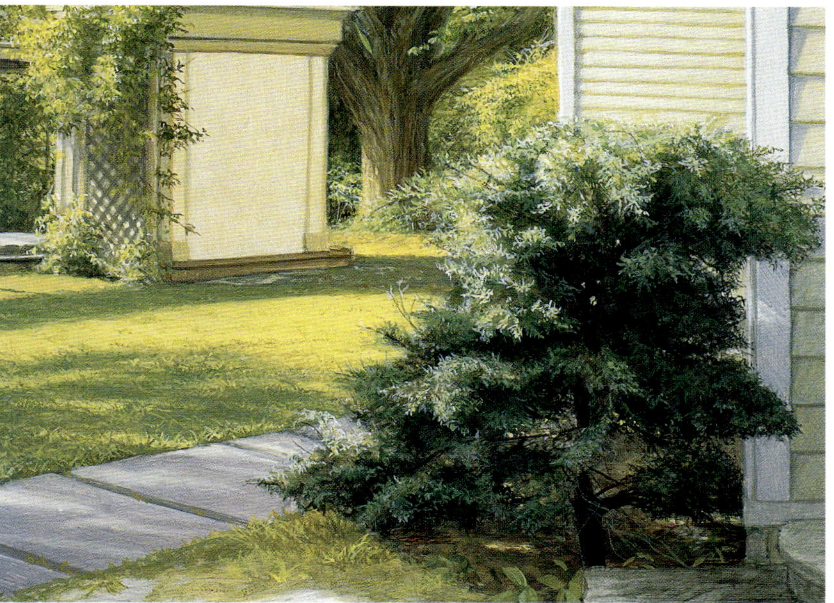



I work from the strongest darks to the lights as I continue to develop the detail of the foliage of the yew. The darkest needles are painted with a mixture of black and blue with a touch of lemon yellow. I paint mid-tones on top of the darks, glazing some of them with the very dark green to make a subtle transition in the darks. I readjust the color from light to dark and back to light until the form and value are accurate. Then I work on the light values in the same way—using light green to paint detail, then glazing some of the foliage with a darker green to get a range of transitional values. My final step is to paint the strongest highlights using a thick white paint mixed with a small amount of cool green.

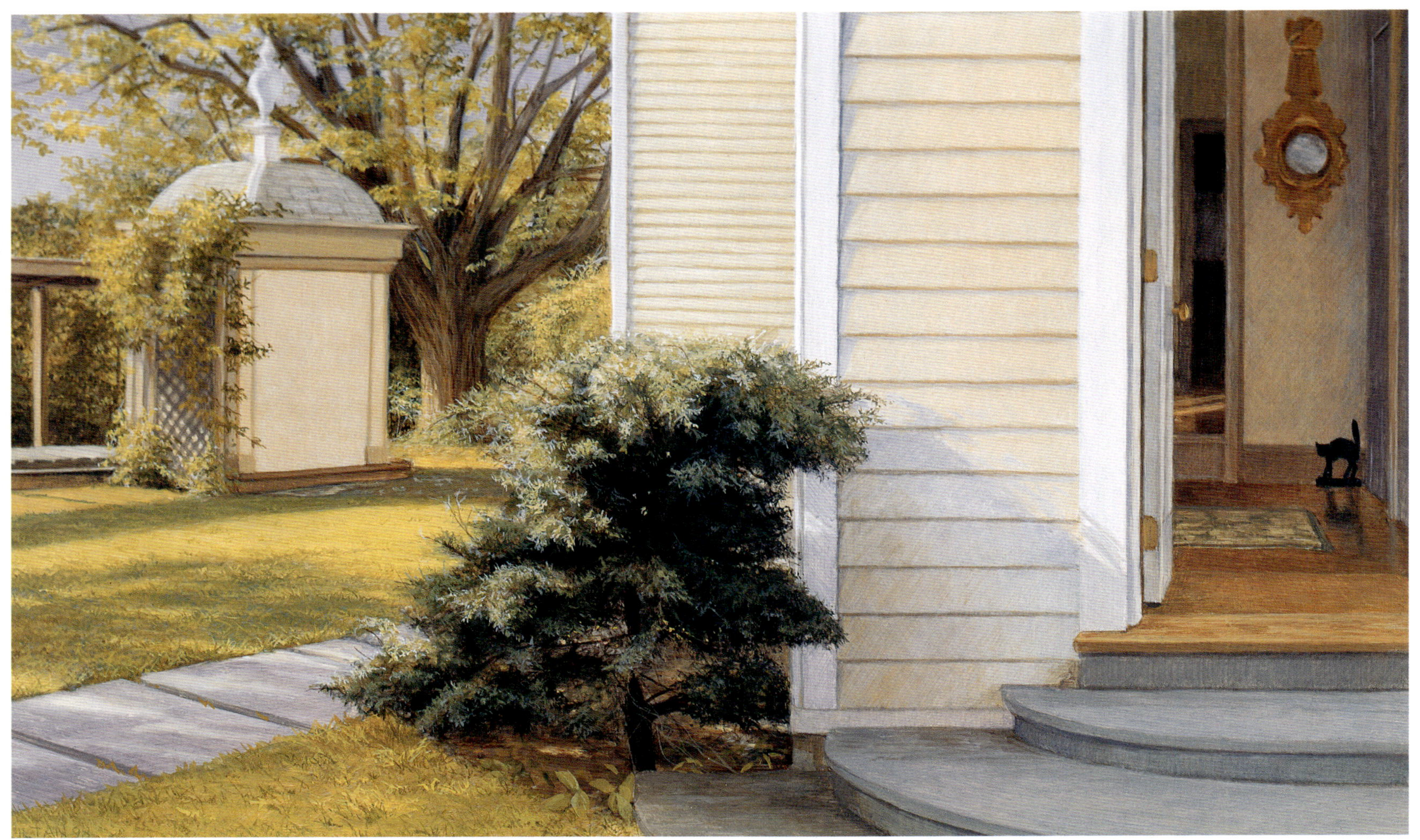

YEW AND OPEN DOORWAY,
GERMANTOWN, NEW YORK
9 × 15¹/₂ inches

Egg tempera is ideal for painting rough textures: it dries quickly, allowing for the layering of a web of brush strokes of different colors; the paint can be carefully scratched, showing the white of the gesso or the color of the underpainting; or paint can be dripped, splattered, or dabbed on with a sponge. Although I prefer using the brush, I recommend experimenting with these techniques, which many contemporary egg tempera painters use.

When I closely study fifteenth-century Italian panel paintings, I see that the artists painted the even tone of architectural elements with broad, blended strokes of a brush, using an opaque color. The paint is applied rather thickly. Since I like to modulate my color, I don't paint smooth surfaces in this manner. Instead, I use many layers of crosshatching with a thin paint that has some white added to it. The opaque white paint makes it easier to paint an even tone.

Tempera is perfect for painting reflective surfaces. Just as a reflection partially obscures the object behind the surface, the translucent tempera paint obscures the underpainting to various degrees. In the following demonstration I paint smooth, rough, and reflective surfaces.

My palette for *House and Tree, Pittsfield, Vermont,* is titanium white, cadmium red light, cadmium yellow medium and light, ultramarine blue, manganese blue, yellow ochre, raw sienna, burnt umber cypress, ivory black, and chrome oxide green.

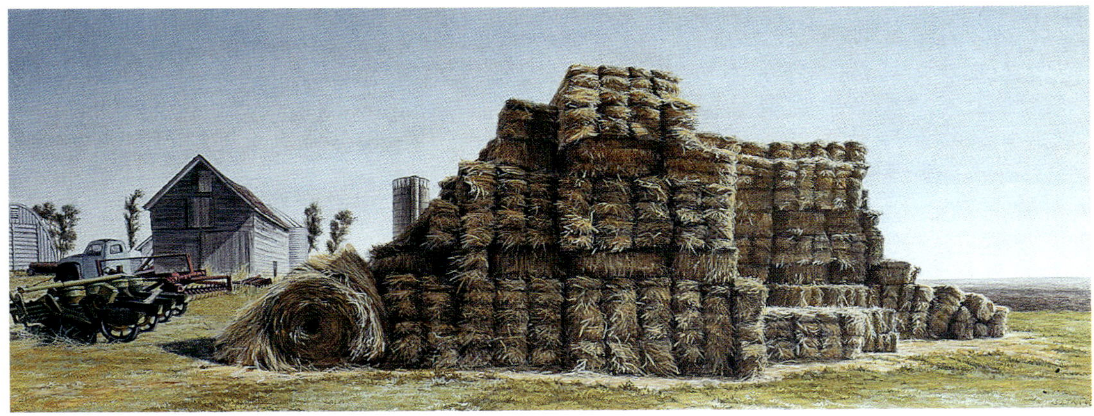

HAY WALL, BELPRE, KANSAS
9 × 24 inches

With many fluid, thin, overlapping brush strokes, I painted the texture of the hay. I used a thicker white paint for the highlights, which I then glazed thinly with yellow paint. The weaving of stroke upon stroke gave the texture the quality of depth.

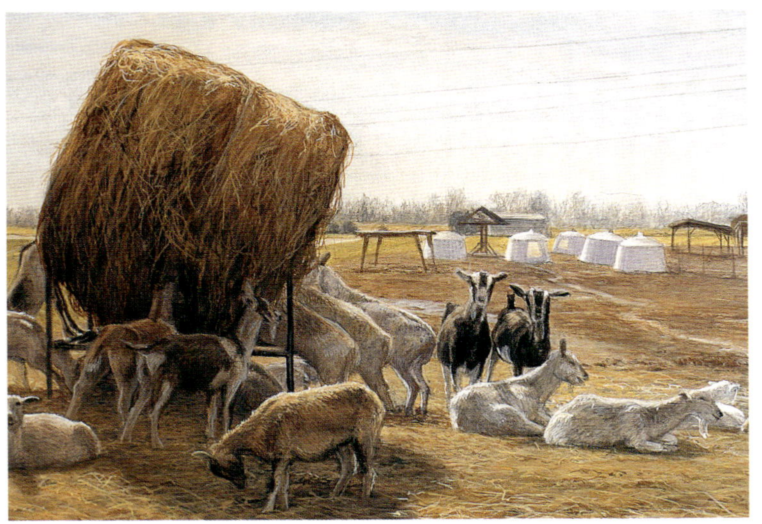

GOATS AND ENERGY PLANT, BATON ROUGE LOUISIANA (detail)

The texture of the goat hair was very different from the texture of hay. To get that texture, I used many short strokes of thin paint, building one on another. The layering of this thin translucent paint gave a furry effect, different from the crisp, clear strokes I used for the hay.

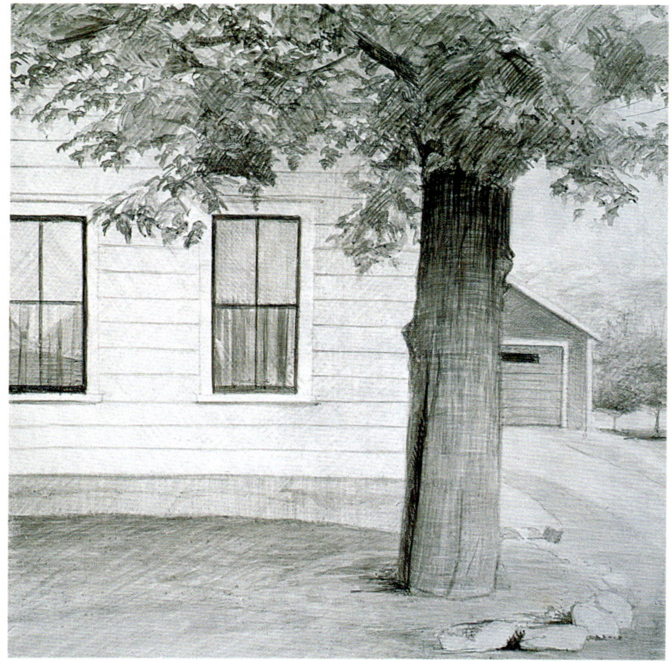



I complete the underdrawing for the painting *House and Tree, Pittsfield, Vermont.* I am interested in establishing value relationships in the underdrawing, including the values of the reflections in the windows. I do not draw the texture of tree trunk or grass, leaving that for the painting.

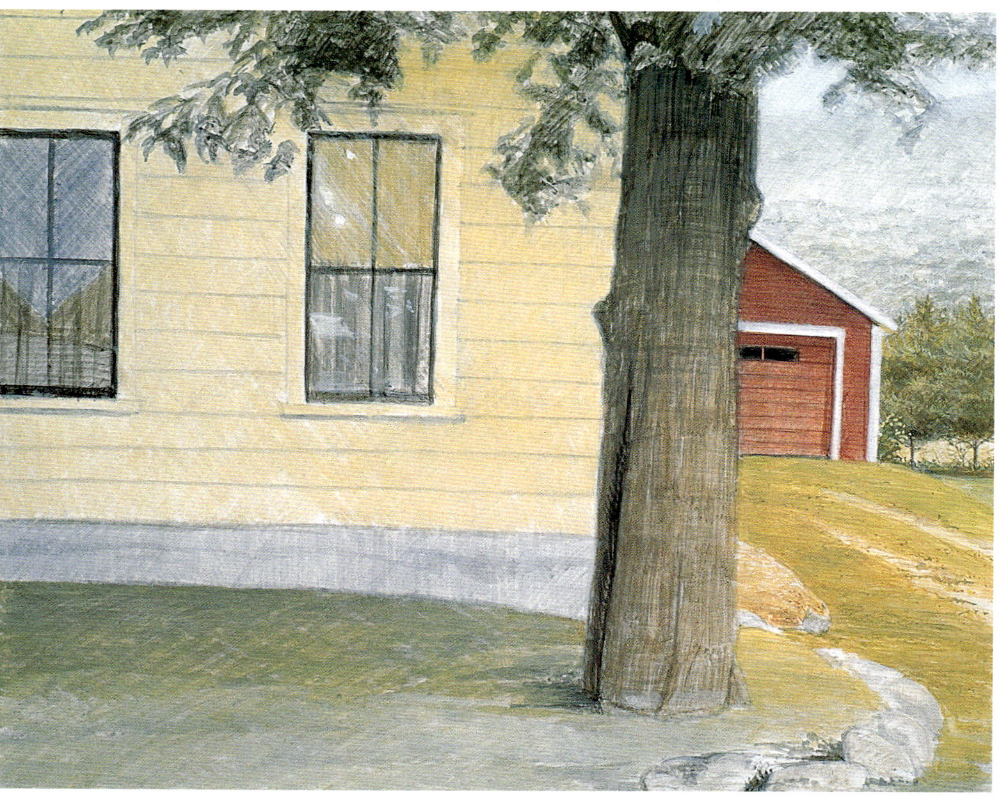



I first complete the distant hill, trees, garage, and grass. I underpaint the house with three values of a yellow mixed with sienna, yellow medium, and white. The tones I mix are slightly lighter than the underdrawing because I can paint a smooth tone more easily with a scumble. Working with a blunt-pointed brush, slightly splayed, allows me to blend smooth tones using many thin layers.

I add the highlights that appear on the right window with white paint. Then, on the upper part of the window, I paint a middle value of ochre and white. On the lower part, which shows curtains, I thinly paint two values of umber, ultramarine blue, and white. On the upper part of the left window I layer a color mixed of ultramarine blue, black, and white. This is a darker value than the final one will be. In the final paint layers, I want to be able to use the cool effect of scumbling for this reflection.

I paint the cement foundation with a color mixed from ultramarine blue, umber, and white. For the tree trunk, I mix a brown with umber, black, and white and paint one layer of this color using vertical strokes.

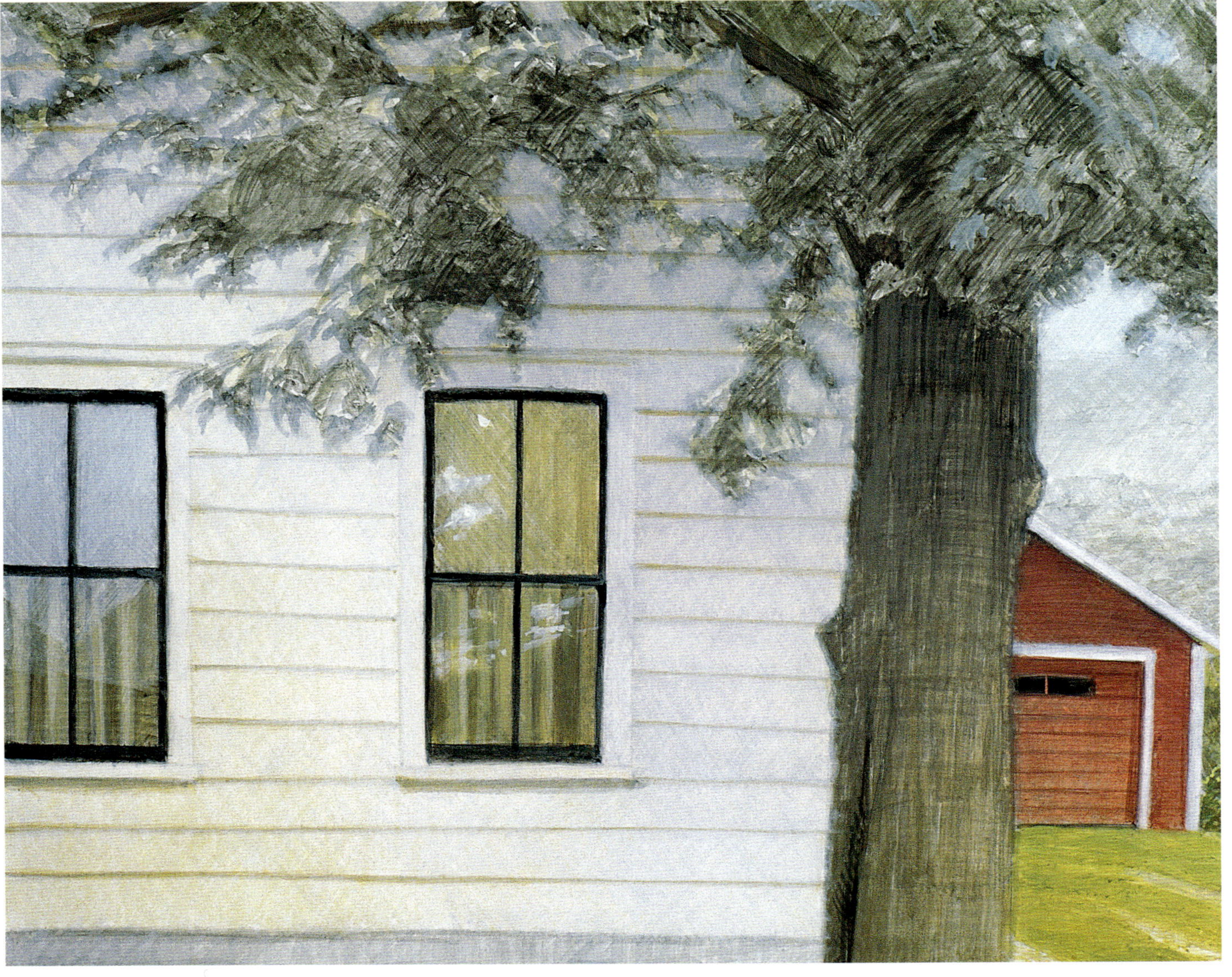



I mix three values of a violet using ultramarine blue, red, and white for the house. The values are lighter than the yellow underpainting in order for the scumble to give a cool tone, and also to go on smoothly. I paint fewer layers of violet on the lower left part of the house to give the effect of a warm reflected light. I begin work on the windows by painting a light value of ochre and white on the lighter parts of the curtains. Then I glaze the curtains with ochre. I paint many layers of white on the upper part of the left window, fewer layers on the lower part, so the curtains show through the reflection. I repaint the brightest reflections on the right window with a thicker white paint.

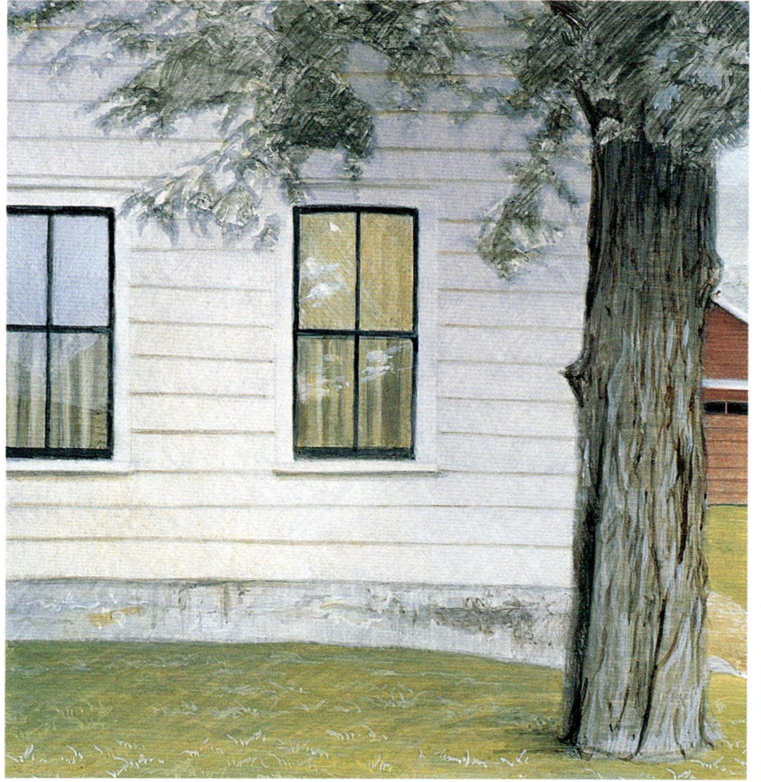



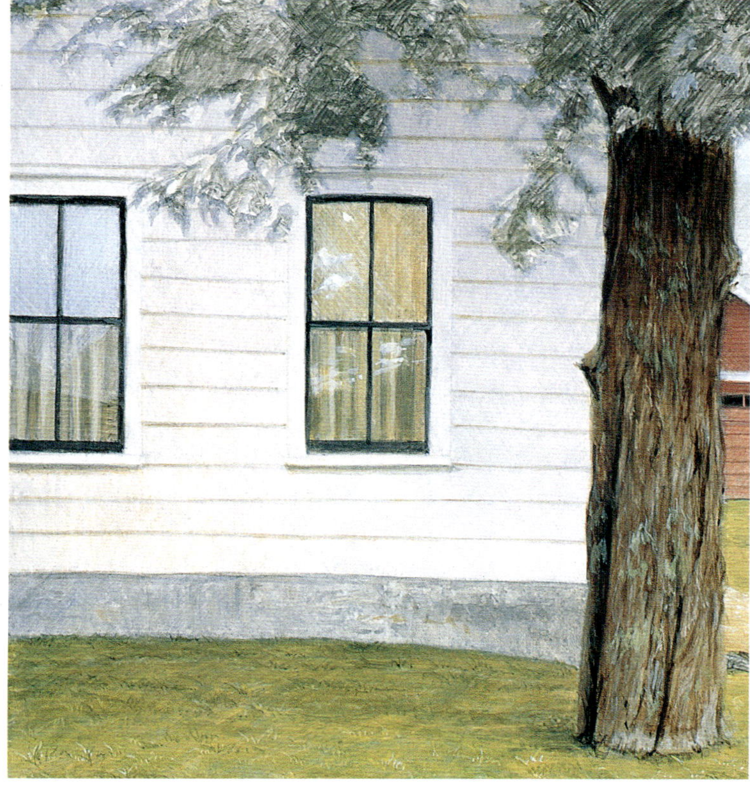



I paint a final layer of a darker violet on the house, deepening the shadowed areas. Then I begin to add textural elements. I add darker and lighter grays to the cement of the foundation to give it a weathered look. For the darks on the tree trunk I paint uneven lines of black and umber to show the pattern of bark. I add the light values of bark with a color mixed with umber, ochre, and white.

Before I paint the texture of grass, I deepen the color of the grass by glazing a green mixed from manganese blue, yellow light, and red. I add the grassy texture with a light value of yellow light and white, using the color more opaquely towards the foreground, which heightens the contrast.

I glaze the tree trunk with thin layers of umber, and emphasize the strongest darks of the bark with black and the strongest lights with umber and white. The last texture that I paint is the greenish lichen growing on the tree. I mix a green with chrome oxide, yellow medium, and white and paint it fairly opaquely on the bark. Finally, I glaze the darkest lichen, in the shadow of the leaves, with black.

I mix a gray using ultramarine blue, umber, ochre, and white which is slightly darker than the gray on the cement. I layer this color to deepen the cement color. I then add more texture with various grays.

I glaze the grass with a mixture of manganese blue and red, which makes the grass a richer color. Then I add more brush marks that represent the grassy texture, using light and dark greens. I use a yellower green in the foreground.

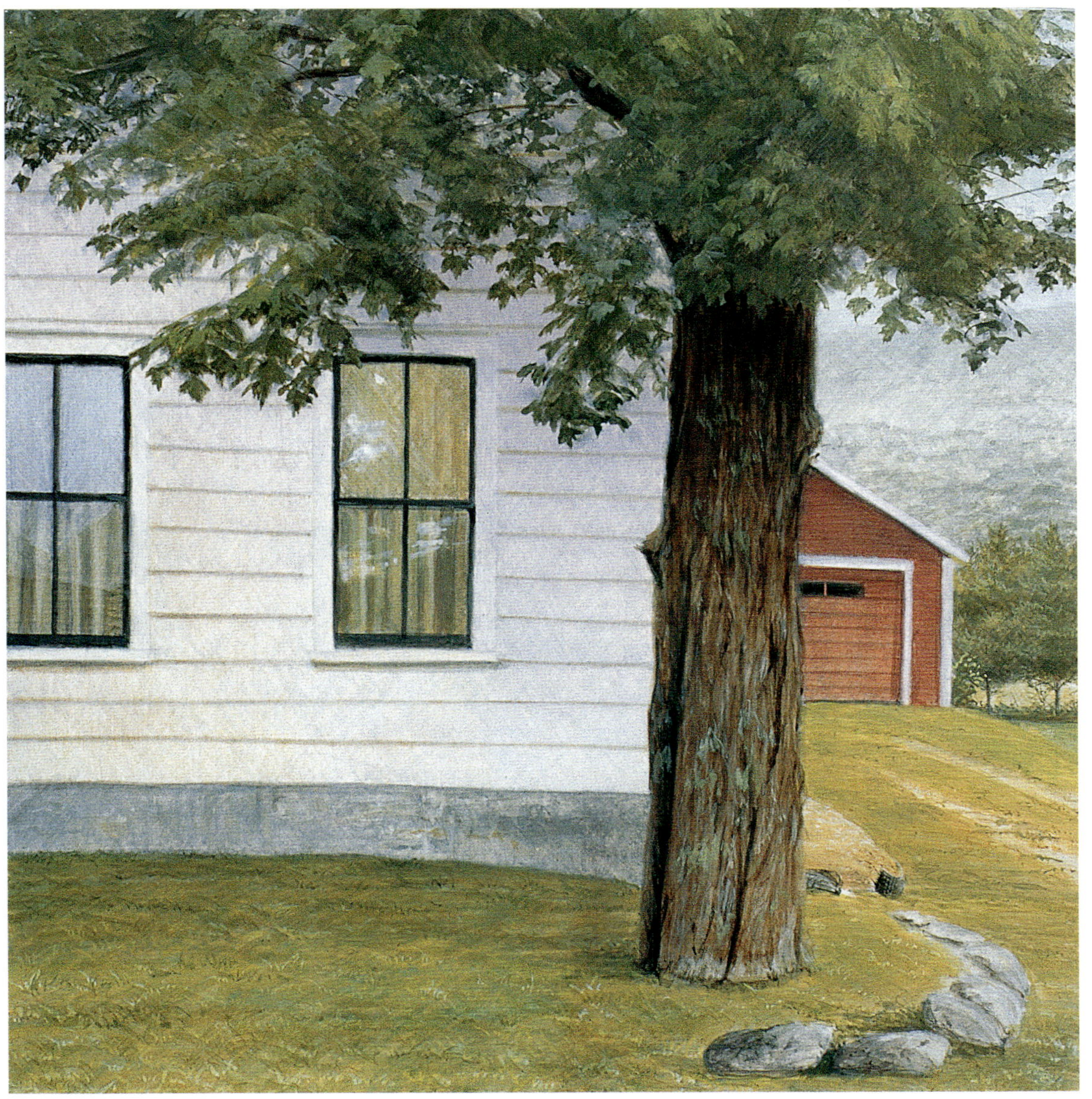

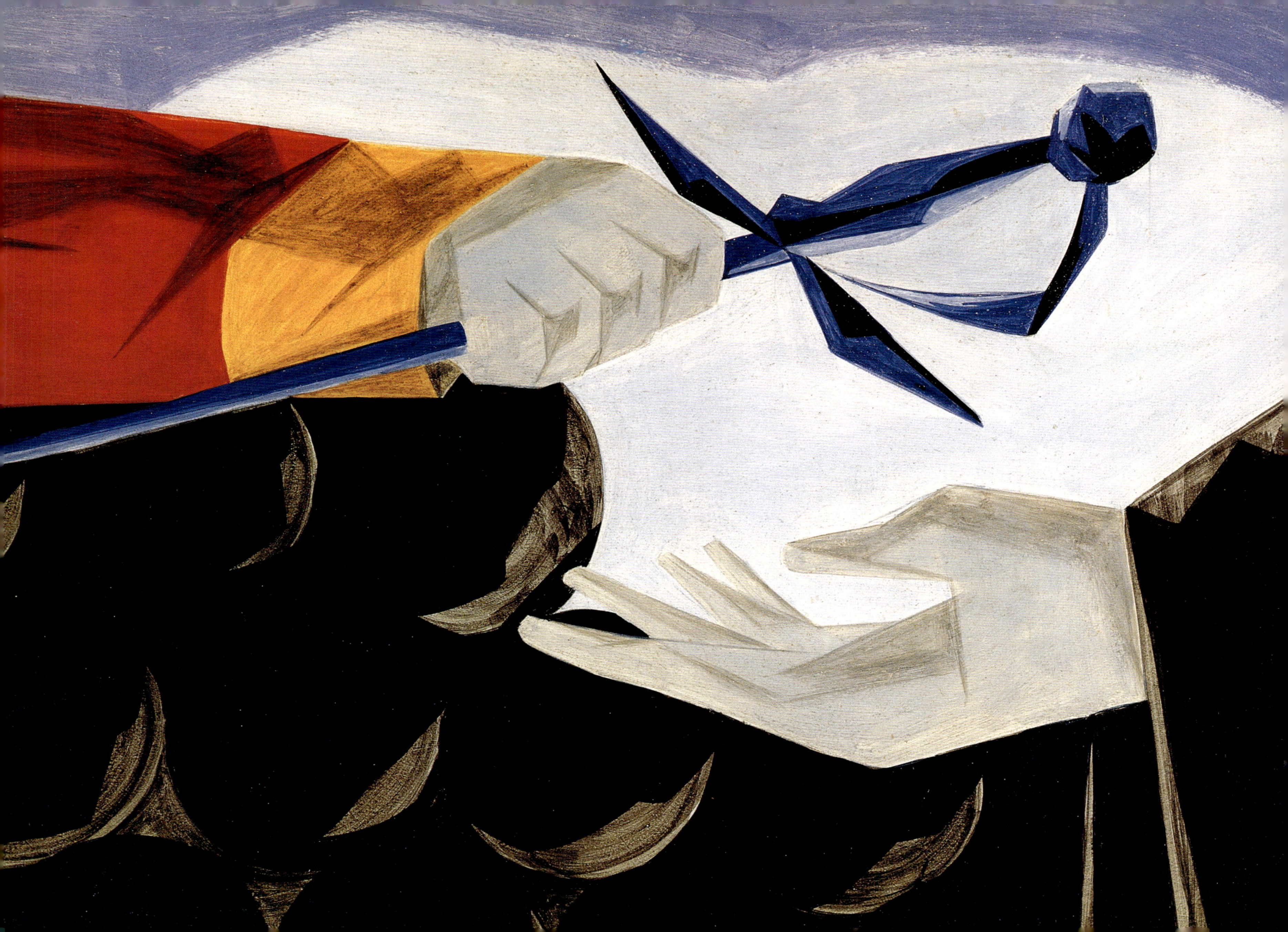

# OTHER APPROACHES

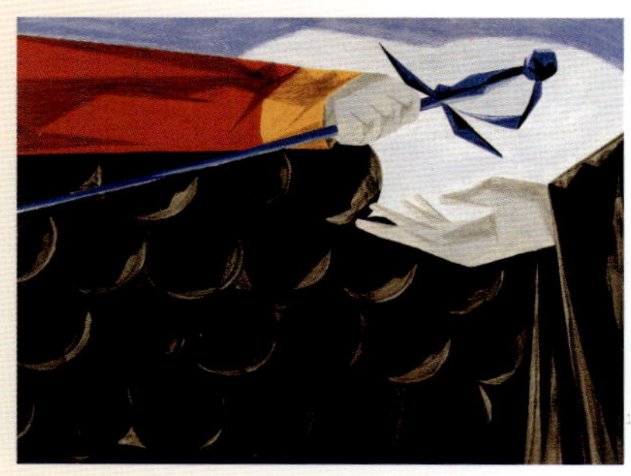

Jacob Lawrence
STRUGGLE SERIES - NO, 13:
PASSING THE SWORD
OF FREEDOM
1955–1956

The powerful composition of this work intensifies the narrative, making the story extremely vivid. This emphasis on story-telling links Lawrence's work to that of the Italian panel paintings, but his flat use of tempera is a departure from that tradition.

As with any other painting medium, egg tempera can lend itself to a variety of approaches. It has been used unconventionally, with the paint fluid and transparent like watercolor, or like gouache, in flat, opaque color areas. It can be applied with tools other than brushes—sponges, rags, palette knives—and splattered or dripped to create textures. The gesso surface of the panel is ideal for scratching or scraping into the paint, which reveals the white of the gesso. It is fun to experiment with various techniques—you may find one that suits your purposes perfectly.

In this chapter, I will describe non-traditional approaches to tempera, and will introduce you to four artists who work with egg tempera: two figure painters, a still-life painter, and an abstract painter. Each artist uses egg tempera a bit differently, just as other artists work with oil or watercolor in individual ways. For instance, none of these artists uses a complete ink underdrawing as I do. These varied techniques give an idea of the wide range of effects that can be created with the tempera medium.

# Other Techniques in Egg Tempera Painting

It is interesting to me that the first widely known American artists to use egg tempera—Thomas Hart Benton and Reginald Marsh (see page 16)—used it in a fluid, watercolor-like fashion, as have other artists such as Peter Hurd. Jacob Lawrence has worked with egg tempera and casein tempera in a flat manner similar to gouache. Benton began to work with tempera in 1925 after coming across Cennini's handbook. Perhaps Benton and these other artists were excited by the possibilities of using this fast-drying, water-based medium because they could layer color quickly without the underlayers lifting or mixing with new layers as happens with watercolor or gouache. Today, of course, we have acrylic paint that shares this characteristic with tempera, although a pigment surrounded by an egg yolk medium and one surrounded by an acrylic medium have different qualities.

Egg tempera can be applied in a free manner with tools other than brushes: palette knives can be used, and rags and sponges make interesting textures. Dripping or splattering paint from a stiff brush adds other textural effects. The only limitation is that the paint should be used thinly because cracking will occur if it is applied thickly.

The paint can also be applied broadly, with a flat brush used in a dry-brush manner. Another way of painting flat color areas is to use a loaded brush and overlapping brush strokes. This works best when the color is lighter than the underpainting so streaks do not show. Renaissance artists used this method of paint application on the architectural elements in their paintings.

Icon painters use a similar approach to broad areas, in a method called *petit lac*. With this "little lake" technique, small pools of color are applied that join to create a large area of flat color. This method is used for the darkest parts of the painting and lighter values are added on top of it, in an actual and metaphoric movement from the dark to the light.

Other methods of applying egg tempera paint (clockwise from upper left): Color applied transparently with a flat 1-inch brush; using sponges cut into 1 1/2-inch squares, thin layers of earth colors and ultramarine blue create an interesting texture; cerulean blue and cadmium lemon yellow applied in alternating layers of hatched strokes yield a lively green which is then scratched with the tip of a razor blade; color applied with paper towels and splattered from a stiff bristle brush.

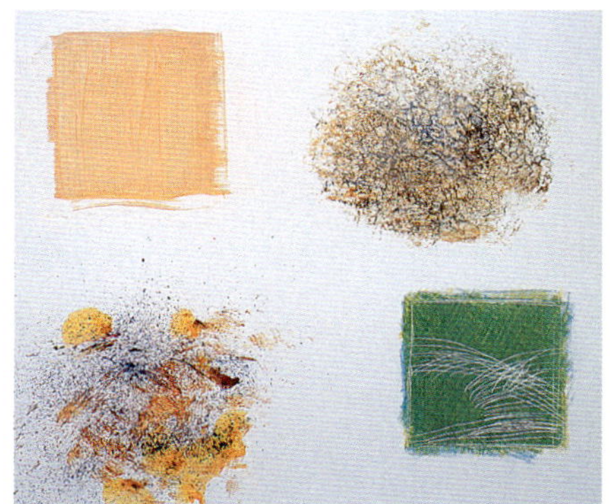

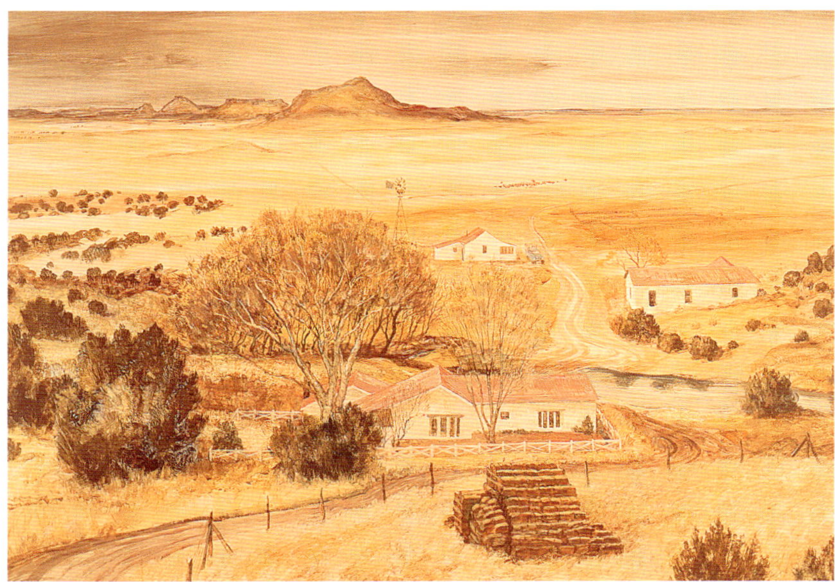

Peter Hurd
THE HEADQUARTERS, DIAMOND A RANCH, WAGON MOUND, MORA COUNTY, NEW MEXICO
1960

Hurd used casein paint for the warm neutral underpainting of this landscape. He then switched to egg tempera for the final paint layers, using the paint in an open and gestural manner.

George Tooker has been painting exclusively with egg tempera for over fifty years. The quiet depth of feeling in his work is intensified by the slow, deliberative tempera process, as are the clear, full forms. Tooker works on uncradled pressed-wood panels that are prepared with two coats of rabbit-skin glue size and six coats of gesso, which are applied to both sides and all the edges of the panel to completely seal it.

Tooker prepares a line drawing of his composition which he transfers to the gessoed panel. He works with an underdrawing less often now, but if he does, he uses India ink. He will sometimes tone the entire panel with a dilute wash of tempered color.

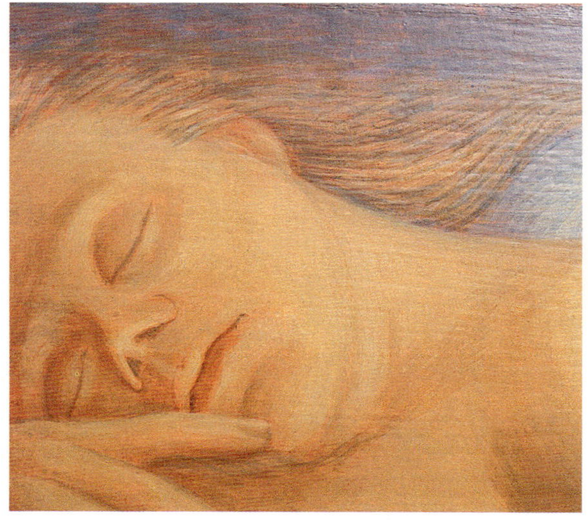

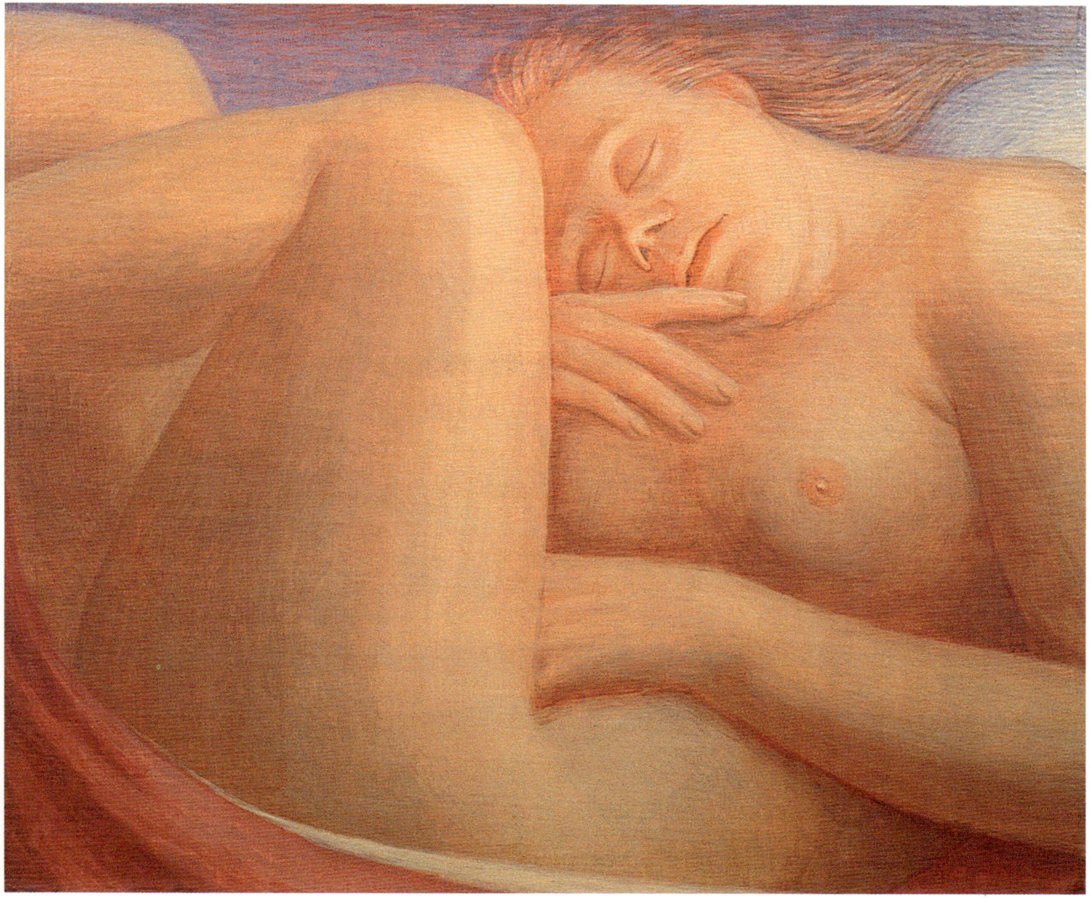

THE UNDERPAINTING FOR *SLEEPING WOMAN*

After transferring his line drawing to the gesso panel, Tooker painted a dilute wash of red earth color, terra pozzuoli, over the entire panel. He then loosely painted broad washes of color to indicate the main forms of the figure. At the point at which this photograph was taken, Tooker had begun to refine and clarify his loose beginning by adding strokes of color which follow the form of the figure. You can see the red of the underpainting showing through the brush strokes and influencing the color of the painting, making its hue very warm.

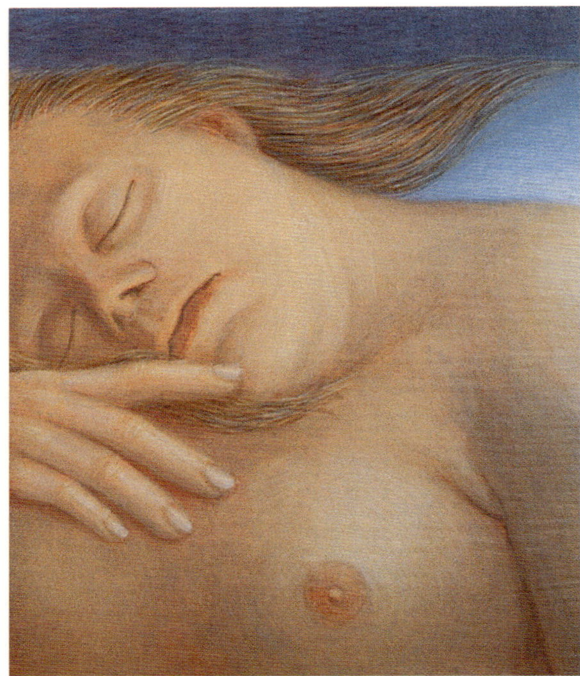

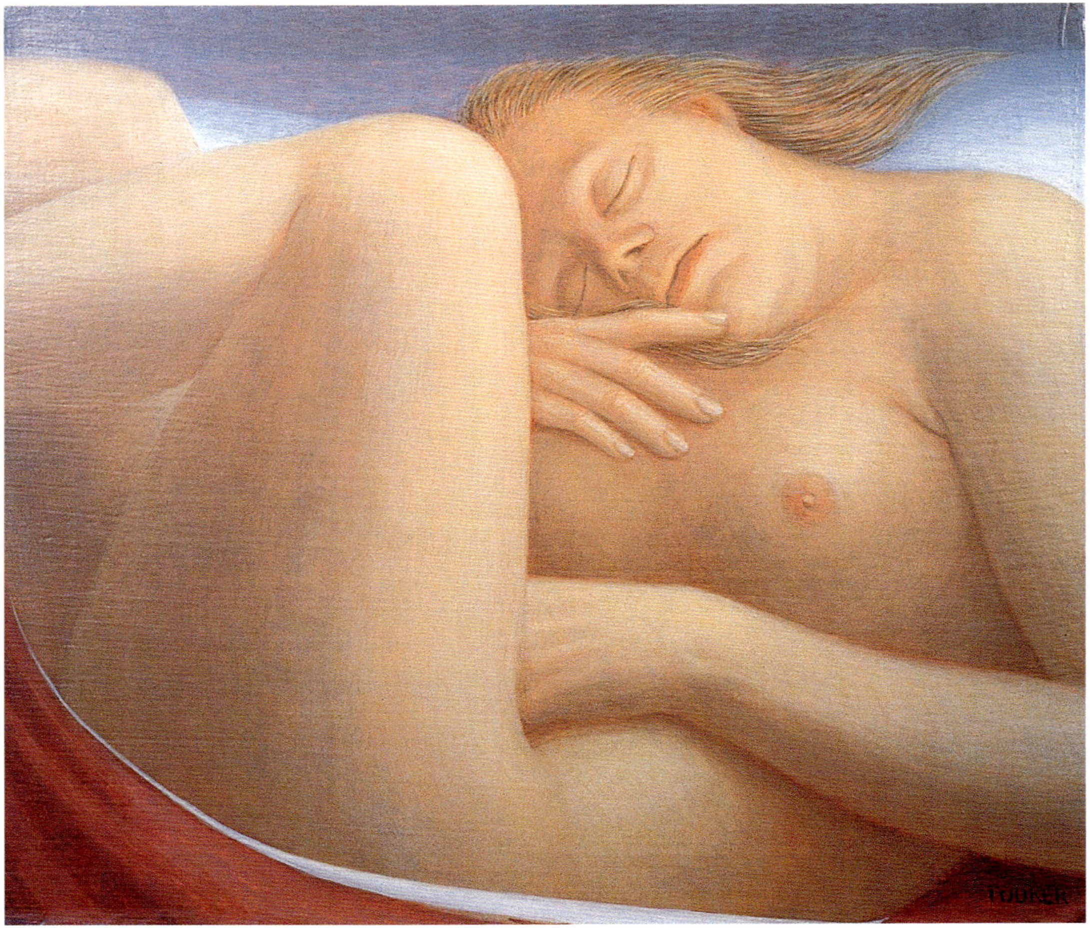

## THE COMPLETED PAINTING

With the many additional layers of paint, the volume of this figure which is cradled in the space of the panel is more developed. The color is cooler and more subtle as color is added, since the underpainting is not having as strong an influence. The earth red color that was used to tone the panel is still visible, however, especially in the blue at the top of the painting.

The glowing quality of light in this painting is characteristic of Tooker's work: it is a light that seems to emanate from the figure. The modeling of the form is very clear, yet soft at the same time, giving an aura of tenderness to the work.

An abstract painter who has worked with many different media, Stan Berning discovered egg tempera three years ago. His paintings make use of an emotive geometry and rich layers of color and contain a conversation between form and process. Berning has found that the glazes painted with egg tempera are finer and more luminous than those of acrylic paint. The medium's crispness works well for his rendering of form. Although he has ground his own pigments in the past, he now uses tube egg-oil emulsions. They dry a bit more slowly than pure egg tempera because of the oil but their slower set-up time allows the paint to be workable for a longer period. He paints on Masonite, or on hollow wood doors for large works, and uses Fredrix dry gesso mix. Here are Berning's notes on his use of tempera painting:

*There are no new, earth shaking techniques which I apply to egg tempera that are different from those that traditionalists apply to their images. It is a matter of attitude. My goal is not to reproduce a vision already imagined but rather to discover the image through the process. Tempera's capacity for a broad range of opacity and transparency, its quick-drying qualities, natural vibrancy, and sensitivity to fine and broad hue adjustment allows me the latitude to "think out loud" on the paint surface. I am aware from the beginning that the crisp delicate nature of the medium, particularly in its final stages, will lead to some precise and controlled areas, so I attempt to keep the process as loose as possible for as long as possible. Not only does this result in some surprisingly energetic surfaces, but also prompts a dialogue that reveals itself in layer upon layer and informs the finished painting.*

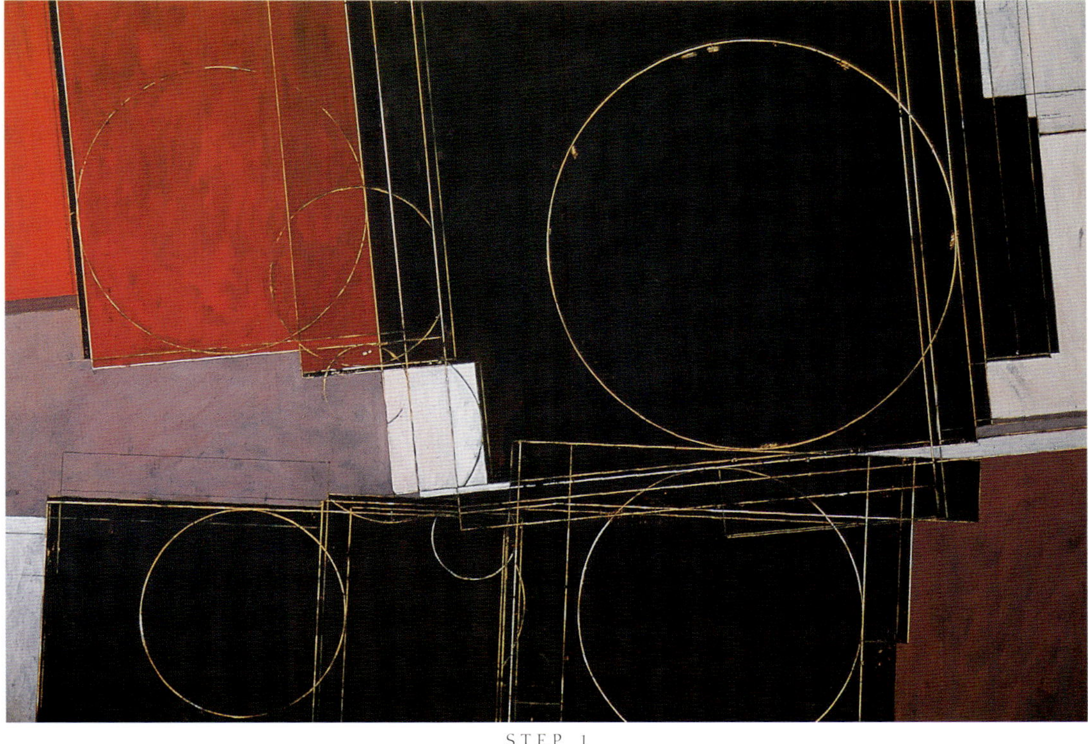

STEP 1

Day 1: I lay down yellow orange mixed wet and heavy for *Fourth Planet #22*. Day 2: Blue, green, orange, red, violet mixed to black. I put the paint on heavily and etch into it to create drawing. I use anything that works, from a dull nail and Q-tips to a plastic pencil tip. Often I'm working the paint very wet using a straight edge or some other tool which picks up paint and marks the surface while I'm using it. Day 3: The lights begin to emerge as I continue to etch and draw.

Day 4: I begin to develop hue adjustments. I am finding areas that I like. Transparent washes come into play. (Because the image is abrupt, primary, and extreme in contrast, I now begin too look for holistic resolves which might unify the image.) Day 5, I lay greens over whites, reds over greens and do lots of work with reds and oranges. Blacks are thin and cold and emphasize the fractured and broken delineation of the composition. (Awkward, lurching, and primary to the extreme, the painting is like a bad cartoon. At this point I am tempted to destroy the image with washes and by aggressively pulling away paint. I have reached a turning point: Go forward or turn in a totally different direction.)

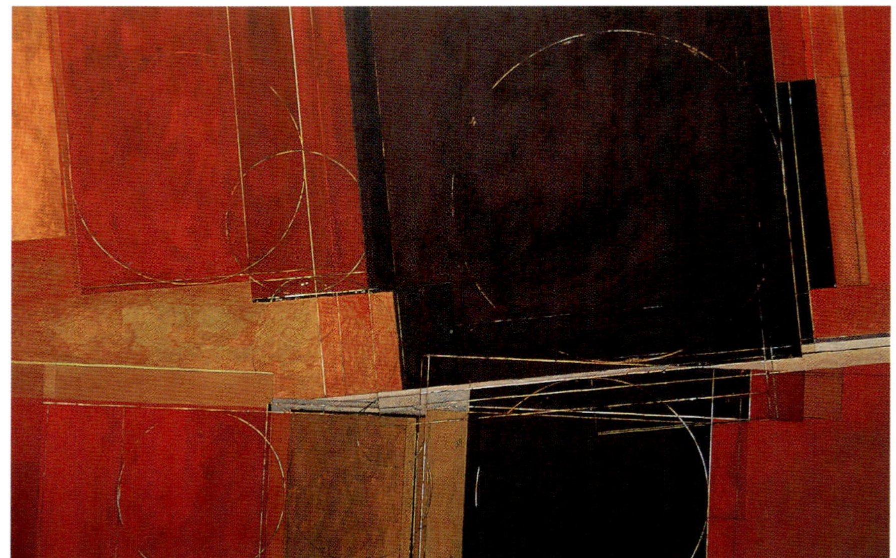



Day 7: I decide to stay with what I have. I soften linear work in the reds by using washes. I warm blacks and give them depth by using washes of violet mixes which achieve an opalescent glow. I extend lights to the lower left but these areas still need a lot of work.

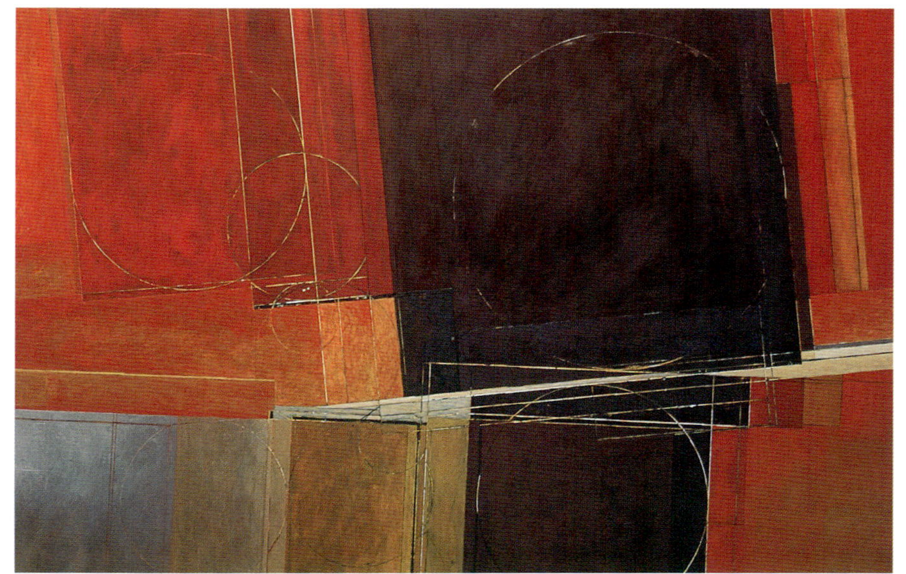

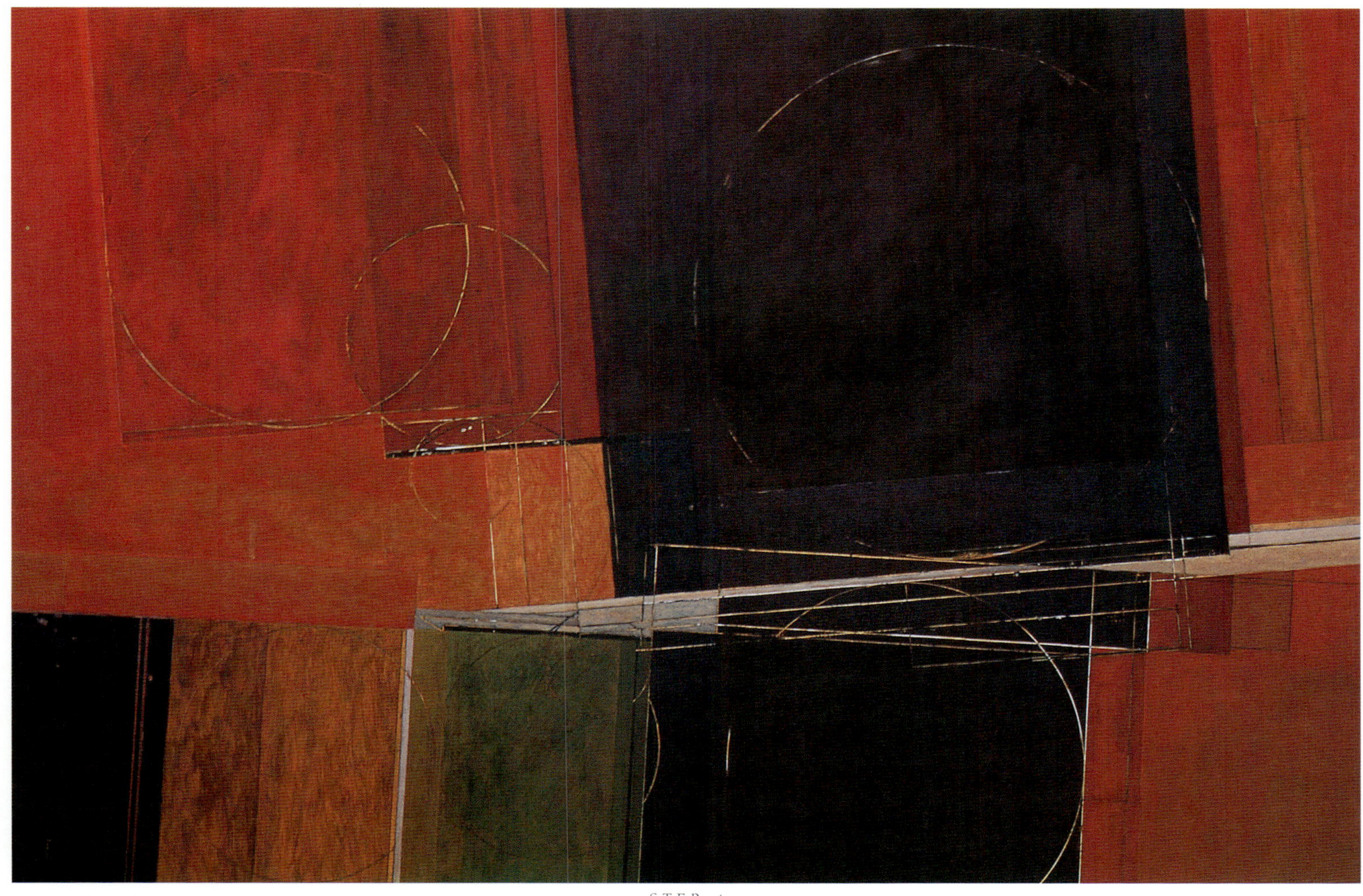



Day 14: Finished. I resolve jarring angles through compositional changes to the areas where reds and blacks meet and by tighter adjustments of hue in the reds. I rework the lower left to lower center over and over again. I find it necessary to bring strong green complements into play and then subdue them with the use of earth tones and more blacks. I adjust the blacks further. The painting's natural vibration has gone from high to medium-low frequency and settled into an attitude of calm elegance—all within a vibrant and muscular image.

Carol Mothner's still-life paintings engage intensely with the visible world. The illusionism in her paintings heightens the sense of wonder. When she first started working with egg tempera three years ago, Mothner felt that she had found a medium that absolutely suited her sensibility since she preferred drawing to any other activity. Her paintings combine traditional and unconventional techniques such as sponging on color and scratching through the paint. She describes her painting process for her work *The Wait*.

Her palette consists of white (two-thirds titanium and one-third zinc whites), mars black, raw umber, cobalt violet, yellow ochre, Venetian red, verdaccio, chromium green, cobalt blue, and cadmium yellow deep. Mothner does not prepare her own panels, but orders them from a local craftsperson.

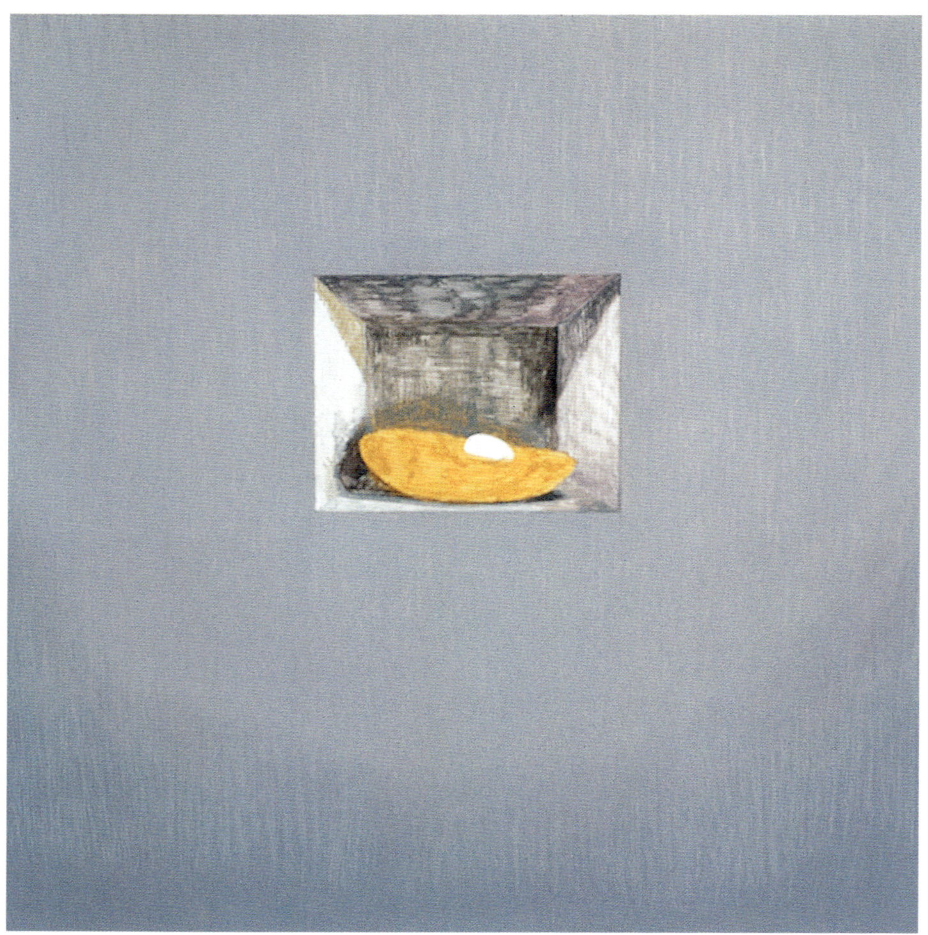

STEP 1

Working from life, I make a very careful drawing in graphite on the panel to minimize the need to make corrections later. I wash the nest in with two thin coats of yellow ochre. All other areas are washed in with a gray made up of different shades of a mixture of cobalt blue, raw umber, and white.

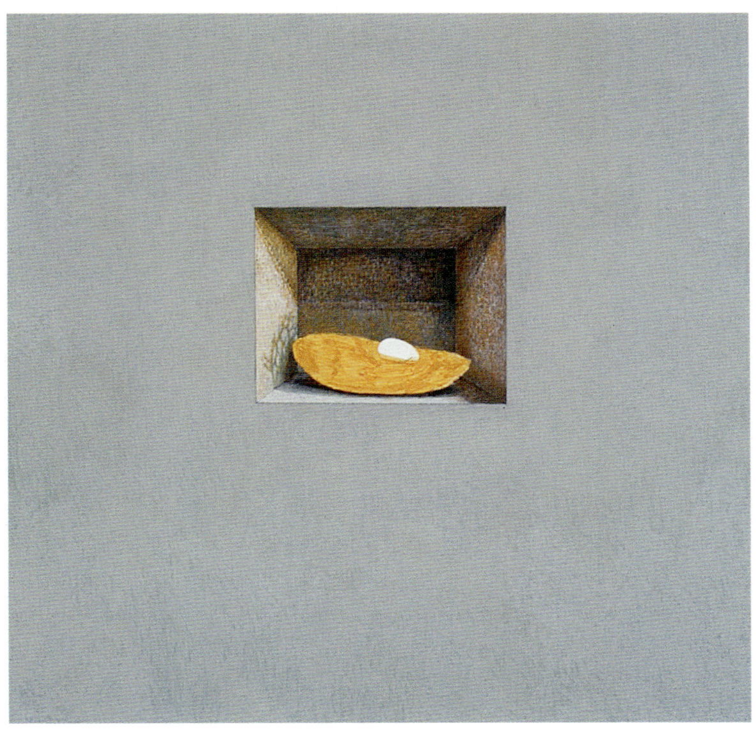

STEP 2

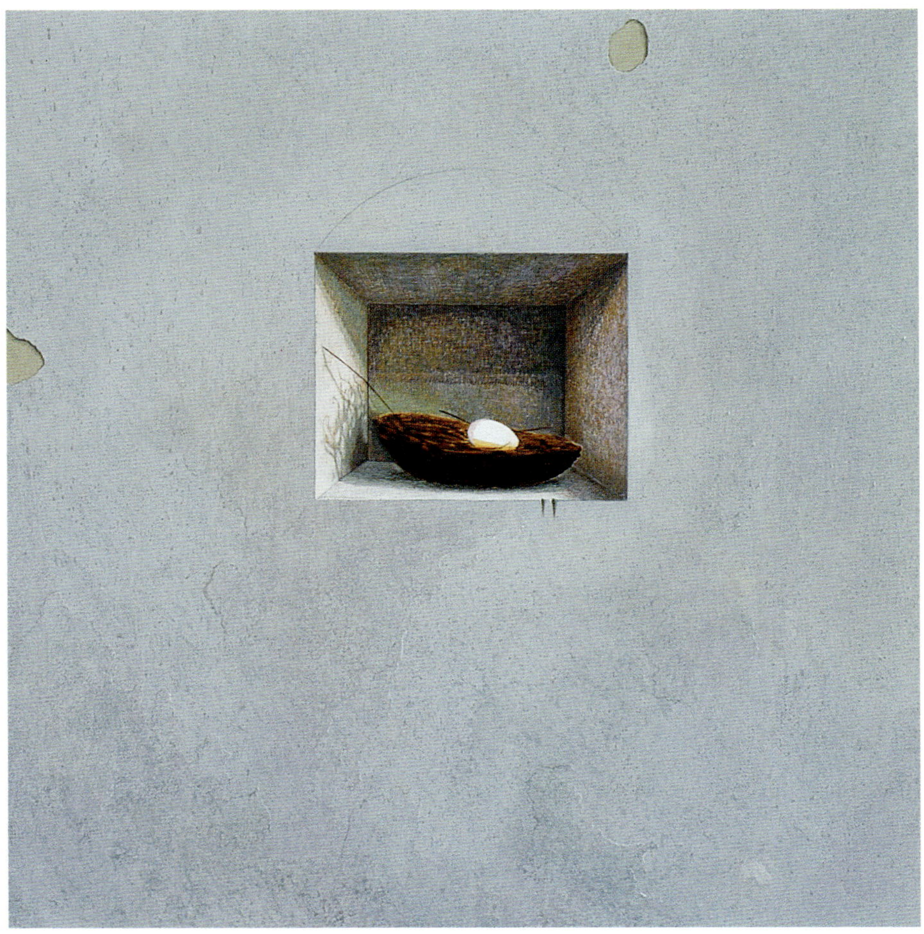

STEP 3

In the niche, with a sable brush, I crosshatch one color at a time. The layered colors are applied thinly starting with cobalt blue, then Venetian red, yellow ochre, chromium green, and finally cobalt violet, and white. I then go back in with cobalt blue and raw umber to push back the darker area. In the lighter areas, I crosshatch layers of yellow ochre and white.

For the wall surrounding the niche I mix some of the previously used gray mix with some yellow ochre, and brush it on thinly so that some of the previous coats show through. Then I mix the same gray with cobalt violet and brush it on thinly. Next I make a mixture of blue, black, white, and cobalt violet. I dip a sponge into this mixture, dry it a bit on a paper towel, and dab it on to the lower part of the wall. I repeat this process three times until I achieve the texture of roughed-up plaster.

Covering the niche area, I next splatter variations of the gray mixture—some browner or greener—onto the wall surrounding the niche. I add highlights of yellow ochre and white to the sides of some of the splatter marks to give the wall a more three-dimensional feeling. The last thing that I work on is the nest and egg, going over the entire nest with a mixture of raw umber and black.

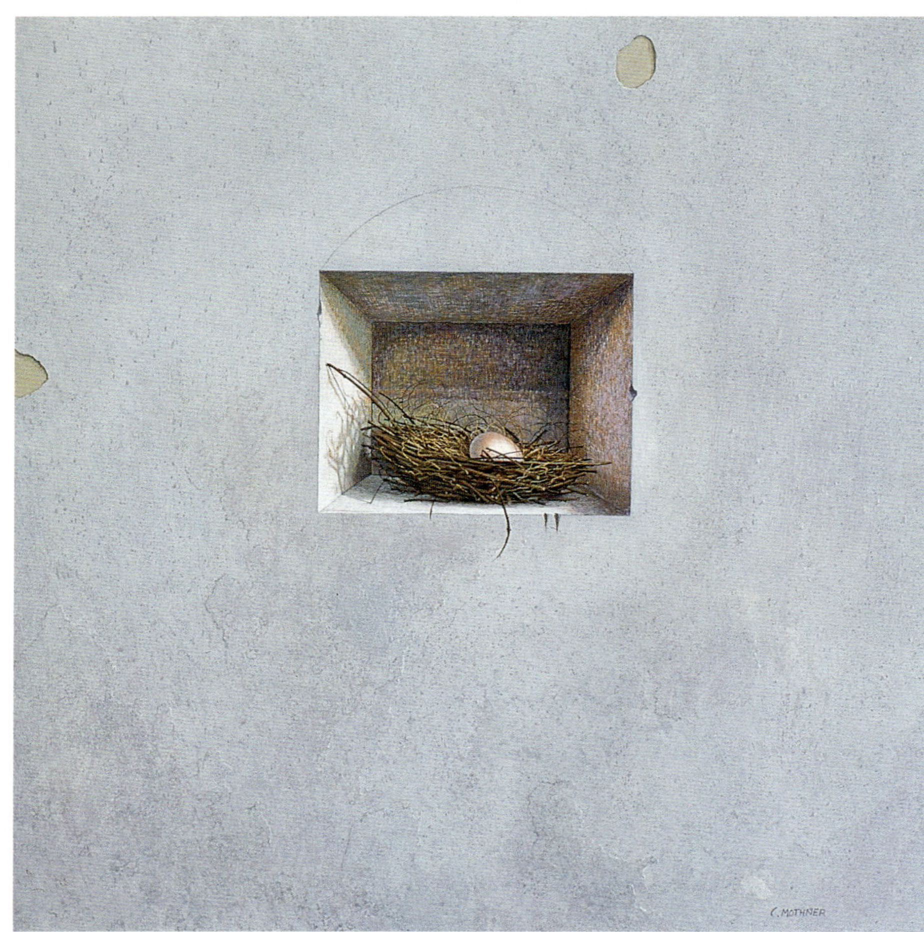

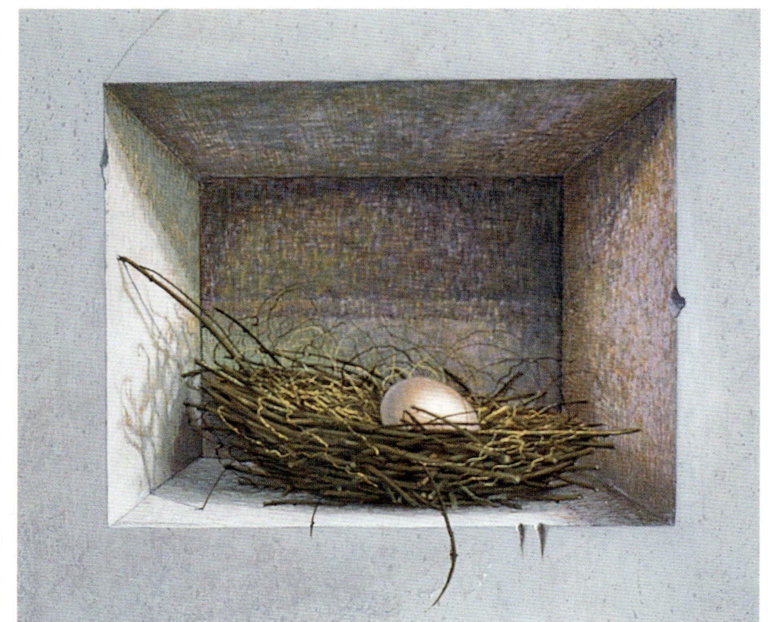



### STEP 4

I continue to develop the nest. In this area I work exactly as I would with oil paint, going in with lights over darks. Each twig is painted individually in varying shades of brown, mixes of ochres, greens, reds, and small amounts of white. When all the twigs have been completed, I go into highlight the inside of the nest and some of the branches that are catching the direct light. I use a dull etching needle to scratch out these areas and a sharp one for some of the tiny lines, thus allowing the yellow ochre underpainting to show through. Where I want branches but may have neglected to put down the ochre, I paint thin lines of white (two layers) and glaze them with ochre mixed with cadmium yellow deep. Because the browns are looking dull at this point, I mix a glaze of verdaccio (a transparent cool brown) with a small amount of vermilion and darken some of the shadows of the nest.

I paint the egg in a traditional egg tempera manner. A wash of chromium green, an ochre glaze, and loose strokes of white are followed by a cobalt violet glaze, some cobalt blue, and verdaccio in the shadow area; and finally a very thin but carefully painted white layer with an extremely thin glaze of Venetian red. The next day, I polish the painting by gently going over the surface with cheesecloth.

Michael Bergt's paintings are closely related to the art of the early Renaissance because his figures point to meanings beyond the mundane; in the Renaissance the figures presented issues of faith, for Bergt they point to the dilemmas of human existence. Bergt's tempera practice incorporates both traditional and unconventional methods, as shown in the following demonstration. Bergt explains his work as follows:

> *Heaven and Earth is a symbolic egg tempera painting with the gesture of the lower figure emulating a deposed Christ as seen in early Flemish painting. The lower figure is half-emerging from the ground like a resurrection, while the "flipped" version of the same figure is floating in the air like an ascension. These figures represent a bridge between the spiritual and material, and heaven and earth.*

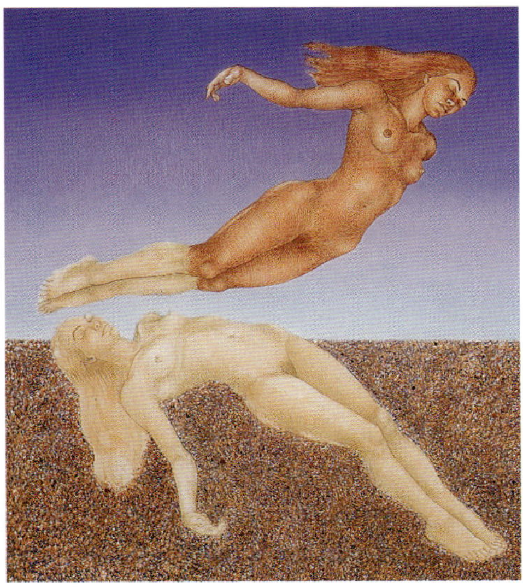

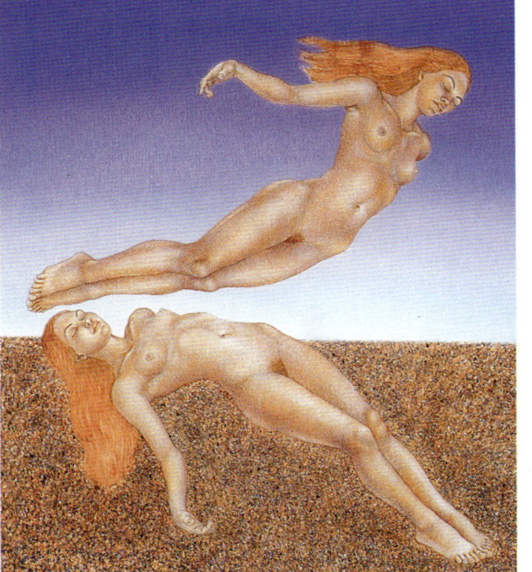

### STEP 1

My painting process begins with transferring a finished preliminary drawing to a prepared gessoed panel. I trace the outline of the drawing and note important elements. I then rub the back of the tracing paper with graphite and transfer my lines to the gesso panel. Initially, a faint pencil outline is all one sees on the white ground of the panel. I proceed to "redraw" the image using a mixture of chromium oxide green and yellow ochre. This color flows more easily than the traditional transparent pigment of terre verte. The forms are modeled with this neutral greenish tone creating a complementary color for the successive layers of colors.

After establishing the greenish underpainting, I prefer to block in the basic colors of the background; this enables me to develop the flesh tones in relation to surrounding color. To create the textured ground, I stippled alternating layers of warm and cool colors with sponges, and applied drips and splatters for added texture. The semi-transparent nature of egg tempera enables me to quickly create a rich and varied surface that is a perfect base for successive layers. The gradation of the sky is achieved by gradually adding white to the deepest blue mixture at the top of the image and working downwards towards the horizon, blending carefully along the way.

### STEP 2

I then cover the cool greenish underpainting of the flesh with a transparent glaze of Italian warm ochre from Zecchi—beginning the alternating layers of opaque and transparent, and warm and cool colors. I apply a flesh tone of reddish color on top of the ochre glaze. I used a burnt sienna, but a red ochre or a mixed red will work as well. I try not to completely obscure the green underpainting with this layer; rather, the intention is to build up thin, semi-transparent layers all blending together to create a complex overlay of colors.

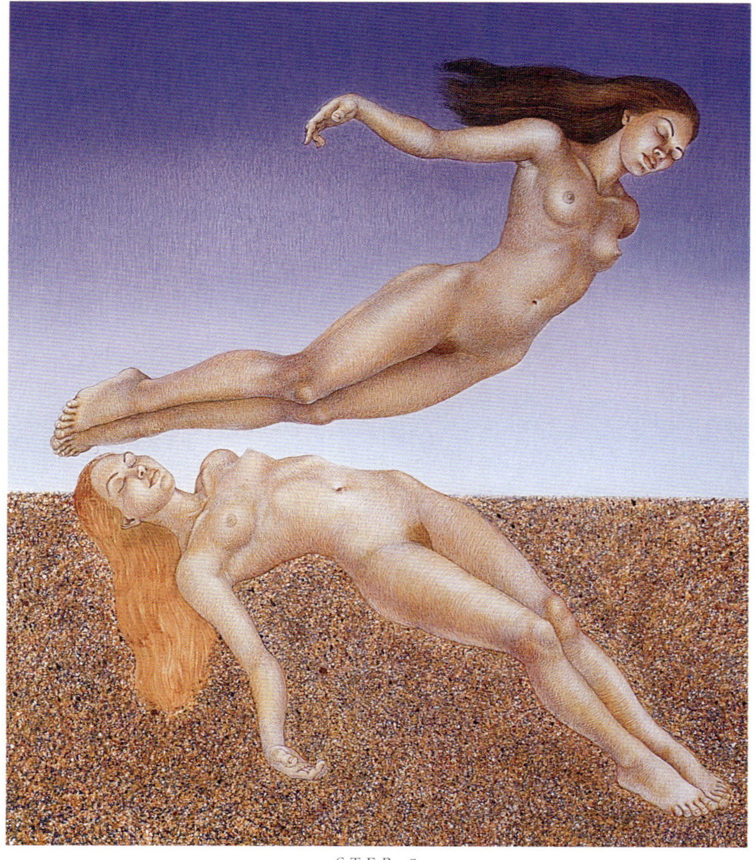

STEP 3

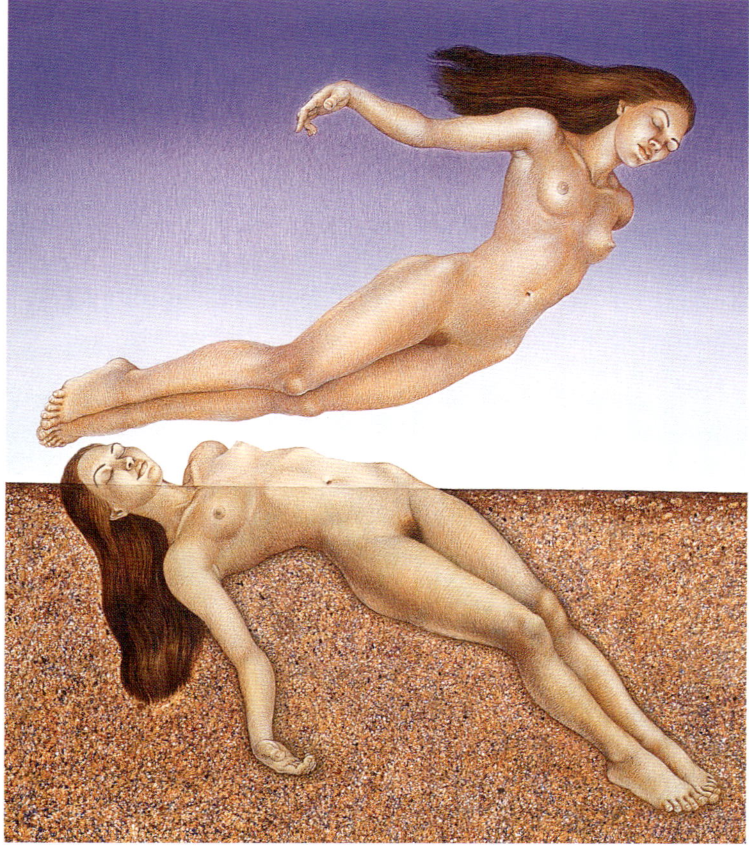

STEP 4

A blended white establishes the highlights and activates the colors. I use a mixture of two-thirds titanium white and one-third zinc white combined with a small amount of green or yellow for this purpose. The mingling of these layers creates a complex variety of values and a very lively surface. I apply this mixture more heavily for the opaque regions, and very thinly into the shadow areas. Initially, the overall effect is a "chalky" color; this is necessary to bring the value up enough to allow a warm glaze over the surface. The glaze I use is either an Italian warm ochre, or a Verona green from Zecchi. Light passing through this glaze enlivens the surface.

With a rich, complex surface established, I am now ready to paint the deeper values. Traditionally, a verdaccio is used for the shadows and darker lines of the figure. Verdaccio is a greenish-brown mixture of black, ochre, and red. (Zecchi in Florence sells a premixed pigment of verdaccio that is used for this purpose). I apply alternating layers of underpainting and glazing throughout the process, but eventually the final touches of shadow and highlights are painted directly, without glazing.

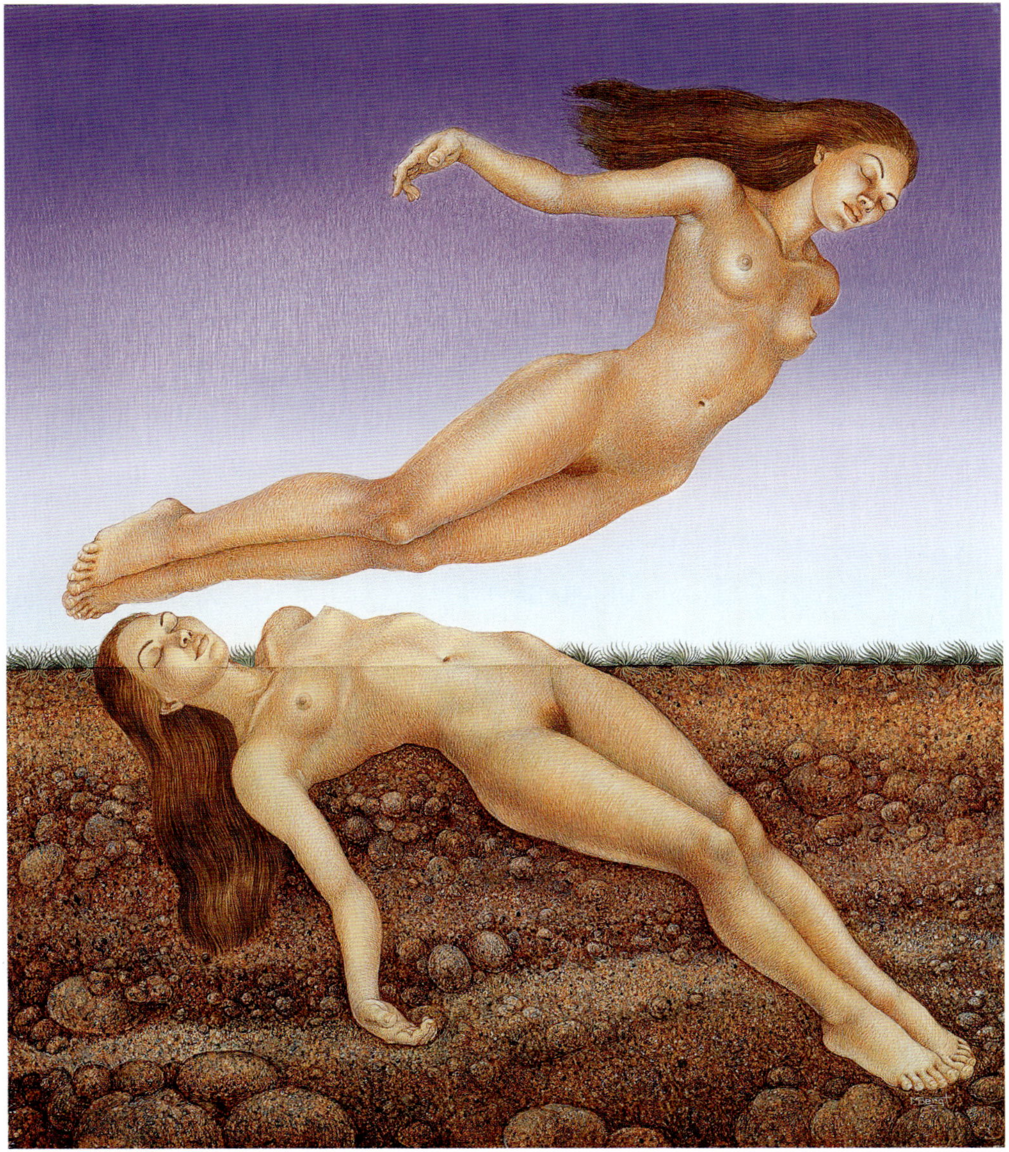

With the shadows established, direct highlights are now possible. I carefully apply the highlights without moving too far into the shadows. The final layer of highlights need not be glazed, so I mix a value appropriate to the surface. Ideally, the final surface should be one of interwoven layers of contrasting colors of warm and cool, transparent and opaque. Shadows are generally more transparent, and highlights opaque. Body color is enlivened through glazing. The final stages of a painting incorporate the subtle adjusting of light and dark, with occasional glazing to unify tones.

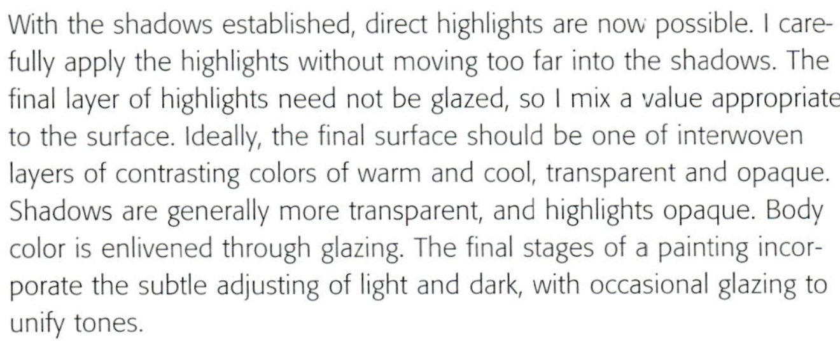

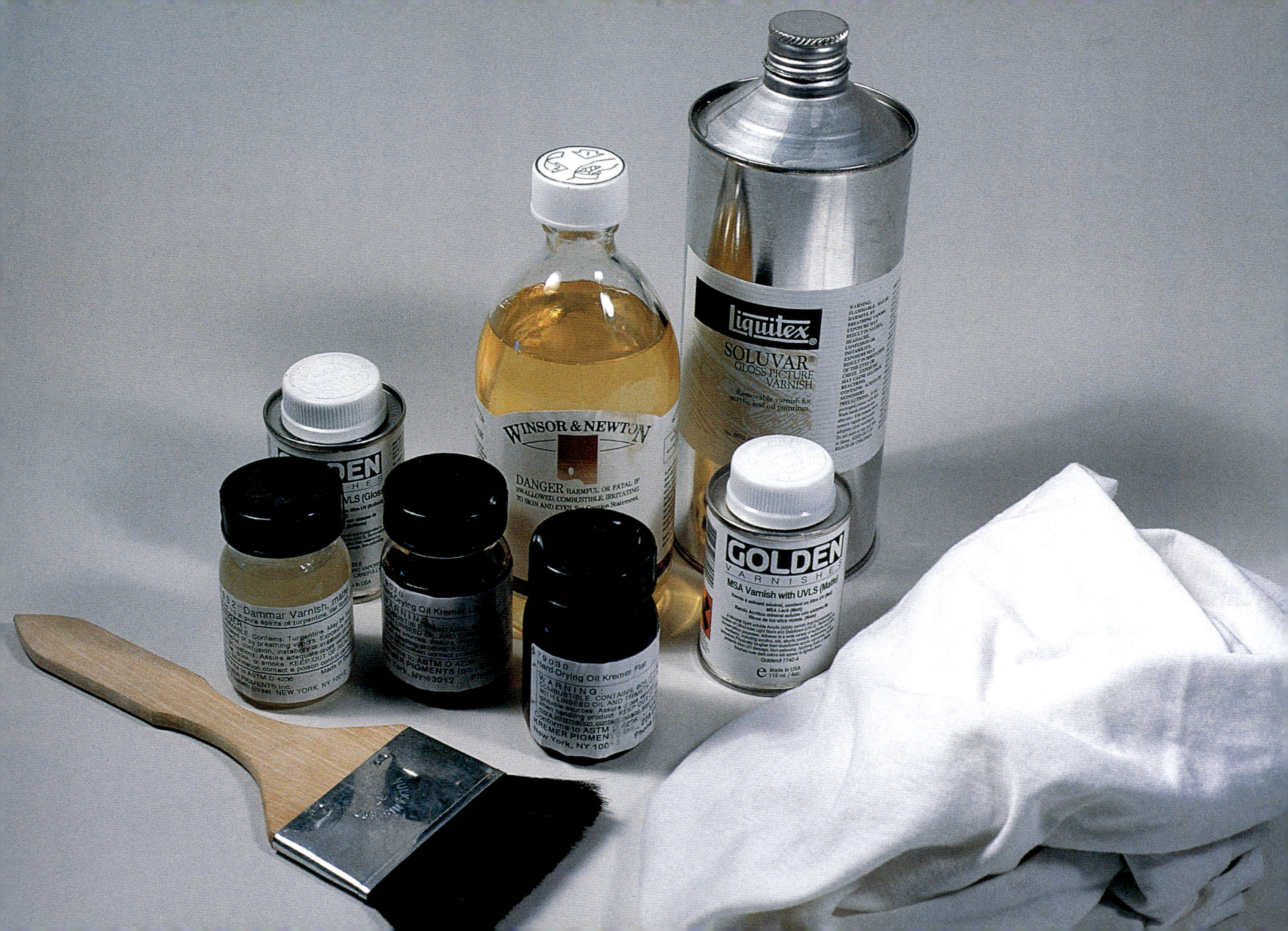

GOLDEN
VARNISHES
UVLS (Gloss)

Liquitex
SOLUVAR
GLOSS PICTURE
VARNISH
Removable varnish for
acrylic and oil paintings.

WINSOR & NEWTON
DANGER HARMFUL OR FATAL IF
SWALLOWED. COMBUSTIBLE. IRRITATING
TO SKIN AND EYES.

GOLDEN
VARNISHES
MSA Varnish with UVLS (Matte)

Dammar Varnish, matte

Hard-Drying Oil Kremer Flat
WARNING
KREMER PIGMENTS
New York, NY 100

# PROTECTING YOUR PAINTING

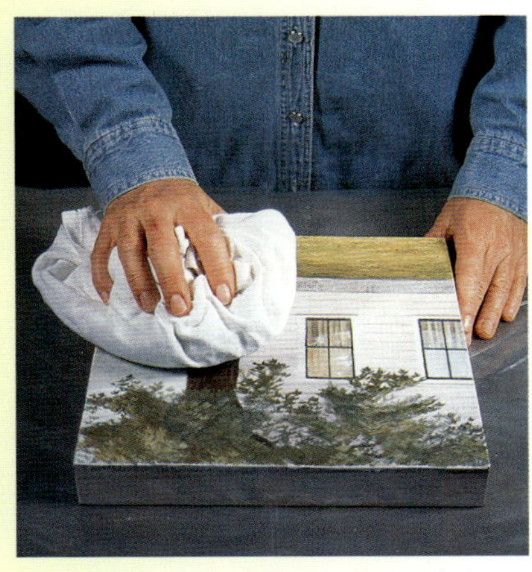

Opposite (from the left): A soft goat-hair varnish brush, various varnishes, a soft cotton rag for burnishing. Above: Burnishing the painting for protection.

**E**gg tempera is a particularly durable and stable medium. Oil paintings can darken with age, other paints often fade, but egg tempera paintings have survived for hundreds of years with the brilliance of their color intact. The final paint layers of these ancient paintings are sometimes abraded or damaged in other ways, but the color itself is not greatly changed unless the artist used fugitive pigments which change over time, usually by turning black.

Once you have finished your egg tempera painting, you are faced with the decision of whether or not to varnish it. A varnish is a liquid solution of resin or acrylic that dries to a hard, transparent film. Whether it is a matte or glossy varnish, it will change the appearance of the painting. Over the years I've had numerous lively discussions with artist friends about the pros and cons of varnishing. The main argument in favor of varnishing a painting is to protect it from dirt; a secondary argument is that the varnish enhances the appearance of the finished painting by evening out the glossy and matte areas. The main argument against varnishing is that this extra protection is not necessary, and only adds to problems of conservation. The even or glossy appearance of the varnished surface can also be a detriment. Kurt Wehlte, in his painting manual, argues against varnishing for any reasons other than the aesthetic one—you like the way it looks. I varnish my oil paintings with an acrylic varnish because it brings out a fresh-looking shine and revives colors that have sunk in.

Egg tempera paintings are a different matter. Conservators are uncertain whether or not Renaissance tempera panel paintings were varnished, even though Cennini mentions varnishing in *The Craftsman's Handbook.* A conservator at the Metropolitan Museum of Art in New York told me that it was not necessary to varnish tempera paintings, and recommended burnishing. Even though Daniel Thompson in *The Practice of Tempera Painting* recommends varnishing, I have taken the conservator's advice and no longer varnish my work for several reasons. Egg tempera paintings take eight to 12 months to cure; if a tempera is varnished before this time has elapsed, the varnish will affect the paint by changing some colors and upsetting the balance of the painting. The varnish may also penetrate the paint, causing problems if the varnish has to be removed.

My paintings often leave my studio before a year has gone by, and I once had a varnishing disaster when a show date was abruptly moved ahead. I tried to rush the varnishing process, not allowing the coats of varnish to dry thoroughly before applying new coats, which caused a terrible puddling of the varnish. I had to remove the varnish, and while doing so I also lifted some delicate paint layers.

Varnishing is a difficult process with tempera; varnish flows smoothly on an oil painting, but sometimes goes on unevenly on tempera, necessitating several coats. Dust sticking to the wet varnish is always a problem. And, very important for my decision, varnish changes the surface of the painting, substituting a glossy smooth finish for the silky sheen and visible touch of the brush strokes of the tempera paint. For me, the beauty of the tempera surface is lost with a varnish.

## BURNISHING THE PAINTING

Burnishing an egg tempera painting will bring out its natural sheen and harden its surface, making it more water-resistant. The painting can be burnished before it is fully cured; I lightly burnish my paintings after two months, when the surface has begun to harden, then polish them more thoroughly a few months later.

I have found that a soft old white cotton tee shirt works very well for burnishing. Silk is also often recommended for this job. Wad the cloth loosely, and with a smooth side against the painting surface, rub it softly over the painting in a circular motion. The gloss of the painting will increase as you work over its surface. If all the areas of the painting are evenly tempered, the gloss will be even across the surface of the panel.

Slight differences in the surface will not harm the painting, but they can help make you more aware which colors require more or less egg yolk for tempering, It is possible to "cheat" at this point and use the medium as a kind of retouch varnish, by painting some very diluted egg yolk medium over parts of the painting that have sunk in and look too matte. You can burnish these areas a few weeks later.

## VARNISHING THE PAINTING

If you decide that you definitely want to varnish your painting, you must wait for eight to 12 months for it to cure fully; waiting a full year is preferable. There are many different varnishes that you can use, from acrylic-based varnishes to various natural resins, in glossy and matte finishes.

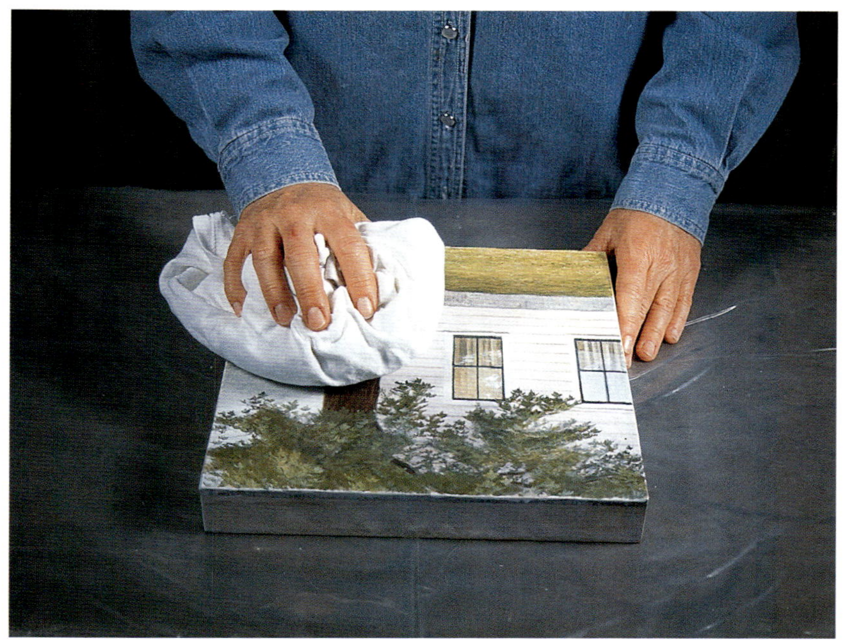

Burnishing the painting.

I suggest that you test a few varnishes on a sample tempera painting because each will look different; each varnish has a different degree of gloss and a slightly different color. The Met conservator mentioned above recommended that if I wanted to varnish, I should use damar varnish. I found damar too glossy and did not like it at all. But, you may like that glossiness.

Damar varnish has a slightly yellow color that I find disturbing on my paintings, as do other natural varnishes such as Kremer's Hard-drying Oil, which consists of a copal resin in linseed oil. Acrylic varnishes do not have this problem—they are very clear. I have used both Soluvar and Golden's MSA (mineral spirits soluble) acrylic varnish. Golden's varnish is the best that I've tried; it adheres quite well to the tempera surface, and is not

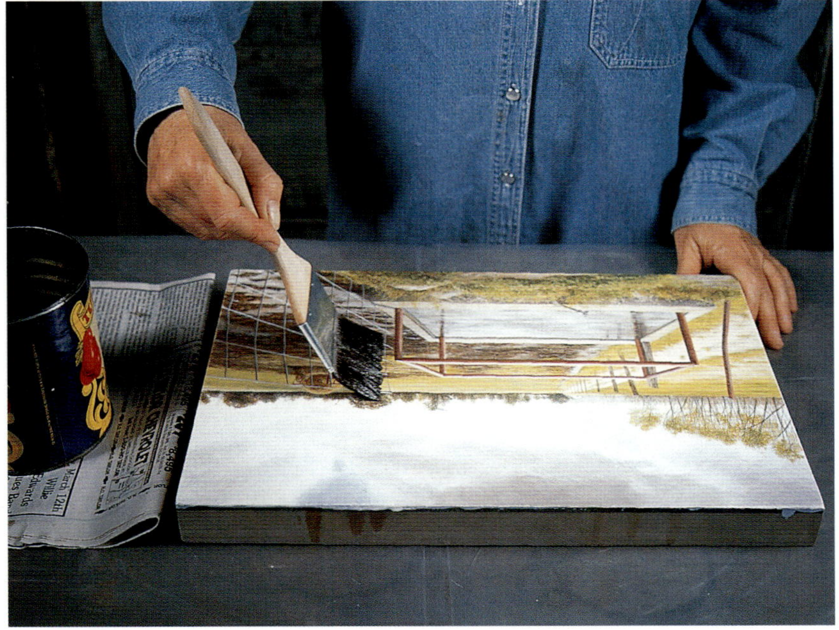

Varnishing the painting.

highly glossy. Of course, you can also use matte varnishes, which don't change the surface appearance of the tempera as much. You cannot apply more than two coats of matte varnish to a painting, however, because the wax additive will make the varnish appear cloudy in thicker layers. A solution to this problem is to use one or two layers of gloss varnish with a final layer of matte varnish.

When your painting has dried for at least eight months, preferably 12, gently clean its surface with a clean rag moistened with mineral spirits. You should be in a room that is clean and free of dust. Spraying the air around your work area with a water mister will help settle the dust. Prepare your varnish in the consistency recommended on the can. I recommend a three-inch-wide soft hair brush for varnishing tempera, (I use a goat hair brush), for a smooth finish. Dip the brush in the varnish, then wipe it against the edge of the container. Apply the varnish thinly across the painting, immediately smoothing it in the opposite direction. Let this first coat dry for at least 24 hours. If you rush, there is a danger of the varnish forming uneven puddles. After a day, apply a second coat. It is better to use several thin coats of varnish than one thick coat. Two thin layers of varnish are sufficient if the surface is evenly glossy, if not, apply another coat, again waiting at least 24 hours between layers.

## THE PROBLEM OF BLOOM

Sometimes an egg tempera painting will get a cloudy substance, a mold, over its surface, caused by moisture or excess egg yolk medium, but it is a fairly rare occurrence; I have never encountered this problem. To avoid problems with bloom it is important to protect your painting from excessive moisture. Never wrap a newly painted picture in a plastic bag—this will encourage mold. When it does appear, George Tooker has recommended carefully brushing the bloom off the surface of the painting with a soft hair brush. Do not wipe the surface, because this can press the bloom into it, but brush it gently.

# Afterword

I am a relative beginner in the egg tempera medium—I've used it for only five years. In preparation for writing this book, I went to the library, came home with piles of books about Renaissance panel paintings and egg tempera painters, and learned more and more about tempera's history and techniques. I spoke with several tempera artists, with whom I shared ideas and technical information. It was exciting, and tremendous fun. I have become more aware of my own painting process as I began to think about the step-by-step development of my work; and my painting process has expanded and changed because of my research. Painting with egg tempera continues to be a wonderful adventure.

One important thing that I've learned is that although tempera is a medium that displays its fullest beauty through a disciplined technique,

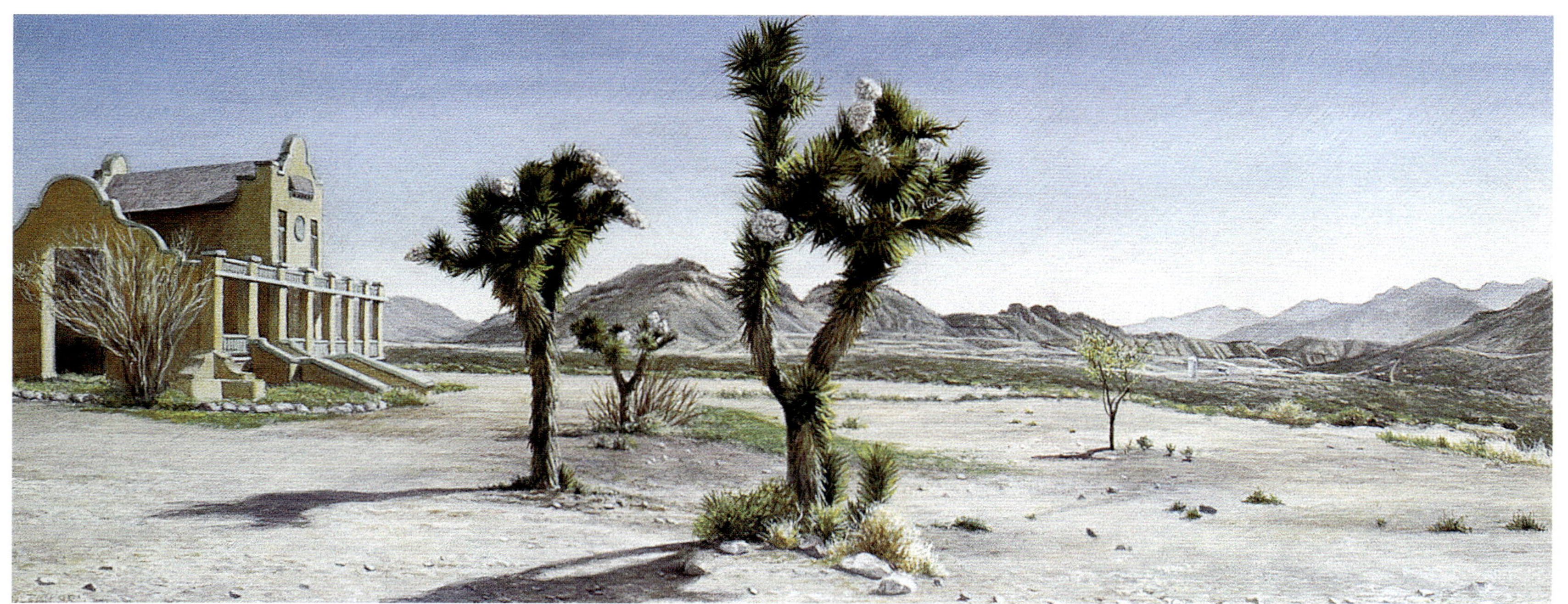

JOSHUA TREES WITH GOLD MINING, RHYOLITE, NEVADA
$6^{1}/_{2} \times 17$ inches

The spiky, dark form of the leaves of the Joshua trees is in dramatic contrast to the surrounding desert. I chose to paint them in the foreground of a landscape that spoke to the past and present of mining. The building was part of an old mining town, long since deserted; in the far distance is a contemporary gold mining operation in which hills are stripped for gold.

that technique has surprising breadth and fluidity. It accommodates many styles and a great range of subject matter. I find particular pleasure in painting images of the present-day working landscape with an ancient medium that was used to picture saints.

Artists have long thought of tempera as a deficient medium, superseded by the more easily manipulated oil paint. Vasari, in his *Lives of the Artists,* described the history of the Renaissance as one of steady progress towards more lifelike effects, which increased as artists took up oil painting. Today, we are no longer bound to the idea of progress or naturalism in art, and many artists are again interested in traditional techniques. Egg tempera, with its clarity and brilliance, is a truly contemporary medium: an old technique made new again.

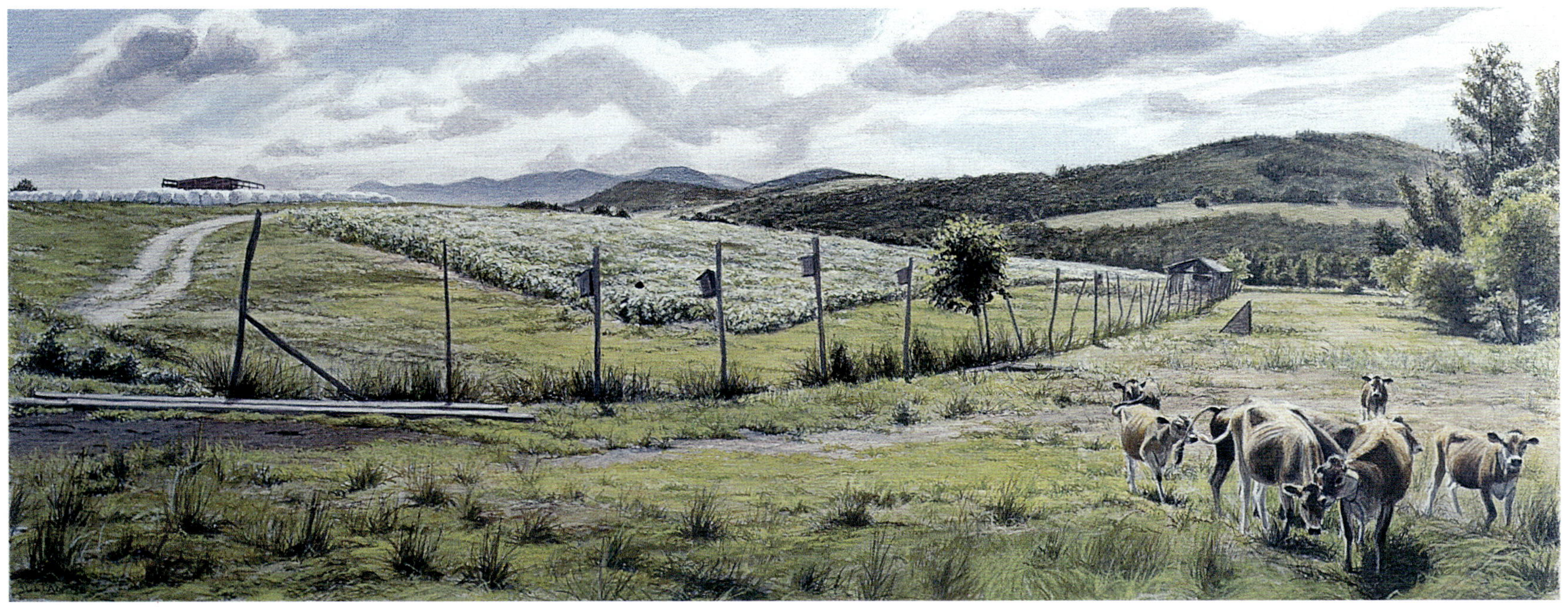

YOUNG CORN AND HEIFERS,
WEST BARNET, VERMONT

Cows are marvelously curious creatures. These young Jersey heifers seem to be trying to communicate across the gulf between Homo sapiens and other mammals. Their golden color adds an additional sparkle to the sun-filled landscape.

# Bibliography


## GENERAL TECHNICAL MANUALS

Doerner, Max. *The Materials of the Artist and Their Use in Painting with Notes on the Techniques of the Old Masters*. New York: Harcourt, Brace and World, 1962. Written by a professor at the Academy of Fine Arts in Munich, and first published in 1921, this book is full of historical and technical information.

Mayer, Ralph. *The Artist's Handbook of Materials and Techniques*. 5th ed. New York: Viking Press, 1991. The bible of contemporary and historical art techniques, this was the book (in earlier editions) that all artists had to have when I was a student.

Wehlte, Kurt. *The Materials and Techniques of Painting*. New York: Van Nostrand Reinhold, 1975. A very complete technical manual. Wehlte, a student and friend of Max Doerner, wrote this book to update and enlarge upon Doerner's work.

It is useful to read several technical manuals, because each has slightly different information, all of it interesting. A bit of advice in one or another could help you solve painting problems. These books describe various types of tempera painting, preparing grounds, the characteristics of various pigments; and they also contain historical notes.

## EARLY PAINTING TREATISES

Cennini, Cennino D'Andrea. *The Craftsman's Handbook*, in Italian, *Il Libro Dell'Arte*. Translated by Daniel V. Thompson Jr. New York: Dover, 1933. This book, written by Cennini around 1400, is the most important painting manual for the study of early Renaissance painting techniques.

*The Strasbourg Manuscript: A Medieval Painter's Handbook*. Translated from the Old German by Viola and Rosamund Borradaile. London: Alec Tiranti, 1966. This treatise on northern European painting techniques was written in the fourteenth or fifteenth century. By reading early painting manuals, you can get an idea of the studio practices of the time. These books have instructions for preparing colors, gilding, and varnishing. This book concentrates on manuscript painting, while Cennini deals primarily with painting on walls or panels.

## BOOKS ABOUT ITALIAN RENAISSANCE PANEL PAINTING

Baxandall, Michael. *Painting and Experience in Fifteenth Century Italy: A Primer in the Social History of Pictorial Style*. Oxford: Clarendon Press, 1972. This book is a fascinating social history. It details artist-client relationships, the purposes of painting, and how fifteenth-century art was judged by contemporaries. It grounds the aesthetics of the period in its culture.

Bomford, David, et al. *Art in the Making: Italian Painting before 1400*. London: National Gallery, 1989. This book has detailed technical and background material about eight panel paintings in the collection of the National Gallery. The panels and frames are discussed, as are the gesso underdrawing, paint layers, and gilding. The numerous photographic details of the panels and microscopic cross sections of paint increase our understanding of the tempera process.

Caroselli, Susan L. *Italian Panel Painting of the Early Renaissance*. Los Angeles: Los Angeles County Museum of Art, 1994. This book is similar to the preceding title in its historical and technical information.

Christiansen, Keith, et al. *Painting in Renaissance Siena 1420–1500*. New York: Metropolitan Museum of Art, 1988. I love this book for its reproductions, which picture some remarkably beautiful works. There are also interesting essays on life and art in Siena in the fifteenth century.

Eastlake, Sir Charles Locke. *Methods and Materials of Painting of the Great Schools and Masters*. New York: Dover, 1960. This book, originally published in 1847 as *Materials for a History of Oil Painting,* has loads of information from original sources about the development of oil painting. Eastlake includes the techniques of the ancients and the early Renaissance and describes changes in tempera technique.

## TWENTIETH-CENTURY INSTRUCTION MANUALS

Bergt, Michael. *A Guide to Egg Tempera Painting*. Santa Fe: Michael Bergt, 1995. A brief but very clear and informative manual written by an artist who has worked exclusively in egg tempera for over 20 years. Available from the author: Rt 6, Box 77, Santa Fe, NM 87501 ($10 including shipping and handling).

Ramos-Poqui, Guillem. *The Technique of Icon Painting*. Kent, England: Burns and Oates/Search Press, 1990. A very clear and well-illustrated description of icon painting which is also useful for secular painting

Schadler, Koo. *Egg Tempera Painting*. Stoddard, N.H.: Koo Schadler, 1998. Another manual by an artist working in egg tempera. It contains a detailed description of gesso making, and other useful information. Available from the author: 60 Queen Street, Stoddard, NH 03464 ($15 including shipping and handling).

Thompson, Jr., Daniel V. *The Practice of Tempera Painting*. New York: Dover Publications, 1962. This instructional manual, originally published by Yale University Press, is the most important contemporary book on egg tempera painting. I learned the technique of tempera from this well-written and clear book. It contains information on gilding that is not covered in my book.

Vickrey, Robert. *New Techniques in Egg Tempera*. New York: Watson-Guptill, 1973. Vickrey's aim in this book is to demonstrate the flexibility of the tempera method, including unconventional uses such as splattering, dripping, and scraping paint.

By reading a variety of egg tempera manuals, you can get an idea of the range of techniques possible with this flexible medium. They will dispel the idea that egg tempera is an academically rigid medium.

## BOOKS ABOUT ARTISTS WORKING WITH TEMPERA

Garver, Thomas H. *George Tooker*. New York: Clarkson N. Potter, 1985. A beautifully written discussion of the artists' work, arranged thematically, with lots of illustrations

Grimes, Nancy. *Jared French's Myths*. San Francisco: Pomegranate Artbooks, 1993. A discussion of the content of French's work: his involvement with Jungian archetypes and William Butler Yeats' theology. Beautiful illustrations.

Kirstein, Lincoln. *Paul Cadmus*. New York: Rizzoli, 1984. A biography of the artist and aesthetic discussion of his works, full of wonderful illustrations.

Wyeth, Andrew. *Two Worlds of Andrew Wyeth: Kuerners and Olsons*. New York: Metropolitan Museum of Art, 1976. This book, the catalogue for an exhibition at the Metropolitan Museum of Art in New York, has as its text an extensive, detailed interview with Andrew Wyeth by Thomas Hoving, at that time the director of the museum.

There is also a video about Paul Cadmus available: *Paul Cadmus: Enfant Terrible at 80* (Homevision, number 3009001).

# Sources

ARTPANEL, 320 Dean Street, Brooklyn, NY 11218. Phone (718) 856-0320. Web site: www.artpanel.com. Manufacturer. ArtPanel makes very high quality ungessoed panels that are ideal for tempera painting—a fiberboard panel and a plywood panel. The fiberboard, Rangerboard, is made of very clean material bound with a urethane resin. The panels come in standard sizes and can also be ordered in custom sizes.

FEZANDIE & SPERRLE, supplied by Benbow Chemical Packaging, 935 Hiawatha Blvd., Syracuse, NY 13208. Phone (315) 474-8236, Fax (315) 478-1307. Catalogue. A very old company that supplies artist's dry pigments.

GUERRA PAINT AND PIGMENT, 510 East 13th Street, New York, NY 10009. Phone (212) 529-0628, Fax (212) 529-0787. E-mail: guerrapaint@mindspring.com. Store and catalogue. Established by an artist, this store has a very long list of pigments dispersed in water, and powdered pigments.

A. HADIK D.B.A. THE GILDER'S STUDIO, 34 Jarvis Street, Sandwich, MA 02563. Phone (508) 833-0782. Manufacturer. This supplier makes custom panels by spraying the gesso onto both sides of untempered pressed-wood panels.

KREMER PIGMENTS, 228 Elizabeth Street, New York, NY 10012. Phone (212) 219-2394, Fax (212) 219-2395. Store and catalogue. Kremer Pigments is a marvelous resource; they have many high quality pigments, including historical colors and a large range of earth colors, and other supplies such as glass jars, brushes, mullers, and chalk and gelatin for gesso. Their catalogues always contain interesting information. They also make several color concentrates (pigments dispersed in water).

PEARL PAINT, 308 Canal Street, New York, NY 10013. Phone to order (800) 451-7327, Phone for customer service (for items not in the catalogue), (800) 221-6845 x2297. Store and catalogue. Pearl is the granddaddy of the discount art suppliers. They carry ready-made supplies, powdered pigments by various companies, whiting, brushes, glass jars, etc.

PERMA COLORS, 226 E. Tremont, Charlotte, NC 28203. Phone and Fax (704) 333-9201, Phone (800) 365-2656. Catalogue. Perma Colors has various supplies including a line of dry pigments, whiting, rabbitskin glue, and brushes. They also make gesso panels and their own dry gesso mix. You have to order at least six panels at a time. The panel that I received was not smoothed, and I had to sand it.

DANIEL SMITH, 4150 First Avenue South, PO Box 84268, Seattle, WA 98124-5568. Phone (800) 426-6740, Fax (800) 238-4065. Store and catalogue. A very good and reasonably priced art supplier, with their own line of pigments and brushes, and other items needed for tempera painting.

SOCIETY OF TEMPERA PAINTERS. PO Box 30766, Santa Fe, NM 87592-0766. Web site: www.eggtempera.com. Founded in 1997 by a group of artists dedicated to the "greater understanding and promotion of tempera painting." They publish a newsletter and have a web site, with interesting information about egg tempera painting. The web site has a useful forum—a place to find answers to questions about the medium, and discussions of mixed techniques such as egg-oil emulsions.

ZECCHI: COLORI—BELLE ARTI, Via dello Studio, 19r, Florence, 50122, Italy. Phone (+39) 055 21 14 70, Fax (+39) 055 21 06 90. Web site: www.supermarket.snf.it/Zecchi/home.htm. Store and catalogue. Zecchi carries an extensive line of modern and historic pigments, as well as other supplies.

# Picture Credits

All paintings by Altoon Sultan, courtesy of Marlborough Gallery, New York.

Page 8:
Giovanni di Paolo, (Giovanni di Paolo di Grazia, active by 1417–died 1482)
THE CREATION AND THE EXPULSION OF ADAM AND EVE FROM PARADISE
Predella panel from an altarpiece,
Tempera and gold on wood
The Metropolitan Museum of Art,
Robert Lehman Collection, 1975.
(1975.1.31) Photograph © 1981
The Metropolitan Museum of Art

Page 10:
Osservanza Master
TEMPTATION OF ST. ANTHONY, 1430
Yale University Art Gallery,
University Purchase from James Jackson Jarves

Page 13:
SHROUD WITH PORTRAIT OF A WOMAN, first century AD
Tempera on linen
The Metropolitan Museum of Art,
Rogers Fund, 1909.
(09.181.8) Photograph © 1996
The Metropolitan Museum of Art

Page 15:
Botticelli (1444/45–1510) and Bartolomeo di Giovanni (1442-1497?)
THE LAST COMMUNION OF SAINT JEROME
Wood, gold, tempera
The Metropolitan Museum of Art,
Bequest of Benjamin Altman, 1913,
and Gift of Daniel Wildenstein, 1989.
(14.40.642, 1989.132)
Photograph © 1990 The Metropolitan Museum of Art

Page 16:
Reginald Marsh
CONEY ISLAND BEACH, 1947
Egg tempera on masonite
Wadsworth Atheneum, Hartford,
Gift of Henry E. Schnakenberg

Page 17:
Andrew Newell Wyeth
NORTHERN POINT, 1950
Egg tempera on gesso panel
36 × 18 3/16 inches
Wadsworth Atheneum, Hartford,
The Ella Gallup Sumner and Mary Catlin Sumner Collection Fund

Page 18:
Paul Cadmus
BOOK BUFF, 1994
Egg tempera on gesso panel
19 × 14 inches
Private Collection,
Courtesy DC Moore Gallery, NYC

Page 19:
Jared French
EVASION, 1947
Egg tempera on gesso panel
21 1/2 × 11 1/4 inches
The Regis Collection, Minneapolis MN,
Photo Courtesy DC Moore Gallery, NYC

Page 19:
George Tooker
DARK ANGEL, 1996
Egg tempera on gesso panel
24 × 19 inches
Courtesy DC Moore Gallery, NYC

Page 44:
Michele da Verona
(circa 1470-1536/44)
THE VIRGIN AND CHILD WITH SAINT ROCH AND SAINT SEBASTIAN
Brush with brown ink,
white and blue gouache
The Metropolitan Museum of Art,
Robert Lehman Collection, 1975. (1975.1.384)
Photograph © 1982
The Metropolitan Museum of Art

Pge 52:
Paul Cadmus
SELF PORTRAIT, 1948
Egg tempera on brown paper
9 1/4 × 7 1/2 inches
Private Collection,
Courtesy DC Moore Gallery, NYC

Page 60:
Carlo Crivelli
SAINT PETER, 1472?
Egg tempera on panel
11 9/16 × 8 3/8 inches
Yale University Art Gallery,
Gift of Hanna D. and Louis M. Rabinowitz

Page 64:
Fra Angelico
SAINT JAMES FREEING HERMOGENES, about 1430
Tempera and gold on wood
10 9/16 × 9 3/8 inches (26.8 × 23.8 cm.)
Kimbell Art Museum, Fort Worth, Texas

Page 66:
Filippino Lippi, (shop of),
CHRIST ON THE CROSS, circa 1495
Egg tempera on panel
Yale University Art Gallery,
University purchase from James Jackson Jarves

Page 104:
Jacob Lawrence
STRUGGLE SERIES - NO. 13: PASSING THE SWORD OF FREEDOM, 1955–1956
Egg tempera on hardboard
12 × 16 inches
Private Collection,
Courtesy DC Moore Gallery, NYC

Page 106:
Peter Hurd
THE HEADQUARTERS, DIAMOND A. RANCH, WAGON MOUND, MORA COUNTY, NEW MEXICO, 1960
Tempera on composition board
26 1/4 × 38 1/4 inches
Hood Museum of Art, Dartmouth College,
Hanover, New Hampshire; anonymous gift

Page 108:
George Tooker
SLEEPING WOMAN, 1998
15 × 18 inches
Courtesy DC Gallery, NYC

Page 111:
Stan Berning
FOURTH PLANET #22, 1998
32 × 48 inches
Courtesy of the artist

Page 114:
Carol Mothner
THE WAIT, 1998
16 × 16 inches
Courtesy Gerald Peters Gallery, Santa Fe, New Mexico

Page 117:
Michael Bergt
HEAVEN AND EARTH, 1998
18 × 16 inches
Courtesy Turner Caroll Gallery, Santa Fe, New Mexico